Editor:
Mary Kaye Taggart

Editorial Project Manager:
Karen J. Goldfluss, M.S. Ed.

Editor-in-Chief:
Sharon Coan, M.S. Ed.

Art Director:
Elayne Roberts

Associate Designer:
Denise Bauer

Cover Artist:
Chris Macabitas

Product Manager:
Phil Garcia

Imaging:
James Edward Grace

Publishers:
Rachelle Cracchiolo, M.S. Ed.
Mary Dupuy Smith, M.S. Ed.

How to Prepare
Your Middle School Students for

Standardized Tests

Author:

Julia Jasmine, M.A.

Teacher Created Materials, Inc.
6421 Industry Way
Westminster, CA 92683
www.teachercreated.com
©1997 Teacher Created Materials, Inc.
Reprinted, 2002
Made in U.S.A.
ISBN-1-57690-132-7

Table of Contents

Table of Contents *(cont.)*

Table of Contents *(cont.)*

Introduction

Traditional standardized tests are back! Returning with them is all of the test anxiety that we thought we had put behind us with the advent of alternative assessment. However, the truth of the matter is that in most cases traditional testing never went away at all. Alternative assessment requirements were simply added to the old methods of assessment. Many school districts continued to use their traditional standardized testing as well as their newer proficiency testing, which they added during the last great assessment upheaval. Teachers and their students felt that they were being "tested to death."

So, if standardized testing never really went away, just what is it that is happening now? It would probably be correct to say that what has returned is the emphasis on standardized testing. National standards are important now, and the states that give the right tests at the right times will receive the most money for education from the federal government.

The most realistic way to look at all of this is that there is not much the individual teacher can do about it either way. It will help our students, however, if we keep in mind that the old objections to standardized testing—the ones that made us seek out alternatives in the first place—are still valid:

- This is a big country with a diverse population, and when tests are "normed," the sample population may not reflect this enormous diversity.

- Students who are not naturally talented in the areas of language and math (who do not excel in what Howard Gardner calls the linguistic and logical/mathematical intelligences in *Frames of Mind: The Theory of Multiple Intelligences* [Basic Books, 1983]) will not do well on achievement tests, even if these students may be immensely talented in other areas.

- Students who do not speak and read English fluently will not do well on the tests.

- Students who live in poverty will not have the experiential background to understand the questions on the test.

There are many people in education who can help to solve these problems:

- The test makers can help by keeping their assessment tools free from bias and basing their norms on a sample that is as representative of our population as possible.

- Educational administrators can help by interpreting the test results correctly, by keeping in mind the student populations that are being tested, and by explaining their interpretations to the public.

- Teachers can help by giving their students the information they need to pass the tests. Some of this information consists of knowledge, but a great deal of it consists of the test-taking skills which are the subject of this book.

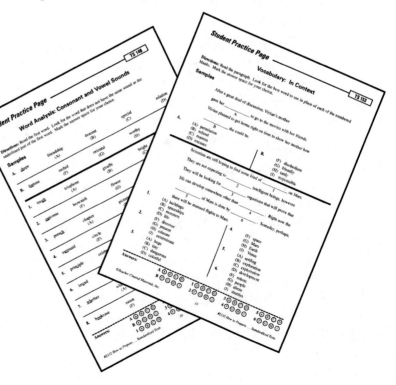

Test Success

At Least Three Requirements

The ability to do well when taking traditional standardized tests requires at least three things:

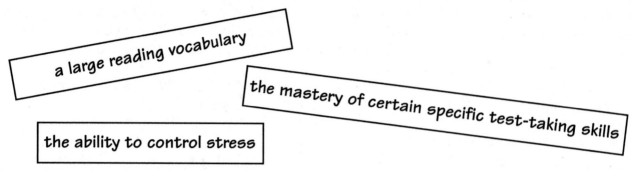

a large reading vocabulary

the mastery of certain specific test-taking skills

the ability to control stress

The vocabulary issue is discussed in detail in the section that follows. The test-taking skills, which will be briefly discussed here and reinforced in each relevant practice section, can be taught by teachers, used by students, and have nothing much to do with the stated purpose of the particular test—to determine a student's level in reading or math, for example. Some tools for controlling stress will also be suggested.

Who Needs Test-Taking Skills?

Certainly, all students need test-taking skills, but "good" students may need them most of all. Without test-taking stability, fluent readers may score low on the incremental skills that have been identified as necessary building blocks for beginning readers, for example. (These incremental skills are still included on some of the tests for fifth through eighth grades.) Fluent readers are well past the place where they labor over, or are even really aware of, beginning sounds, ending sounds, and vowel sounds. They just read. Similarly, students with excellent skills in logic and problem solving may not show much success on problems involving the basic math facts that are often learned by rote. Depending on the test you will be giving, you may need to teach some phonics and math skills almost as separate subjects.

The students who use these incremental skills without really noticing them are, of course, the very students you would like to have excel when they take whatever test your school or district has decided to give. They should be able to carry a record of success with them in their school careers, and you should get credit for teaching them. This is particularly important in an educational climate where school districts, schools, and individual teachers are judged on their students' test results which are often emblazoned across the newspapers to generate public reactions.

What Are These Skills?

The skills students need at all grade levels in order to do well on standardized tests include the ability to follow complicated and often confusing directions, the ability to scale back what they know and focus on just what is asked, the ability to choose among confusing distracters (multiple-choice answers), and the ability to maintain concentration during boring and tedious repetition. Since you have probably spent years perfecting your ability to give clear and easily understood directions, you probably love it when your students bring their existing knowledge to bear on a new problem, you most likely give students clear answer choices from which to choose, and you undoubtedly do not want to change your basic teaching style to one that is boring and repetitious, you will need another approach.

Test Success *(cont.)*

What to Do and How to Do It

You can teach your students to translate the test directions into the words that you use and that they can more easily understand. Although you will not be able to deviate from the script during the actual testing, you can certainly stop on any practice page and rephrase the directions for the sample questions. Say, for example, "This means . . . ," or "I usually say . . . ," or "When you hear this, it means . . . ." (Remind your students that you will not be able to do this during actual tests.) You can show them how to restrict their responses. (They should read the answer choices before they begin to elaborate on the questions in their own minds.) You can turn the tedium into a game. You could also teach test-taking skills during a separate segment of your school day and set up some kind of a reward system to help students stay focused. The material that follows in this book will help you to do this without having a negative impact on your curriculum or individual teaching style.

Inform the Students

Be sure to explain to the students what you are doing and why. Tell them that you will be teaching test-taking skills to them, establishing a room environment much like what they will experience during a real test, and often reading from a script. Assure them that the experience will reduce their stress levels and make them successful test-takers. (Assure yourself that the experience will reduce your stress level too and make you look good when the scores are published in your local newspaper or produced as part of your own yearly evaluation.)

Address the Issue of Stress

Give your students some tools for handling the stress that accompanies test taking. Talk about routine habits that they can develop: getting enough sleep, eating a good breakfast, and getting some exercise after school. Small children usually understand that they feel better after they use their large muscles by running, jumping, climbing, and so on. Pre-adolescents and adolescents are going through similar growth spurts. They need ample opportunities to exercise. A routine of school, homework, television, and bed simply will not give their large muscles the relief they need in order to relax. Consider sending home a letter asking parents to become part of the testing team by encouraging their students to develop these helpful habits.

Allow self-directed activities and free movement around your classroom when you are not presenting teacher-directed activities. Cooperative group activities are always appropriate and will give your students a chance to interact in different ways. By including a variety of teaching strategies, you will prevent the school day from turning into one long paper-and-pencil session.

Tell the students that they can use their imaginations to see themselves doing well on the tests. Many athletes use this technique and have written or talked about it at length. They visualize themselves hitting balls, making baskets, and winning races. Read some of these accounts to your students and encourage them to see themselves feeling calm, thinking clearly, and marking the correct answers.

Use exercises such as deep breathing and stretching at regular intervals during the day. Then, when the testing time arrives, your students will know how to do these exercises and will not be distracted because of the novelty of these activities.

The Vocabulary Piece

Reading Vocabulary

The size of your students' reading vocabularies will be a deciding factor in how well they score on standardized achievement tests. The term *reading vocabulary* is used here to mean a body of words that students read and comprehend without effort, words that have concepts connected to them. Ideally, students' reading vocabularies should encompass all of the words that they will meet in the tests. They must know not only the target words in vocabulary questions but also all of the words used in the stories and all of the words used in the distracters (multiple-choice answers). For example, if students cannot correctly read all of the possible answers in a question about spelling, they will not be able to answer the question successfully.

Depending on the format of the test you are giving, you may be able to encourage your students to answer all of the questions that contain words that they know and then go back and figure out the words that they did not recognize. However, because of time constraints, you may not always be able to offer them this option.

Some Methods to Use

Whatever vocabulary-building skills you are using, consider adding some of these practice methods to increase your students' reading vocabularies. **Flash cards** are a wonderful, if old-fashioned, tool. **Oral discussion** of words is a handy method that can be used as a part of instruction in any subject matter. Consider posting *lists* of words to accompany a social studies or science lesson or to provide a recall tool for the words you talked about in an oral discussion. Use word games to reinforce and expand your students' vocabularies. Finally, give your students a **visual context** for as many words as possible. Although some of these skills may be associated in your mind with the primary classroom, they are effective at any age and will be particularly appropriate in classrooms where students speak more than one language.

Flash Cards

Gather words for vocabulary flash cards from all of the sources that are available to you. Just write the words on ordinary 3" x 5" or 5" x 7" (7.6 cm x 12.7 cm or 12.7 cm x 17.8 cm) index cards. You can fill spare moments by using these cards in a teacher-directed activity. Or, put packs of the flash cards in your activity centers for your students to use in partner or small group work. Also, you can have classroom aides, volunteers, or cross-age tutors use the flash cards with individuals or small groups.

Depending on how many words you manage to gather, you can pack them according to categories: History, Geography, Science, Math, and so on. (See "Some Sources for Words" starting on page 11.)

The Vocabulary Piece *(cont.)*

Oral Discussion

This is the easiest of all the methods, requiring no supplies or setup. Just stop and talk about the words you are hearing or reading. (Consider reinforcing this method by jotting the words down on the chalkboard as you talk about them.) For example, if someone reads, hears, or says the word stream, you could initiate discussion with the following questions.

What is a stream?

How does a stream compare to a river?

What is a creek?

Who has ever seen a stream, a river, or a creek?

What did it (they) look like?

What are the differences among streams, rivers, and creeks and bodies of water like oceans or lakes?

Who has seen an ocean or a lake?

What did it (they) look like?

The added benefit of this method is that each word automatically has a basic concept attached to it.

Lists

If you had been making a list of the preceding oral discussion, you would have these words:

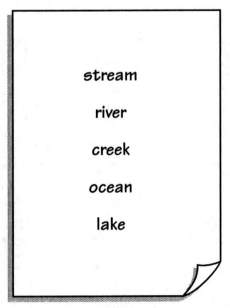

stream

river

creek

ocean

lake

The Vocabulary Piece (cont.)

Lists (*cont.*)

Depending on the original source of the word stream—if it is part of a science lesson about bodies of water, for example—and depending on how many other words you stop to discuss, you might come up with quite an extensive list of words. You might have added pond, bay, sea, canal, gulf, and so on. List all of these words on a chart titled "Bodies of Water." Post it somewhere in the classroom and review it occasionally.

Word Games

There are many types of word games to choose from, and all of them remove vocabulary study from the area of work into the realm of play. It is probably a good idea not to stress the educational value of the games but instead just let the students think they are having a wonderful time. Consider investing in a couple of Scrabble games for your classroom. Keep a supply of quadrille paper (1/4" graph paper) on hand and let the students construct their own original crossword puzzles and word searches. If a student gives you a puzzle, make enough copies for everyone in the class or keep a stack with your games. Just make sure that the puzzle creators include answer keys.

Invent, or ask your students to invent, your own vocabulary version of the popular television game Jeopardy. If your students are interested in this, have them write a definition on one side of a card and a word on the other side. Whoever is acting as the master of ceremonies will read the definition and the contestant who is called on will say, "What is . . . ?" They can create various categories to correspond with your current curriculum and stage whole-class games. This is a great rainy day activity.

Visual Context

Provide your students with a visual context for the words that they learn by showing and discussing as many videos and movies as you can fit into your busy day. Show science films, social studies films, math films, and films based on classic or modern stories. In order to make this method work, you will need to look at the movie or video with your class. Make a practice of stopping the projector or VCR to talk about the words. No matter what kind of a film or video you are watching, if your class had participated in the science lesson mentioned earlier you could stop it and say:

> Look. This is an example of a river. That is what a river looks like in a city (or in a rural setting). I'll rewind the tape so that we can look at it again. Remember, we wrote the word "river" on our chart of Bodies of Water. (Have someone get the chart and point out the written word.)

> There is a "citadel." Remember, that's the word everyone missed when we played Jeopardy. Well, that is what a citadel looks like. Who remembers how to spell it? Please write it on the board.

Try not to be pressured into feeling guilty for showing videos and movies to your students. Some people feel that anything visual is merely entertainment and object to this in the classroom. If you are faced with this kind of criticism, you can counter it by pointing out that you are using the visual experiences as part of your instructional method to maximize your students' success on the upcoming standardized tests by helping them to increase their vocabularies. If necessary, invite your critics to sit in on a lesson in which you do vocabulary exercises using visual aids.

The Vocabulary Piece *(cont.)*

Some Sources for Words

You can get your words from anywhere and everywhere. For purposes of standardized testing, in addition to what might be called **"grade-level words,"** your students will need to know **subject-specific words**, words that may be **outside of their personal experiential backgrounds**, **plural forms of words, words with affixes, compound words, contractions, synonyms and antonyms, words with more than one meaning**, and **prepositions and their meanings**. They will also need a strategy for dealing with a variety of **proper names** and know how the word **"blank"** is used in many standardized test questions.

Grade-Level Words

If you are using a basal reader series, a good source of grade-level words is the word list that usually appears at the back of the book or in the teacher's materials. You should also provide yourself with the word lists from the preceding books in the series. For example, if you are using a sixth grade reader, get the word lists from the fourth and fifth grade readers. Consider getting the word lists from the books that follow as well. If these lists are not provided, call the publisher's customer representative and ask for them.

If you are using other kinds of reading materials—a literature-based program for example—skim through the books and pull the words that you think are the most relevant. Also, get words from other standard lists: contact publishers and ask for the word lists for their basal series; use the Dolch list which you can probably find in a teacher supply store; use the EDL list which contains the words appearing at different grade levels in the most used basal reader series; purchase some of the teacher and/or parent resource books containing basic word lists. Also, if you are fairly new to the field of teaching, talk to teachers on your staff who have been teaching for a while and who may be willing to share their resources. They probably have words lists tucked away in their files, dating from the last time the educational pendulum swung in the direction of standardized testing.

Subject-Specific Words

Since students understand big words as easily as little ones, use the special vocabularies of the subjects you deal with as you teach. Talk about "numerals" as well as "numbers." Use words like "addend," "sum," "difference," and "product" routinely so that your students will be used to them. Talk about "transportation" and "communication" during social studies. Say that you are going to "observe" or "experiment" when beginning a science activity. Add math words, science words, and social studies words to your flash cards and lists. Most math, science, and social studies texts include glossaries. These are excellent sources for important words.

The Vocabulary Piece *(cont.)*

Words Based on Experiential Background

Students need to comprehend the meanings of many words that will not be part of their experiential backgrounds. For example, rural students will need some conceptual context for words such as "subway" and "skyscraper." Suburban students may need to recognize the meanings of such words as "apartment" and "taxi." Urban students, especially those who live in the inner city, should be given some idea of what split-level tract houses and suburban shopping malls look like along with the more obviously rural stables and pastures.

Students in many parts of the South and Southwest may need to be given some information about snow. They may know that it is white, but they will not necessarily know that it is cold. Students who live away from the coasts may have no concepts to go with the word "ocean," and students who live on the Great Plains may need to be given some idea of what mountains look like.

Keep in mind that it is always safer to assume that students *do not* have an experiential background than that they do. Just because you live thirty miles from the ocean or the mountains does not mean that your students have ever been to those places.

Lists of words based on experiential background (or the lack of it) will be lists that you develop for your own situation, based on the needs that you identify. The methods described in developing visual contexts for words (see page 10) will be of use here, as will oral discussion. Choose films that will fill in some of your students' blank places. Once you decide on the words you need, you can apply the other methods for reinforcement by making lists and flash cards.

If you are in a situation that allows for field trips, these will help your students to develop experiential backgrounds and enrich their vocabularies. When you know where you are going, prepare a list of words that reflect the things that you think you will see and give a copy of the list to each student. Make sure that they can read the words on the list by reviewing and discussing them as often as is necessary. (Add some pictures to help those students who speak little English to remember the words.) Take the lists with you. Have your students look for the things on the list and check off the ones they find. They can also add words to their lists. (Remember to take pencils.) When you get back from the field trip, talk about what all of the words mean and add them to your flash cards and/or make a list titled "Our Field Trip."

Note: On pages 190–202 you will find a list of selected words that may be added to your spelling program throughout the year. Since these words often appear on standardized tests, it would benefit your students to become familiar with them prior to taking a test.

The Vocabulary Piece *(cont.)*

Plurals

On standardized tests, students are expected to be able to differentiate between the singular and plural forms of both written words and words given orally and then to use these differences in comprehension questions. Recognition of singular and plural forms of words becomes particularly important in the test section dealing with language usage. In this section students will be expected to identify cases in which subjects and verbs do or do not agree.

When you talk about words, talk about their plurals too. Add plurals to your flash cards and word lists.

Words with Affixes and Inflectional Endings

Students need to be able to read and know the meanings of words with affixes because they will be asked to recognize the **root** word. For example, if the given word is "careful" and two of the distracters are "care" and "car," the student who cannot read the given word with comprehension will not know which answer to choose.

Students also must know the meanings of the suffixes themselves and understand how they affect the meanings of the root words. Remember that the "s" or "es" that forms a plural on the end of a word is sometimes considered a suffix and sometimes an inflectional ending. Teach your students about these two types of endings.

Have your students add prefixes and suffixes to words for practice. Talk about comparatives and superlatives and have the students add "er" and "est" to words that they already know (for example: slow, slower, slowest).

Compound Words

Compound words are made up of two parts that can each stand alone. Students must be able to distinguish compound words from words with prefixes and suffixes. Have your students brainstorm a list of compound words and use them to make lists and packs of flash cards. Help them to get started with sports words: baseball, basketball, football, etc.

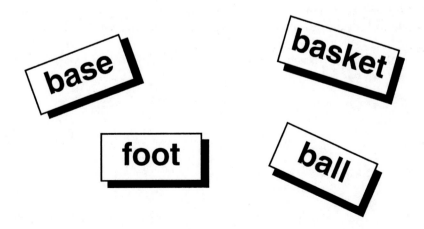

The Vocabulary Piece *(cont.)*

Contractions

The students will be expected to know the words that are represented by common contractions. Do not forget "let's," "I'll," "won't," and "you're." Put a contraction on one side of a flash card and the words it represents on the other side so that your students can quiz each other.

Synonyms and Antonyms

Both synonyms and antonyms for words can be generated during oral discussions. Make a game of listing them and talk about the fact that synonyms mean the same (or almost the same) as a given word and antonyms mean the opposite.

Words with More Than One Meaning

Words of this type are best demonstrated with an example of a test item.

Fill in the circle next to the answer that fits best in the blanks in both sentences.

The children _____ into the pool.

The _____ flew into the barn.

- ○ bird
- ○ jumped
- ○ dove
- ○ played

Some of the words fit into one sentence or the other but only one word fits into both sentences.

Prepositions

In order to be successful when taking standardized tests, students need to know (read and understand the meanings of) all of the common prepositions. One easy way to deal with this need is to approach it in terms of opposites: up/down, in/out, over/under, around/through, before/after, to/from, and so on.

If you make flash cards of these words, add a graphic of some kind to help your students remember the words.

The Vocabulary Piece (cont.)

Proper Names

Your students will encounter many proper names in sentences and stories, and not all of these will be of the "Dick and Jane" variety. Many unusual names are used as well as many that reflect a range of ethnic diversity. Meeting an unfamiliar proper name, especially as the very first word of a sentence or story, often has the effect of stopping students in their tracks. You can teach them to substitute the word "blank" (see next section) for the names they do not know. You can also make them familiar with the written forms of the names of all of the students in your classroom and point out all of the proper names when you read stories.

Not being able to read proper names correctly is a real problem only when the gender of the person named is vital for comprehension. For example: If a statement read, "Bruce and John are smiling," and the pictures show one boy smiling, a boy and a girl smiling, and two boys smiling, it would be imperative that the test taker know that "Bruce" and "John" are both boys' names. There is not much you can do about this except expose your students to a number of proper names. (In addition, you should probably make your students aware of the fact that hair length is usually used to show the difference between boys and girls in the pictures that show only faces on the tests.)

"Blank"

The use of the word "blank" is both a test-taking and a vocabulary issue. Many oral questions are asked using the word "blank" and many written questions are set up with a blank (_____) in them. For example, you might be asked to say, "Read the selection and the sentence below it. Choose the answer that goes in the blank."

It was hard to get anything _____ at my house last Saturday morning. It was my brother's birthday and he was really excited. But then, Javier is always excited about something!

- ○ doing
- ○ does
- ○ done
- ○ had done

(This is a simplified example, but the following method works in more complicated instances as well.)

The Vocabulary Piece *(cont.)*

Teach your students to read the statement to themselves using the word "blank":

It was hard to get anything *"blank"* at my house last Saturday morning.

Then have them read the statement putting each answer choice in place of the blank:

It was hard to get anything *doing* at my house last Saturday morning.

It was hard to get anything *does* at my house last Saturday morning.

It was hard to get anything *done* at my house last Saturday morning.

It was hard to get anything *had done* at my house last Saturday morning.

Stress the importance of reading all of the choices in this way and also of checking back in the story before making a decision. The sentence should not only make sense, but it should also reflect comprehension of the story.

If your students do not recognize the proper name "Javier," have them read the story to themselves like this:

But then, *"Blank"* is always excited about something!

Maximizing Vocabulary Results

Send the word lists home with the students:

- Make them part of your homework.
- Use them for spelling words.
- Check out the packs of flash cards to your students in the same way you might check out library books.
- Use the words as the basis for storywriting.

Have contests with prizes (stickers, candy, free time, etc.):

- Who can read a pack of words?
- Who can read the most packs of words?
- Who can tell the meanings of these words?
- Who can add a new word to this list?
- Who can say a synonym word for each of these words?
- Who can write a synonym word for each of these words?

The Vocabulary Piece *(cont.)*

Have the students teach each other:

- As soon as one student has mastered a list or a pack of words, have him or her teach those words to another student.
- As soon as one student has mastered a list or a pack of words, have him or her teach those words to a small group of students.

Have the students play and/or create games:

- Give your students cards to make double sets of word packs. Have them use the double packs to play "Memory."
- Play "20 Questions" with words from your lists. (I'm thinking of a word on our list of math words . . . .)
- Give your students the opportunity to make up word games and to teach them to the class.

Encourage the students to create their own word banks:

- Let the students make dictionaries in three-ring binders. They can add notes, definitions, and pictures to help them remember words. If you want (and if paper is plentiful) let them put only one entry on each page so that they can resort the pages when new words are added to keep their words in alphabetical order.
- Make available file boxes such as those made for recipe cards. Have the students write their words and definitions on index cards and file them in alphabetical order. Add divider cards with tabs showing the letters of the alphabet to help organize this process. Relevant facts can also be added to the definitions to provide context.

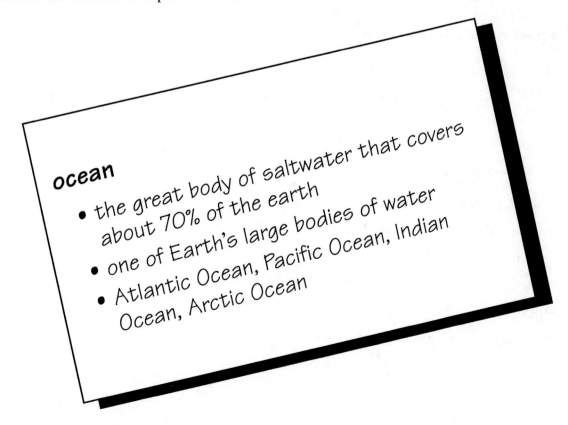

ocean
- the great body of saltwater that covers about 70% of the earth
- one of Earth's large bodies of water
- Atlantic Ocean, Pacific Ocean, Indian Ocean, Arctic Ocean

The Vocabulary Piece *(cont.)*

Have the students use the word lists for writing stories:

- Challenge the students to use as many of the words on a list as they can in a story.

- Tell them to highlight all of the words in a story that are on one or more of the lists in the classroom.

- Let the students use a list of sports words to write a sports story and/or a science list to write a science fiction story.

Tell your students to use the word lists for reading activities:
- Have them read newspaper articles and highlight all of the "list" words they find.

- Divide up a newspaper and have a group search for "list" words to highlight. Count the words and declare the group with the most highlighted words the winner.

An On-Going Process

Keep in mind that gathering words for your word lists is an on-going process. Try to add to your list every day and use the various methods suggested in this section. Many of the methods can be approached as sponge activities to make your school day more fun. They will also help your students ease into a richer reading vocabulary that will increase their chances for success on standardized tests.

How to Use This Book

Where to Start

1. Consult the appropriate chart for the test you will be giving. (See "Skills Charts" beginning on page 21 for some general information.)

2. Look down the list of skills that appear on that test. You will find page numbers referring you to the Student Practice Pages (SPP) and Teacher Scripts (TS) that address the skill. If you will be giving the TAAS "Grade 7" test, for example, you will find that the first skill listed is Language Arts: Sentences. If you are giving the revised edition of the CTBS "Book C" test, the first skill listed is Vocabulary: Synonyms. If you are using "Book 7-Revised Edition" of the Iowa Test of Basic Skills (ITBS), the first skill listed is Reading: Vocabulary.

3. Identify the pages you will be using.

> **Note:** Abbreviated cross-references have been provided throughout the Student Practice Pages and the Teacher Scripts. To find the teacher page for any Student Practice Page (pages 32–147), see the box at the top of the student page marked TS (Teacher Script). To locate the student page for any Teacher Script (pages 148–187), see the box next to the skill title marked SPP (Student Practice Page).

Making Practice Test Booklets/Scripts/Answer Keys

❑ Use the pages you have identified to make a practice test booklet for each of your students.

❑ Put your practice test booklets together by following these steps:
- Make one copy of each of the student practice pages you selected.
- Don't forget the Student Cover Sheet.
- Assemble the student practice pages in the order they appear on the chart.
- Number the pages in the upper right-hand corner.
- If you want students to stop at the bottom of the page, add a stop sign. If you want them to go right on, draw an arrow.
- When the pages are arranged and numbered and you have added any symbols you need, make enough copies for your students and staple the pages together in booklet form. Don't forget to make one or two extra for yourself.

❑ Put your Teacher Script booklet together by following these steps:
- Identify and copy the Teacher Script for each Student Practice Page you selected.
- Several scripts appear on each script page. If you do not need one or more of the scripts on a page you have selected, draw an "X" through the part you will not be using. Or use a highlighter pen to highlight the ones you will be using.
- Assemble the script pages in the same order as the Student Practice Pages.
- A Teacher Script Cover Sheet is provided.
- Compare your script pages to the student booklet and write the page numbers from the student practice pages on the appropriate blanks in your script.
- Staple the script pages together in booklet form.

❑ An answer key has been provided on pages 207–224. You may work directly from this answer key or make an answer key for each page by marking the correct answers in one of your extra student practice booklets.

How to Use This Book *(cont.)*

Follow-Up

❑ As you use the practice pages, if you come across a skill that is hard for your students, try these ideas:

- Teach the skill in various ways in your regular curriculum.
- Create additional supplementary practice pages of your own.
- Retest at a later date, using the practice page in this book.

Teaching the Test-Taking Skills

❑ Set aside a block of time each day to teach test skills using the booklets you have made.

❑ Provide time for using the restroom before you start. Anxious students need to use the restroom more often.

❑ Make your room environment as test-like as possible.

- If your desks are pushed together in groups, have students move them apart.
- Put a "Testing—Do Not Disturb" sign on the door.
- Explain "test etiquette" to your students:

  -No talking

  -Attentive listening

  -Following directions (such as, "Stop working and put your pencil down.")
- Spend some time explaining the rows of answer spaces at the bottom of each practice page. These are designed to approximate the answer sheets students will use for the "real" tests. Show students how to keep their places by checking back and forth between the numbers on the practice key and the numbers on the practice page.

❑ Provide a strip of construction paper for each student to use for a marker. These can double as bookmarks when your testing practice is finished for the day. Make extras for replacements.

❑ Provide scratch paper and encourage students to use it. This is really necessary for math questions and can come in handy for some language arts items too.

❑ Establish a routine for replacing broken pencils. Give each student two to start with and have a back-up pencil supply handy. Ask students to raise a hand with the broken pencil in it so you can give them new ones and take the broken ones without any fuss. Ask a student or two to take on the job of keeping the pencils sharpened. If your school is short of funds for classroom supplies, send home a letter asking parents to provide pencils. And try to stay calm. Pencils break. Students who are worried about your reaction to their broken pencils will not do as well on the test. You can't relieve all test anxiety, but you can remove "pencil anxiety."

❑ Explain to students that you will be reading from a script and repeating directions and questions in a way that may not sound like your usual teaching style.

Explain typical test symbols such as the arrow that means "continue" and the Stop Sign, usually at the bottom of a page, that means "Do not go on until you are told."

If applicable to the test pages you are using, explain the answer choice that indicates that the correct answer does not appear. This choice is sometimes found on the math pages.

Skills Charts

Find the Right Test

Look at the charts on pages 21–31 and the headings on the charts themselves to find the type of test (CTBS, ITBS, MAT, etc.) that you will be giving and the edition (Revised Edition, Fourth Edition, etc.)

In General

In general, the older editions of the tests consist of one booklet for grades three through five. This is often called "Book C." The later editions of the tests are often separated and numbered by grade level: Book 6, Book 7, and Book 8. The Texas Assessment of Academic Skills (TAAS) tests at grades seven and nine.

If you are on the low end of the grade level range for a test (giving any of the older editions at grade 5, for example), prepare your students for the fact that there will be a lot of material that they will not be familiar with and will not be expected to know.

Note that on pages 21–30 the numbers in parentheses represent the grade levels of the tests.

Test Editions and Levels

CAT	*Third Edition*	*[Level]*		*Fourth Edition*	*[Level]*
	Book C (5–8)	[16,17]		Book 6 (6)	[16]
				Book 7 (7)	[17]
				Book 8 (8)	[18]
CTBS	*Old Edition*	*[Level]*		*Revised Edition*	*[Level]*
	Book C (5–8)	[G, H]		Book C (5–8)	[15, 16, 17/18]
ITBS	*Old Edition*	*[Level]*		*Revised Edition*	*[Level]*
	Book C (6–8)	[12, 13, 14]		Book 6 (6)	[12]
				Book 7 (7)	[13]
				Book 8 (8)	[14]
MAT	*Third Edition*	*[Level]*		*Fourth Edition*	*[Level]*
	Book C (5–8)	[intermediate]		Book 6 (6)	[I2]
				Book 7 (7)	[I3]
				Book 8 (8)	[I4]
NJ EWT	Grade 8				
SAT	Book C (5–8)				
SAT 9	Intermediate 3 through Advanced 2 (fall, Grade 7—Spring, Grade 8)				
TAAS	Grade 7				
	Grade 9				

A Look at Skills Tested in CAT

Third Edition Book C (5–8)		Fourth Edition Book 6 (6)	
Skill	**Page**	**Skill**	**Page**
Word Analysis		**Vocabulary**	
Consonants/Vowels	32, **148**	Synonyms/Antonyms	34, 35, **149**
Roots/Affixes	33, **148**	In Context	40–42, **152, 153**
Vocabulary		Derivations	43, **153**
Synonyms	34, **149**	**Reading Comprehension**	
Antonyms	35, **149**	Passages	45–69, **157**
Multiple Meanings	38, 39, **151**	**Spelling**	
Affixes	37, **151**	Spelling Skills	70–75, **158–160**
In Context	40–42, **152, 153**	**Language Mechanics**	
Reading Comprehension		Punctuation	79–82, **162–164**
Passages	45–69, **157**	Capitalization and Punctuation	83, **164**
Spelling		**Language Expression**	
Spelling Skills	70–75, **158–160**	Usage	87–89, **166, 167**
Language Mechanics		Sentences	93–95, **168, 169**
Capitalization	76–78, **161, 162**	Paragraphs	96, 97, **170**
Punctuation	79–82, **162–164**	**Math Computation**	
Capitalization and Punctuation	83, **164**	Computation Skills	122–131, **179–181**
Language Expression		**Math Concepts/Applications**	
Usage	87–89, **166, 167**	Numeration	132, **182**
Sentences	93, **168**	Geometry	136–140, **184**
Sentence Combining	94, **169**	Measurement	136–141, **184**
Topic Sentences	96, **170**	Problem Solving	142–147, **185–187**
Sentence Sequence	97, **170**	**Work-Study Skills**	
Math Computation		Library/Dictionary Skills	112, **174**
Addition	122, 123, **179**	Reference Sources	112, **174**
Subtraction	124, 125, **179**	Table of Contents	114, **175**
Multiplication	126, **180**		
Division	128, 129, **180**		
Math Concepts/Application			
Numeration	132, **182**		
Number Sentences	133, **182**		
Number Theory	134, **183**		
Problem Solving	142–147, **185–187**		
Measurement	136–141, **184**		
Geometry	136–140, **184**		
Work-Study Skills			
Library Skills	112, **174**		
Outlines	117, **176**		
Maps	120, **178**		

A Look at Skills Tested in CAT

<table>
<tr><td colspan="2">Fourth Edition
Book 7 (7)</td><td colspan="2">Fourth Edition
Book 8 (8)</td></tr>
<tr><td>Skill</td><td>Page</td><td>Skill</td><td>Page</td></tr>
<tr><td colspan="2">Vocabulary</td><td colspan="2">Vocabulary</td></tr>
<tr><td>Synonyms/Antonyms</td><td>34, 35, 149</td><td>Synonyms/Antonyms</td><td>34, 35, 149</td></tr>
<tr><td>In Context</td><td>40–42, 152, 153</td><td>In Context</td><td>40–42, 152, 153</td></tr>
<tr><td>Derivations</td><td>43, 153</td><td>Derivations</td><td>43, 153</td></tr>
<tr><td colspan="2">Reading Comprehension</td><td colspan="2">Reading Comprehension</td></tr>
<tr><td>Passages</td><td>45–69, 157</td><td>Passages</td><td>45–69, 157</td></tr>
<tr><td colspan="2">Spelling</td><td colspan="2">Spelling</td></tr>
<tr><td>Spelling Skills</td><td>70–75, 158–160</td><td>Spelling Skills</td><td>70–75, 158–160</td></tr>
<tr><td colspan="2">Language Mechanics</td><td colspan="2">Language Mechanics</td></tr>
<tr><td>Punctuation</td><td>79–82, 162–164</td><td>Punctuation</td><td>79–82, 162–164</td></tr>
<tr><td>Capitalization and Punctuation</td><td>83, 164</td><td>Capitalization and Punctuation</td><td>83, 164</td></tr>
<tr><td colspan="2">Language Expression</td><td colspan="2">Language Expression</td></tr>
<tr><td>Usage</td><td>87–89, 166, 167</td><td>Usage</td><td>87–89, 166, 167</td></tr>
<tr><td>Sentences</td><td>93–95, 168, 169</td><td>Sentences</td><td>93–95, 168, 169</td></tr>
<tr><td>Paragraphs</td><td>96, 97, 170</td><td>Paragraphs</td><td>96, 97, 170</td></tr>
<tr><td colspan="2">Math Computation</td><td colspan="2">Math Computation</td></tr>
<tr><td>Computation Skills</td><td>122–131, 179–181</td><td>Computation Skills</td><td>122–131, 179–181</td></tr>
<tr><td colspan="2">Math Concepts/Applications</td><td colspan="2">Math Concepts/Applications</td></tr>
<tr><td>Numeration</td><td>132, 182</td><td>Numeration</td><td>132, 182</td></tr>
<tr><td>Geometry</td><td>136–140, 184</td><td>Geometry</td><td>136–140, 184</td></tr>
<tr><td>Measurement</td><td>136–141, 184</td><td>Measurement</td><td>136–141, 184</td></tr>
<tr><td>Problem Solving</td><td>142–147, 185–187</td><td>Problem Solving</td><td>142–147, 185–187</td></tr>
<tr><td colspan="2">Work-Study Skills</td><td colspan="2">Work-Study Skills</td></tr>
<tr><td>Parts of a Book</td><td>114, 115, 175</td><td>Library/Dictionary Skills</td><td>112, 174</td></tr>
<tr><td>Maps</td><td>120, 178</td><td>Outlines</td><td>117, 176</td></tr>
<tr><td></td><td></td><td>Bibliography</td><td>119, 177</td></tr>
</table>

A Look at Skills Tested in CTBS

Book C (5–8)		**Revised Edition** **Book C (5–8)**	
Skill	**Page**	**Skill**	**Page**
Vocabulary		**Vocabulary**	
Synonyms	34, **149**	Synonyms	34, **149**
Affixes	37, **151**	Antonyms	35, **149**
Multiple Meanings	38, 39, **151**	Affix Meanings	37, **151**
In Context	40–42, **152**, **153**	Multiple Meanings	38, 39, **151**
Reading Comprehension		In Context	40–42, **152**, **153**
Passages	45–69, **157**	Derivations	43, **153**
Critical Reading	45–69, **157**	**Reading Comprehension**	
Spelling		Passages	45–69, **157**
Spelling Skills	70–75, **158–160**	Critical Reading	45–69, **157**
Language Mechanics		**Spelling**	
Capitalization	76–78, **161**, **162**	Spelling Skills	70–75, **158–160**
Punctuation	79–82, **162–164**	**Language Mechanics**	
Capitalization and Punctuation	83, **164**	Punctuation	79–82, **162–164**
Language Expression		Capitalization and Punctuation	83, **164**
Usage	87–89, **166**, **167**	**Language Expression**	
Sentences	93–95, **168**, **169**	Usage	87–89, **166**, **167**
Sentence Combining	94, **169**	Sentence Forms	93–95, **168**, **169**
Paragraphs	96, 97, **170**	Sentence Parts	93–95, **168**, **169**
Organization	97, **170**	Sentence Combining	93–95, **168**, **169**
Math Computation		Paragraph Study	96, 97, **170**
Addition	122, 123, **179**	**Math Computation**	
Subtraction	124, 125, **179**	Addition	122, 123, **179**
Multiplication	126, 127, **180**	Subtraction	124, 125, **179**
Division	128, 129, **180**	Multiplication	126, 127, **180**
Math Concepts/Applications		Division	128, 129, **180**
Numeration	132, **182**	**Math Concepts/Applications**	
Number Sentences	133, **182**	Numeration	132, **182**
Number Theory	134, **183**	Geometry	136–140, **184**
Measurement	136–141, **184**	Measurement	136–141, **184**
Geometry	136–140, **184**	Problem Solving	142–147, **185–187**
Problem Solving	142–147, **185–187**	**Work-Study Skills**	
Work-Study Skills		Library/Dictionary Skills	112, **174**
Parts of a Book	114, 115, **175**	Index	115, **175**
Dictionary Skills	116, **176**	Outlines	117, **176**
		Maps/Graphs	120, 121, **178**

A Look at Skills Tested in ITBS

Third Edition Book C (6–8)		Fourth Edition Book 6 (6)	
Skill	**Page**	**Skill**	**Page**
Vocabulary		**Vocabulary**	
Synonyms	34, **149**	Vocabulary Skills	34–43, **149–153**
Reading Comprehension		**Reading Comprehension**	
Facts	45–69, **157**	Passages	45–69, **157**
Inferences	45–69, **157**	**Spelling**	
Generalizations	45–69, **157**	Spelling Skills	70–75, **158–160**
Spelling		**Language Arts**	
Spelling Skills	70–75, **158–160**	Capitalization and Punctuation	83, **164**
Language Mechanics		Usage and Expression	87–89, **166, 167**
Capitalization	76–78, **161–162**	Sentences	93–95, **168, 169**
Punctuation	79–82, **162–164**	Paragraphs	96, 97, **170**
Language Expression		**Math Computations**	
Usage	87–89, **166, 167**	Addition	122, 123, **179**
Correct Words	90, **167**	Subtraction	124, 125, **179**
Sentences	93–95, **168, 169**	Multiplication	126, 127, **180**
Paragraphs	96, 97, **170**	Division	128, 129, **180**
Math Computation		**Math Concepts/Applications**	
Addition	122, 123, **179**	Concepts/Estimation	132–135, **182, 183**
Subtraction	124, 125, **179**	Problem Solving	142–147, **185–187**
Multiplication	126, 127, **180**	Data Analysis	142–147, **185–187**
Division	128, 129, **180**	**Work-Study Skills**	
Fractions	122–129, **179, 180**	Dictionary/Guide Words	112, 116, **174, 176**
Decimals	122–129, **179, 180**	Key Terms	118, **177**
Math Concepts/Application		Maps	120, **178**
Numeration	132, **182**		
Number Sentences	133, **182**		
Whole Numbers/Integers	135, **183**		
Fractions	122–131, **179–181**		
Decimals/Percents	122–131, **179–181**		
Measurement	136–141, **184**		
Geometry	136–140, **184**		
Math Problem Solving			
Addition/Subtraction	142–147, **185–187**		
Multiplication/Division	142–147, **185–187**		
Multi–Step	142–147, **185–187**		
Work-Study Skills			
Maps	120, **178**		
Graphs/Tables	121, **178**		
Dictionary Skills	112, 113, **174**		
Index	115, **175**		
Reference Materials	112, **174**		

A Look at Skills Tested in ITBS

A Look at Skills Tested in MAT

Third Edition Book C (5–8)		Fourth Edition Book 6 (6)	
Skill	**Page**	**Skill**	**Page**
Vocabulary		**Vocabulary**	
Vocabulary Skills	34–43, **149–153**	Vocabulary Skills	34–43, **149–153**
		Multiple Meaning Words	38, 39, **151**
Reading Comprehension		**Reading Comprehension**	
Passages	45–69, **157**	Passages	45–69, **157**
Spelling		**Spelling**	
Spelling Skills	70–75, **158–160**	Spelling Skills	70–75, **158–160**
Language Mechanics		**Language Mechanics**	
Capitalization and Punctuation	83, **164**	Capitalization and Punctuation	83, **164**
Language Expression		**Language Expression**	
Usage	87–89, **166, 167**	Usage	87–89, **166, 167**
Grammar and Syntax	91, 92, **168**	Sentences	93–95, **168, 169**
Paragraphs	96, 97, **170**	Paragraphs	96, 97, **170**
Math Computation		**Math Computation**	
Addition	122, 123, **179**	Addition	122, 123, **179**
Subtraction	124, 125, **179**	Subtraction	124, 125, **179**
Multiplication	126, 127, **180**	Multiplication	126, 127, **180**
Division	128, 129, **180**	Division	128, 129, **180**
Fractions/Decimals	122–129, **179, 180**		
Math Concepts/Applications		**Math Concepts/Applications**	
Numeration	132, **182**	Concepts	132–135, **182, 183**
Geometry	136–140, **184**	Problem Solving	142–147, **185–187**
Measurement	136–141, **184**	**Work-Study Skills**	
Problem Solving	142–147, **185–187**	Using a Dictionary	112, 116, **174, 176**
Graphs and Charts	142–147, **185–187**		
Work-Study Skills			
Reference Sources	112, **174**		
Index	115, **175**		
Library Catalog Card	112, **174**		
Dictionary Skills	112, 116, **174, 176**		

A Look at Skills Tested in MAT

A Look at Skills Tested in NJ EWT

Grade 8

Skill	Page
Reading Comprehension	
Narrative Text	44–65, **154–157**
Informational Text	44–65, **154–157**
Persuasive/Argumentative Text	44–65, **154–157**
Everyday Text	44–65, **154–157**
Spelling	
Spelling Skills	70–75, **158–160**
Language Mechanics	
Capitalization and Punctuation	84, **165**
Language Expression	
Usage	87–89, **166, 167**
Sentence Completion	95, **169**
Sentence Construction	91–93, **168**
Transitions	98, **170**
Writing Tasks	
Solving a Problem	109, **173**
Cause and Effect	110, **173**
Opinion	111, **173**
Math Concepts/Applications	
Operations	122–131, **179–181**
Measurement	136–141, **184**
Geometry	136–140, **184**
Patterns and Relationships	142–146, **185–187**
Data Analysis	142–146, **185–187**
Pre–Algebra	147, **187**

A Look at Skills Tested in SAT/SAT 9

SAT Grade C (5–8)		SAT 9 Intermediate 3 Through Advanced 2 Fall, Grade 7—Spring, Grade 8	
Skill	**Page**	**Skill**	**Page**
Vocabulary		**Vocabulary**	
Word Meaning	36, **150**	Reading Vocabulary	34, 35, 37–43, 149,
Context Clues	40–42, 152, **153**	**151–153**	
Multiple Meaning Words	38, 39, **151**	**Reading Comprehension**	
Comprehension		Initial Understanding	45–69, **157**
Listening	44, **154**	Interpretation	45–69, **157**
Stories	45–69, **157**	Critical Analysis	45–69, **157**
Spelling		Reading Strategy	40–42, **152, 153**
Spelling Skills	70–75, **158–160**	Listening	44, **154**
Language Mechanics		**Writing Assessment**	
Capitalization	76–78, **161, 162**	Open–Ended Assessment	99–111, **171–173**
Punctuation	79–82, **162–164**	**Mathematics**	
Usage	87–89, **166, 167**	Problem Solving	142–147, **185–187**
Language Expression		Procedures	132–135, **182–183**
Sentence Structure	93–95, **168, 169**	**Spelling**	
Sentence Combining	94, **169**	Spelling Skills	70–75, **158–160**
Math Computation		**Language**	
Addition and Subtraction	122–125, **179**	Mechanics	76–83,**161–164**
Multiplication	126, 127, **180**	Expression	87–89, 93, 94, **166–169**
Division	128, 129, **180**	Organization	96, 97, **170**
Ratios and Percents	130, 131, **181**	**Study Skills**	
Math Concepts/Applications		Using Information	112, 114–116, 119, **174,**
Numeration	132, **182**	**175, 177**	
Number Theory	133, **182**	Resource Materials	112, 120, **174, 178**
Geometry	136–140, **184**	Outlining	117, **176**
Measurement	136–141, **184**	**Science**	
Problem Solving	142–147, **185–187**	Scientific Inquiry	45–47, **157**
Study Skills		Conceptual Understanding	45–47, 52, 53, **157**
Dictionary Skills	112, 116, **174, 176**	Life Science	45–47, 52, 53, **157**
Reference Skills	112, **174**	Physical Science	142, **185**
Library/Dictionary Skills	112, **174**	Earth–Space Science	64, 65, **157**
Reference Sources	112, **174**	**Social Science**	
Parts of a Book	114, 115, **175**	History	118, **177**
Outlines	117, **176**	Geography	120, **178**
		Civics	111, **173**

A Look at Skills Tested in TAAS

Grade 7		Grade 9	

Note: The TAAS (Texas Assessment of Academic Skills) Grade 9 Test is included here because it is usually given at the beginning of the ninth grade year as a pre-test to establish a baseline.

Word Analysis: Consonant and Vowel Sounds

Directions: Read the first word. Look for the word that does not have the same sound as the underlined part of the first word. Mark the answer space for your choice.

Samples

A. <u>sh</u>ape	friendship (A)	descent (B)	special (C)	relation (D)
B. f<u>or</u>tune	orchid (F)	oriental (G)	worthy (H)	portrait (J)

1. tou<u>gh</u>	telephone (A)	giraffe (B)	bright (C)	telegraph (D)
2. <u>ou</u>tcome	brownish (F)	flower (G)	brought (H)	fountain (J)
3. prea<u>ch</u>	chapter (A)	picture (B)	chasm (C)	rancher (D)
4. m<u>er</u>maid	circle (F)	burned (G)	heard (H)	terrify (J)
5. prin<u>c</u>iple	celebrate (A)	dedicate (B)	deceive (C)	except (D)
6. int<u>e</u>nd	cookie (F)	elephant (G)	carpet (H)	success (J)
7. <u>wh</u>ether	whistle (A)	wholly (B)	awhile (C)	whirlwind (D)
8. b<u>oo</u>kcase	moon (F)	would (G)	football (H)	precook (J)

Answers:

A Ⓐ Ⓑ Ⓒ Ⓓ   2 Ⓕ Ⓖ Ⓗ Ⓙ   5 Ⓐ Ⓑ Ⓒ Ⓓ   8 Ⓕ Ⓖ Ⓗ Ⓙ

B Ⓕ Ⓖ Ⓗ Ⓙ   3 Ⓐ Ⓑ Ⓒ Ⓓ   6 Ⓕ Ⓖ Ⓗ Ⓙ

1 Ⓐ Ⓑ Ⓒ Ⓓ   4 Ⓕ Ⓖ Ⓗ Ⓙ   7 Ⓐ Ⓑ Ⓒ Ⓓ

Word Analysis: Root Words and Affixes

Directions: Read the underlined word. Look for the root word or affix of the word. Mark the answer space for your choice.

Samples

A. readable	ad (A)	dab (B)	read (C)	able (D)
B. submarine	sub (F)	mar (G)	mari (H)	ine (J)

Look for the root word of the word that is underlined.

1. overdone	erd (A)	do (B)	done (C)	over (D)
2. frightful	rig (F)	right (G)	ful (H)	fright (J)

Look for the prefix of the word that is underlined.

3. preshrunk	runk (A)	shrunk (B)	pre (C)	pres (D)
4. television	tele (F)	vision (G)	sion (H)	levi (J)

Look for the suffix of the word that is underlined.

5. fearless	fea (A)	les (B)	ess (C)	less (D)
6. collection	on (F)	coll (G)	tion (H)	lect (J)

Answers:

A (A) (B) (C) (D)   1 (A) (B) (C) (D)   3 (A) (B) (C) (D)   5 (A) (B) (C) (D)

B (F) (G) (H) (J)   2 (F) (G) (H) (J)   4 (F) (G) (H) (J)   6 (F) (G) (H) (J)

Vocabulary: Synonyms

Directions: Read the phrase. Look for the word that has the same or almost the same meaning as the underlined word. Mark the answer space for your choice.

Samples

A. somber look
- (A) angry
- (B) surprised
- (C) yearning
- (D) melancholy

B. champion a cause
- (F) support
- (G) win
- (H) oppose
- (J) challenge

1. seek sanctuary
- (A) benefits
- (B) happiness
- (C) protection
- (D) directions

2. lasting amity
- (F) jealousy
- (G) friendship
- (H) hatred
- (J) indifference

3. heavy onus
- (A) burden
- (B) package
- (C) rain
- (D) clouds

4. sufficient ground
- (F) scanty
- (G) luxurious
- (H) unnecessary
- (J) enough

5. mischievous child
- (A) happy
- (B) impish
- (C) unfortunate
- (D) intelligent

6. was biased
- (F) impartial
- (G) prejudiced
- (H) sincere
- (J) negative

7. great potential
- (A) difficulty
- (B) promise
- (C) need
- (D) pleasure

8. quick response
- (F) answer
- (G) respect
- (H) agreement
- (J) repose

9. flimsy material
- (A) beautiful
- (B) expensive
- (C) ugly
- (D) weak

10. surprising clutter
- (F) neatness
- (G) organization
- (H) mess
- (J) decoration

Answers:
A (A) (B) (C) (D)   2 (F) (G) (H) (J)   5 (A) (B) (C) (D)   8 (F) (G) (H) (J)
B (F) (G) (H) (J)   3 (A) (B) (C) (D)   6 (F) (G) (H) (J)   9 (A) (B) (C) (D)
1 (A) (B) (C) (D)   4 (F) (G) (H) (J)   7 (A) (B) (C) (D)   10 (F) (G) (H) (J)

Vocabulary: Antonyms

Directions: Read the phrase. Look for the word that has the opposite meaning of the underlined word. Mark the answer space for your choice.

Samples

A.   bashful attitude
  (A) modest
  (B) bold
  (C) unpleasant
  (D) self-conscious

B.   become ecstatic
  (F) elated
  (G) comfortable
  (H) interested
  (J) miserable

1.   tropical weather
  (A) arid
  (B) monotonous
  (C) sweltering
  (D) steamy

6.   melodramatic performance
  (F) overemotional
  (G) theatrical
  (H) frightening
  (J) realistic

2.   absolutely tranquil
  (F) placid
  (G) beautiful
  (H) dedicated
  (J) hysterical

7.   counterfeit money
  (A) fake
  (B) real
  (C) extra
  (D) surplus

3.   finally eliminated
  (A) abolished
  (B) included
  (C) petrified
  (D) disregarded

8.   total triumph
  (F) success
  (G) victory
  (H) failure
  (J) labor

4.   adverse circumstances
  (F) neutral
  (G) troubling
  (H) fortunate
  (J) confusing

9.   agile movements
  (A) nimble
  (B) quick
  (C) secret
  (D) awkward

5.   acquire information
  (A) lose
  (B) gain
  (C) gather
  (D) organize

10.   professional athlete
  (F) amateur
  (G) successful
  (H) paid
  (J) individual

Answers:

A Ⓐ Ⓑ Ⓒ Ⓓ   2 Ⓕ Ⓖ Ⓗ Ⓙ   5 Ⓐ Ⓑ Ⓒ Ⓓ   8 Ⓕ Ⓖ Ⓗ Ⓙ

B Ⓕ Ⓖ Ⓗ Ⓙ   3 Ⓐ Ⓑ Ⓒ Ⓓ   6 Ⓕ Ⓖ Ⓗ Ⓙ   9 Ⓐ Ⓑ Ⓒ Ⓓ

1 Ⓐ Ⓑ Ⓒ Ⓓ   4 Ⓕ Ⓖ Ⓗ Ⓙ   7 Ⓐ Ⓑ Ⓒ Ⓓ   10 Ⓕ Ⓖ Ⓗ Ⓙ

Vocabulary: Word Meanings

Directions: Listen carefully as each question is read aloud. Then read along in your booklet as the answer choices are read aloud. Mark the answer space for your choice.

Samples

A.
- (A) rides
- (B) walks
- (C) drives
- (D) flies

B.
- (F) valuable
- (G) typical
- (H) radical
- (J) unique

1.
- (A) vegetable
- (B) animal
- (C) tree
- (D) metal

6.
- (F) special
- (G) irritated
- (H) calm
- (J) attractive

2.
- (F) perseverance
- (G) ability
- (H) independence
- (J) personality

7.
- (A) right
- (B) easy
- (C) fun
- (D) safe

3.
- (A) increase
- (B) decrease
- (C) intensify
- (D) cooperate

8.
- (F) close
- (G) suitable
- (H) friendly
- (J) cherished

4.
- (F) attic
- (G) clothing
- (H) gem
- (J) flower

9.
- (A) sweat
- (B) happen
- (C) end
- (D) breathe

5.
- (A) intelligent
- (B) wealthy
- (C) stubborn
- (D) polite

10.
- (F) crowd
- (G) majority
- (H) crusade
- (J) few

- -

Answers:

A Ⓐ Ⓑ Ⓒ Ⓓ	**2** Ⓕ Ⓖ Ⓗ Ⓙ	**5** Ⓐ Ⓑ Ⓒ Ⓓ	**8** Ⓕ Ⓖ Ⓗ Ⓙ
B Ⓕ Ⓖ Ⓗ Ⓙ	**3** Ⓐ Ⓑ Ⓒ Ⓓ	**6** Ⓕ Ⓖ Ⓗ Ⓙ	**9** Ⓐ Ⓑ Ⓒ Ⓓ
1 Ⓐ Ⓑ Ⓒ Ⓓ	**4** Ⓕ Ⓖ Ⓗ Ⓙ	**7** Ⓐ Ⓑ Ⓒ Ⓓ	**10** Ⓕ Ⓖ Ⓗ Ⓙ

Vocabulary: Affixes

Directions: Read the pair of words. Look for the word or words that best tell the meaning of the underlined affix. Mark the answer space for your choice.

Samples

A. <u>under</u>tow   <u>under</u>age

- (A) bottom
- (B) below
- (C) less than
- (D) equal to

B. sugar<u>less</u>   weight<u>less</u>

- (F) smaller
- (G) result of
- (H) without
- (J) enough

---

1. <u>il</u>literate   <u>il</u>legal

- (A) very
- (B) all
- (C) not
- (D) most

5. enchant<u>ment</u>   disappoint<u>ment</u>

- (A) state of being
- (B) possibility of
- (C) lack of any
- (D) tendency toward

---

2. <u>micro</u>scope   <u>micro</u>chip

- (F) very large
- (G) very small
- (H) very far
- (J) very near

6. cheer<u>ful</u>   wonder<u>ful</u>

- (F) more than one
- (G) relating to
- (H) full of
- (J) lack of any

---

3. <u>tele</u>phone   <u>tele</u>scope

- (A) useful
- (B) useless
- (C) from a star
- (D) at a distance

7. lov<u>able</u>   admir<u>able</u>

- (A) relating to
- (B) being worthy of
- (C) beforehand
- (D) later than

---

4. <u>super</u>colossal   <u>super</u>natural

- (F) best
- (G) worst
- (H) more than
- (J) less than

8. paint<u>er</u>   perform<u>er</u>

- (F) able to
- (G) unable to
- (H) away from
- (J) one who

Answers:

A (A) (B) (C) (D)   2 (F) (G) (H) (J)   5 (A) (B) (C) (D)   8 (F) (G) (H) (J)

B (F) (G) (H) (J)   3 (A) (B) (C) (D)   6 (F) (G) (H) (J)

1 (A) (B) (C) (D)   4 (F) (G) (H) (J)   7 (A) (B) (C) (D)

Vocabulary: Multiple Meanings

Directions: Read the pair of word meanings. Look for the word that agrees with both meanings. Mark the answer space for your choice.

Samples

A. to jump and a place to keep valuables

    (A) leap   (B) safe   (C) jump   (D) vault

B. to walk heavily and wood sawed into boards

    (F) slats   (G) lumber   (H) plod   (J) trudge

1. a place to learn and a group of fish

    (A) classroom   (B) school   (C) pod   (D) swarm

2. to slide by accident and a small piece of paper

    (F) fall   (G) stumble   (H) slip   (J) page

3. written information and to observe

    (A) bulletin   (B) look   (C) poster   (D) notice

4. a bed of flowers and to grow plants

    (F) plot   (G) farm   (H) garden   (J) raise

5. one's viewpoint and to tip at an angle

    (A) slant   (B) opinion   (C) lean   (D) judgment

6. a piece of ground and to plan in secret

    (F) scheme   (G) plot   (H) land   (J) yard

7. to move toward a goal and to smooth out wrinkles

    (A) iron   (B) push   (C) press   (D) flatten

8. a political group and a celebration

    (F) faction   (G) gathering   (H) gala   (J) party

Answers:

A (A) (B) (C) (D)   2 (F) (G) (H) (J)   5 (A) (B) (C) (D)   8 (F) (G) (H) (J)

B (F) (G) (H) (J)   3 (A) (B) (C) (D)   6 (F) (G) (H) (J)

1 (A) (B) (C) (D)   4 (F) (G) (H) (J)   7 (A) (B) (C) (D)

Vocabulary: Multiple Meanings

Directions: Read the pair of sentences. Find the word that fits in both blanks. Mark the answer space for your choice.

Samples

A. He left a_____to let his mother know where he was going.

The musician hit a wrong_____.

   (A) letter
   (B) tone
   (C) message
   (D) note

B. The_____was closed for a week after the fire.

I hope I_____this test.

   (F) road
   (G) pass
   (H) understand
   (J) forest

1. They will_____the best person to do the job.

Her neck got stiff from sitting in a cold_____.

   (A) hire
   (B) draft
   (C) find
   (D) breeze

2. She arranged a_____of peach blossoms in the vase.

He will_____the seeds with the hose.

   (F) bouquet
   (G) water
   (H) branch
   (J) spray

3. "This road is so bumpy it will_____your bones," he said.

The jam is in that tall_____.

   (A) shake
   (B) rattle
   (C) jar
   (D) container

4. Many people are very influenced by their_____group.

We saw him_____down the street to find out if the bus was coming.

   (F) age
   (G) look
   (H) peer
   (J) income

5. The young shepherd always_____the sheep.

He sometimes_____to overeat.

   (A) wants
   (B) tends
   (C) minds
   (D) inclines

6. The pirates will_____them on that lonely island.

She has a new_____sweater.

   (F) strands
   (G) purple
   (H) abandon
   (J) maroon

Answers: A (A)(B)(C)(D) 1 (A)(B)(C)(D) 3 (A)(B)(C)(D) 5 (A)(B)(C)(D)
B (F)(G)(H)(J) 2 (F)(G)(H)(J) 4 (F)(G)(H)(J) 6 (F)(G)(H)(J)

Vocabulary: In Context

Directions: Read each sentence. Use the other words in the sentence to help you figure out the meaning of the underlined words. Mark your answer choice below.

Samples

A. She looked so <u>woebegone</u> as she waved from the door that we had a hard time leaving. <u>Woebegone</u> means—

   (A) sad

   (B) angry

   (C) surprised

   (D) pleased

B. As the roller coaster car strained to reach the top of the rise, Anne gasped in <u>trepidation</u> of the long plunge down. <u>Trepidation</u> means—

   (F) hope

   (G) fear

   (H) memory

   (J) satisfaction

1. The emergency crew worked feverishly to <u>resuscitate</u> the child that they had pulled the pool. <u>Resuscitate</u> means—

   (A) rescue

   (B) find

   (C) revive

   (D) protect

4. Very few people travel far enough to visit such a <u>remote</u> village. <u>Remote</u> means—

   (F) poor

   (G) miserable

   (H) faraway

   (J) lovely

2. The villain's <u>malice</u> could be seen in his evil expression. <u>Malice</u> means—

   (F) affection

   (G) surprise

   (H) plot

   (J) hatred

5. His <u>gallant</u> action in the face of danger saved the lives of many people. <u>Gallant</u> means—

   (A) selfish

   (B) brave

   (C) regrettable

   (D) ridiculous

3. Her <u>affluence</u> was evident in her rich clothes and luxurious home. <u>Affluence</u> means—

   (A) wealth

   (B) education

   (C) intelligence

   (D) influence

6. The <u>monotonous</u> repetition made the job of sorting screws and nails almost unbearable. <u>Monotonous</u> means—

   (F) exciting

   (G) dull

   (H) lively

   (J) necessary

Answers:

A (A) (B) (C) (D) 1 (A) (B) (C) (D) 3 (A) (B) (C) (D) 5 (A) (B) (C) (D)

B (F) (G) (H) (J) 2 (F) (G) (H) (J) 4 (F) (G) (H) (J) 6 (F) (G) (H) (J)

Student Practice Page ——————— TS 152

Vocabulary: In Context

Directions: Read the sentence or paragraph. Look for the best word to use instead of the blank. Mark the answer space for your choice.

Samples

A. The temperature was below freezing. The dog was so wet and cold that his whole body_____.

  (A) cooled   (C) quivered
  (B) collapsed   (D) creaked

B. It was going to be a long day. Jack decided to_____himself by eating a really good breakfast.

  (F) fortify   (H) deceive
  (G) weaken   (J) dilute

1. "This is really important," said Margot. "If you_____my secret, I will never be able to forgive you."

  (A) ignore   (C) forget
  (B) reveal   (D) explain

2. The tourists in the museum all gasped in admiration. "That painting is_____!" they exclaimed.

  (F) large   (H) disgusting
  (G) tiny   (J) exquisite

3. The astronomer was excited as he used his new_____ for the first time to observe the comet.

  (A) microscope   (C) telescope
  (B) gyroscope   (D) stethoscope

4. "I cannot believe that your dog ate your homework again," said the teacher. "Your story is too_____."

  (F) interesting   (H) complicated
  (G) implausible   (J) shocking

5. The boys were overjoyed to smell the aroma of pizza when they opened the front door. They were_____after a day without food.

  (A) invigorated   (C) ravenous
  (B) challenged   (D) bursting

6. Instead of allowing one exception after another, our club decided to_____the rules to fit what we really do.

  (F) amend   (H) abandon
  (G) enforce   (J) tell

7. After she spilled water on the stickers, she found that they would not_____to the pages of her album.

  (A) collect   (C) press
  (B) adhere   (D) detach

8. "I cannot eat cooked parsnips," said Gail. "They are the one vegetable that I really_____!"

  (F) relish   (H) enjoy
  (G) abhor   (J) ignore

Answers: A Ⓐ Ⓑ Ⓒ Ⓓ   2 Ⓕ Ⓖ Ⓗ Ⓙ   5 Ⓐ Ⓑ Ⓒ Ⓓ   8 Ⓕ Ⓖ Ⓗ Ⓙ
B Ⓕ Ⓖ Ⓗ Ⓙ   3 Ⓐ Ⓑ Ⓒ Ⓓ   6 Ⓕ Ⓖ Ⓗ Ⓙ
1 Ⓐ Ⓑ Ⓒ Ⓓ   4 Ⓕ Ⓖ Ⓗ Ⓙ   7 Ⓐ Ⓑ Ⓒ Ⓓ

Vocabulary: In Context

Directions: Read the paragraph. Look for the best word to use in place of each of the numbered blanks. Mark the answer space for your choice.

Samples

After a great deal of discussion, Vivian's mother

gave her _____ to go to the movies with her friends.
                   A

Vivian planned to get home right on time to show her mother how

_____ she could be.
          B

A.		B.	
(A) permission		(F) disobedient	
(B) refusal		(G) friendly	
(C) reasons		(H) tardy	
(D) excuses		(J) responsible	

Scientists are still hoping to find some kind of _____ on Mars.
                                                        1

They are not expecting to _____ intelligent beings, however.
                                    2

They will be looking for _____ organisms that will prove that
                                3

life can develop somewhere other than _____ . Right now the
                                              4

_____ of Mars is done by _____ . Someday, perhaps,
          5   6

there will be manned flights to Mars.

1.		4.	
(A) buildings		(F) space	
(B) spaceships		(G) Mars	
(C) monsters		(H) Earth	
(D) life		(J) Venus	
2.		5.	
(F) discover		(A) settling	
(G) present		(B) exploration	
(H) educate		(C) exploitation	
(J) exterminate		(D) development	
3.		6.	
(A) huge		(F) robots	
(B) tiny		(G) people	
(C) dangerous		(H) aliens	
(D) colorful		(J) shuttles	

Answers: A Ⓐ Ⓑ Ⓒ Ⓓ   1 Ⓐ Ⓑ Ⓒ Ⓓ   3 Ⓐ Ⓑ Ⓒ Ⓓ   5 Ⓐ Ⓑ Ⓒ Ⓓ
          B Ⓕ Ⓖ Ⓗ Ⓙ   2 Ⓕ Ⓖ Ⓗ Ⓙ   4 Ⓕ Ⓖ Ⓗ Ⓙ   6 Ⓕ Ⓖ Ⓗ Ⓙ

Vocabulary: Derivations

Directions: Read each question. Fill in the answer space for the answer you think is correct.

Samples

A. Which of these words probably comes from the Latin word <u>imitāri</u> meaning <u>copy</u>?

 (A) imitate
 (B) immaculate
 (C) immature
 (D) immediate

B. Which of these words probably comes from the Hindi word <u>jangal</u> meaning <u>forest</u>?

 (F) janitor
 (G) January
 (H) jaunty
 (J) jungle

1. Which of these words probably comes from the French word <u>mirer</u> meaning <u>to be reflected</u>?

 (A) mire
 (B) mirth
 (C) mirage
 (D) merger

2. Which of these words probably comes from the Latin word <u>ornare</u> meaning <u>to adorn</u>?

 (F) ordinary
 (G) ornament
 (H) origin
 (J) ornery

3. Which of these words probably comes from the Spanish word <u>rancho</u> meaning <u>a farm</u>?

 (A) ranch
 (B) rancid
 (C) rancor
 (D) rank

4. Which of these words probably comes from the Middle English word <u>vanite</u> meaning <u>emptiness</u>?

 (F) vane
 (G) vanity
 (H) vandal
 (J) vantage

5. Which of these words probably comes from the Middle English word <u>senat</u> meaning <u>old</u>?

 (A) sandal
 (B) senor
 (C) sense
 (D) senate

6. Which of these words probably comes from the Tibetan word <u>yag</u> meaning <u>wild ox</u>?

 (F) yak
 (G) yam
 (H) yank
 (J) yap

Answers:
A (A) (B) (C) (D) 1 (A) (B) (C) (D) 3 (A) (B) (C) (D) 5 (A) (B) (C) (D)
B (F) (G) (H) (J) 2 (F) (G) (H) (J) 4 (F) (G) (H) (J) 6 (F) (G) (H) (J)

Reading Comprehension: Listening

Directions: Listen carefully as each story is read aloud. Then listen to each question. Read along in your booklet as the answer choices are read aloud. Fill in the circle for the best answer to each question.

Samples

A.

- (A) pulled on his knee pads
- (B) pulled on his elbow pads
- (C) laced up his rollerblades
- (D) put on his helmet

B.

- (F) ride a bike
- (G) skate
- (H) visit a friend
- (J) play ball

1.

- (A) Detroit City College
- (B) United Nations University
- (C) American University
- (D) The passage does not say.

6.

- (F) newspaper article
- (G) fictional story
- (H) letter
- (J) television news bulletin

2.

- (F) citizens of Michigan
- (G) other diplomats
- (H) people of the United States
- (J) people at the United Nations

7.

- (A) entertain
- (B) inform
- (C) describe
- (D) persuade

3.

- (A) spring
- (B) summer
- (C) fall
- (D) winter

8.

- (F) happy
- (G) eerie
- (H) triumphant
- (J) angry

4.

- (F) soil
- (G) rain
- (H) leaves
- (J) dew

9.

- (A) confused
- (B) confident
- (C) apathetic
- (D) patient

5.

- (A) The seeds came up.
- (B) The leaves spread out.
- (C) The flower buds formed.
- (D) A butterfly dropped down.

10.

- (F) Green Fields
- (G) Juan's Day in the Country
- (H) Alone at Last!
- (J) Where Am I?

Answers:

A (A) (B) (C) (D) **2** (F) (G) (H) (J) **5** (A) (B) (C) (D) **8** (F) (G) (H) (J)

B (F) (G) (H) (J) **3** (A) (B) (C) (D) **6** (F) (G) (H) (J) **9** (A) (B) (C) (D)

1 (A) (B) (C) (D) **4** (F) (G) (H) (J) **7** (A) (B) (C) (D) **10** (F) (G) (H) (J)

Reading Comprehension: Passages

Samples

Anthropology is the study of human beings. (*Anthropo* means humans and *logy* means study of.) It is concerned with all aspects of human development. Because of this broad approach, it is generally divided into two branches: cultural anthropology and physical anthropology.

Cultural anthropology is the study of people who are alive today, and it has traditionally focused on the societies of the world which have little (or at least less) technology. It is the study of the broad area of learned behavior occurring only among humans. A cultural anthropologist making a study of an Eskimo village, for example, would study clothing, food, religious practices, and a wide range of Eskimo behaviors.

Physical anthropology is the study of the biological features of humans. Physical anthropologists trace and follow the development of the bones and skulls that they find to put together the fascinating story of human variation and human development. Their study can include people who are alive today, but often it deals with people who lived and died long ago.

Because human beings are so complex, however, it is impossible to separate completely the subject matters of these two branches. The *biocultural* approach to anthropology, which combines the physical and the cultural features, offers the best overall look at human beings.

1. What is the topic of the selection?
    (A) cultural anthropology
    (B) physical anthropology
    (C) anthropology in general
    (D) anthropologists

2. Physical anthropology is concerned with . . .
    (F) all aspects of human development.
    (G) the history of human biology.
    (H) food and religious practices.
    (J) the broad area of learned behavior.

3. The author takes the position that it is impossible to completely separate physical and cultural anthropology because . . .
    (A) both branches deal with people who are alive today.
    (B) both branches deal with people who left only bones to study.
    (C) human beings are so complex.
    (D) human beings always have a culture.

4. The author's purpose in this passage is to . . .
    (F) establish a basis for considering both the physical and cultural branches of anthropology.
    (G) restrict the topic to just the physical aspects of anthropology.
    (H) restrict the topic to just the cultural aspects of anthropology.
    (J) propose an entirely new way of looking at the science of anthropology.

5. In this passage, the term *biocultural* means. . .
    (A) an approach that stresses the physical aspects of anthropology.
    (B) an approach that stresses the cultural aspects of anthropology.
    (C) a combination of the traditional and modern approaches to anthropology.
    (D) a combination of the physical and cultural approaches to anthropology.

Answers:

1 Ⓐ Ⓑ Ⓒ Ⓓ   4 Ⓕ Ⓖ Ⓗ Ⓙ
2 Ⓕ Ⓖ Ⓗ Ⓙ   5 Ⓐ Ⓑ Ⓒ Ⓓ
3 Ⓐ Ⓑ Ⓒ Ⓓ

Comprehension/Passages: Section One/Page 1

Directions: Read the passage and the questions that follow. Choose the best answer to each question and fill in the circle for your answer choice.

What exactly is memory? People talk about it all the time as if they know exactly what it is and what makes it work. People invent clever <u>mnemonic</u> (ne-mon-ic) devices to aid memory, and other people learn them. "<u>M</u>y <u>v</u>ery <u>e</u>legant <u>m</u>other <u>j</u>ust <u>s</u>erved <u>u</u>s <u>n</u>ine <u>p</u>izzas" is a mnemonic device for remembering the names of the nine planets of our solar system in order from the sun. Can you remember the names of the planets from the underlined letters in the words of this sentence? (They are <u>M</u>ercury, <u>V</u>enus, <u>E</u>arth, <u>M</u>ars, <u>J</u>upiter, <u>S</u>aturn, <u>U</u>ranus, <u>N</u>eptune, and <u>P</u>luto.) And tomorrow will you use the mnemonic device to remember the names of the planets or the names of the planets to recall the sentence making up the mnemonic device? Very often, unfortunately, the mnemonic device may be harder to remember than the original information.

A number of people have designed systems to help other people remember. You can look through the course catalogs of university extensions and community colleges and usually find at least one weekend course designed to help you improve your memory. Many of these courses are compilations of methods that have been used and tested for efficacy over a long period of time and have become accepted standards in the memory field. The person giving the course has simply pulled them all together and will deliver them to the students in a convenient and clever package. Some of the courses, however, are based on the inventions and/or research of the people presenting them and may or may not have any basis in science. Some of the people giving the courses may know a great deal about memory and about the brain. Others may just know a great deal about separating people from their money.

In view of these facts, what should you do if memory is a problem for you? It is probably a good idea to try the old-fashioned home remedies first because your memory is undoubtedly not as bad as you think it is. If you really had no memory, you would not be able to recognize your mother or your father or your own face in the mirror every morning!

People used to think that memorizing poems and famous sayings "trained" the memory. No one seems to really believe this anymore, but it can do no harm and will provide you with something with which to amuse yourself and others if you are ever trapped in an elevator during a long power failure.

Some people say you can help yourself remember names, for example, by learning <u>association techniques</u> that encourage you to connect one thing with another. A lady named Mrs. Trumpet might have a large nose. If you form a mental picture of this woman blowing her nose, say the association technique experts, the next time you see her, you will remember her name. However, unless you are very good at this technique, you may find yourself calling her "Mrs. Elephant," which will make both her and you extremely uncomfortable!

If all else fails, you can simply admit that you have a poor memory. You can say, "I'm so sorry, but I simply cannot remember names. Would you please tell me yours again?" and unless you are talking to the president of the United States, the person will probably understand. If you see the president often and this is a problem, you should probably take that memory class that begins on the last day of the month. Now, let's see:

> Thirty days hath September,
> April, June, and November.
> All the rest have thirty-one
> Except for February. . . .

GO→

Comprehension/Passages: Section 1/Page 2

1. This page could best be described as . . .

   (A) a scientific explanation of memory.
   (B) a light-hearted look at memory.
   (C) an explanation of how to overcome serious memory defects.
   (D) a justification for living with the effects of a poor memory.

2. Which of these statements from the passage is a fact?

   (F) Very often, unfortunately, the mnemonic device may be harder to remember than the original information.
   (G) It is probably a good idea to try the old-fashioned home remedies first because your memory is undoubtedly not as bad as you think it is.
   (H) Some people say you can help yourself remember names, for example, by learning *association techniques* that encourage you to connect one thing with another.
   (J) If you see the president often and this is a problem, you should probably take that memory class at the community college.

3. The statement "My very elegant mother just served us nine pizzas" was designed to help people remember . . .

   (A) the days of the week in order.
   (B) the months of the year in order.
   (C) the names and order of our solar system's planets.
   (D) the number of stars in the Milky Way.

4. Which is the last technique the author advises trying?

   (F) memorizing poems and sayings
   (G) learning association techniques
   (H) admitting you have a poor memory
   (J) taking a memory class

5. You can conclude from this passage that . . .

   (A) there are no absolutely certain cures for a poor memory.
   (B) most people are satisfied with their ability to remember.
   (C) scientists know at least one sure cure for a poor memory.
   (D) memorizing poetry is a good way to improve your memory.

6. What do you think would happen if a person lost his or her memory temporarily?

   (F) It would be easy to cope with everyday life.
   (G) It would be exciting to find out what had happened before.
   (H) It would be funny because no one would know what would happen next.
   (J) It would be scary because the person would not know who he or she was.

7. *Mnemonic* refers to something that . . .

   (A) helps or is designed to help the ability to remember.
   (B) is connected with a serious incurable illness.
   (C) has to do with a clever or interesting saying.
   (D) makes people forget the information they have learned.

8. In this passage, the term *association techniques* means . . .

   (F) ways of connecting one thing with another.
   (G) ways of forming clubs or other organizations.
   (H) useful things to know about forming friendships.
   (J) useful ways to handle people that you do not like.

GO→

Answers:

1 (A) (B) (C) (D)   4 (F) (G) (H) (J)   7 (A) (B) (C) (D)

2 (F) (G) (H) (J)   5 (A) (B) (C) (D)   8 (F) (G) (H) (J)

3 (A) (B) (C) (D)   6 (F) (G) (H) (J)

Comprehension/Passages: Section 1/Page 3

Directions: Read the passage and the questions that follow it. Choose the best answer to each question and fill in the circle for your answer choice.

"So how are we going to make the cafeteria look spooky?" Jack asked as he looked around at the huge empty room. "The Halloween Dance is just a few days away, and we don't even have one idea."

"Yes, we do," said Gloria crossly. "We have lots and lots of ideas. You just don't like any of them." She frowned at Jack. "We are part of the entertainment committee too, you know." She nodded at José and Bianca who nodded back. They all glared at Jack.

"They are dumb ideas," said Jack. "Who wants stupid old pumpkins and scarecrows? We told the Student Council that we would think of something really different for this dance."

"Then come up with an idea, Jack," said Bianca. "At least we have all made suggestions. You just keep saying you can't think of anything. That is no help at all."

"We could have a Ghost Dance," Jack said. "Everyone could wear a sheet and we could turn out all the lights and . . . ."

"You know Mr. McGuire won't let us do that," said José. "We have to have the lights on, and besides no one will want to wear a sheet."

"That's the truth, said Gloria. "I have a new dress that I want to wear. I'm not going to cover it up with a sheet!"

"I have a suggestion," Bianca said finally. "Let's go home now. Tonight, everyone think of one really good idea. Write it on a piece of paper but don't sign it. The ideas will be <u>anonymous</u>. Then tomorrow we will read all of the ideas and choose one of them."

After a certain amount of grumbling, the members of the entertainment committee picked up their books and went home to think and plan.

The next morning they slipped their written plans through the crack at the bottom of Bianca's locker. After school they met again in the deserted cafeteria.

"Here are our suggestions," said Bianca, laying a neat stack of folded papers on the table. "I asked Mrs. Murdoch in the computer lab to enter them and print them off so that we wouldn't know who wrote them. Shall we start? Let's each read one." Bianca unfolded the first computer print-out and began to read it aloud.

"I think we should have a Dress-Up Dance. We could all come dressed as the people we want to be when we grow up," read Bianca from the first piece of paper. "The decorations should be grown-up too. Nothing too scary or funny. Pumpkins, maybe, and stalks of corn."

Gloria unfolded her piece of paper. "I think we should have a Future Dance," she read. "We could all come dressed as the people we want to be when we grow up. The theme could be futuristic too. Nothing scary or funny. Signs, maybe, with the names of jobs and professions on them."

It was José's turn. He unfolded his piece of paper and read: "Let's have a Career Dance. We could all wear the clothes that would go with something we want to be when we grow up. We could have some great prizes too, like Most Authentic, Most Valuable, and Most Likely to Happen. We could have each person cast a vote."

Jack's turn came last. "I think everyone should dress up as the people they want to be in the future," he read. "We could decorate with spaceships and time machines and have some great games. We could ask everyone to invent a futuristic dance or dance move and have a contest for the best one."

GO→

Comprehension/Passages: Section 1/Page 4

The members of the entertainment committee looked at each other for a minute, suspiciously. Then they all started to laugh. "Well," said Jack. I guess we had a lot of ideas in common after all. What a great dance this is going to be!"

They got right to work. They asked the art teacher for strips of paper and poster paint so that they could decorate them with the names of possible careers. Some of the career names they chose were doctor, lawyer, teacher, computer programmer, dentist, meteorologist, anthropologist, coach, football player, actor, basketball player, baseball player, and musician. They got large appliance boxes from a local store and constructed a "Time Machine" and a "Spaceship." They posted signs around the school that said:

Come as What You Want to Be

Music/Prizes/Fun for All!

Friday, October 31

After School in the Cafeteria

They wrote fliers to send home and made enough copies for all of the homeroom classes. At the bottom of the fliers, they added a note asking parents to sign up to send, bring, and/or serve refreshments.

That Thursday afternoon all of the members of the committee stayed late after school. They had asked their parents and older brothers and sisters to join them when they finished school and work to help decorate the cafeteria.

"Too many cooks spoil the broth," laughed Bianca's mother as she bumped into José's father while they were both tacking up signs around the <u>perimeter</u> of the room.

"But many hands make light work," said Gloria's mother as she and Jack's mother put the finishing touches on the refreshment table.

"Don't look a gift horse in the mouth," advised Bianca's father when the committee discovered that one side of the box that they were going to use for the spaceship was broken. "Just turn the box over and use the other side."

"Right!" agreed Jack's father. "A bird in the hand is worth two in the bush!"

"This was so much fun," said Gloria.

"As much fun as the dance will be, probably," agreed Jack.

"Let's all go have hamburgers," suggested José.

"Oh, yes," Bianca agreed.

So they all went out for hamburgers and the parents had as much fun as the kids.

The next day at 2:45, the teachers excused the students fifteen minutes early so that they could all put on their costumes. At 3:00 the principal, who was dressed like Darth Vader, opened the doors of the cafeteria. One of the teachers, who was dressed as Mary Poppins, turned on the music. Jack's father, who was dressed like a football player, invited the students to start dancing. Bianca, who was dressed in a khaki shirt and shorts and carried a small plastic pick and a whisk broom, danced with José, who had a guitar slung over his shoulder. Gloria, who wore a skirt and sweater and carried some books, danced with Jack, who wore a white coat and had a stethoscope around his neck.

Everybody had a great time. When the dance was over, the entertainment committee stayed to help the clean-up committee because they wanted to make the afternoon last as long as possible. They threw away most of the decorations, but each one of the committee members kept one sign. Guess which signs the members of the entertainment committee kept.

GO→

Comprehension/Passages: Section 1/Page 5

9. The best title for this story would be . . .

    (A) Everybody Can Help.
    (B) Career Day.
    (C) The Halloween Dance.
    (D) Parent Participation.

10. The members of the entertainment committee asked their families for help because . . .

    (F) there was a lot to do and not much time.
    (G) they were not very good at their jobs.
    (H) they thought that their families did not have enough to do.
    (J) they wanted to be taken out to eat when the job was done.

11. How do the other committee members feel toward Jack at the beginning of this story?

    (A) supportive
    (B) irritated
    (C) sympathetic
    (D) agreeable

12. This story is about . . .

    (F) things that could not happen.
    (G) places that could not exist.
    (H) animals acting like people.
    (J) people who could be real.

13. By the end of the story, the students on the entertainment committee . . .

    (A) seem to dislike each other.
    (B) appear to be very good friends.
    (C) probably don't know each other very well.
    (D) have evidently never worked together before.

14. Which is the best summary of this story?

    (F) The entertainment committee finally agrees on a theme for the dance, gets busy and, with some help from their families, puts together a successful school event.
    (G) The entertainment committee wastes a great deal of time arguing about a theme for the Halloween dance but finally comes through.
    (H) The entertainment committee makes many beautiful signs for the dance including the names of careers such as doctor, lawyer, teacher, anthropologist, and football coach.
    (J) The parents of the students on the entertainment committee enjoy helping put up the decorations for the dance and then take the committee out to eat.

15. The members of the entertainment committee laughed after all of their suggestions had been read aloud because . . .

    (A) nothing had been solved after all.
    (B) they still had to make all kinds of decisions.
    (C) all of the suggestions were so much alike.
    (D) all of the suggestions were funny.

16. The most outspoken person on the entertainment committee is . . .

    (F) José.
    (G) Mr. McGuire.
    (H) Jack.
    (J) Gloria.

GO→

Answers:

9 (A) (B) (C) (D)   12 (F) (G) (H) (J)   15 (A) (B) (C) (D)

10 (F) (G) (H) (J)   13 (A) (B) (C) (D)   16 (F) (G) (H) (J)

11 (A) (B) (C) (D)   14 (F) (G) (H) (J)

Comprehension/Passages: Section 1/Page 6

17. Which of the parents' comments means that you should not be too critical of something that is given to you?

    (A) "Too many cooks spoil the broth."
    (B) "Many hands make light work."
    (C) "Don't look a gift horse in the mouth."
    (D) "A bird in the hand is worth two in the bush."

18. What is the mood at the end of the story?

    (F) happy
    (G) sad
    (H) angry
    (J) excited

19. What is the setting of most of this story?

    (A) a classroom
    (B) the school cafeteria
    (C) the student's homes
    (D) the art room

20. Which of these statements is true?

    (F) Jack and José both like to argue about everything.
    (G) Bianca's mother and José's father did not agree about where to put the decorations.
    (H) Bianca's and Jack's fathers agreed about using the broken box to make the spaceship.
    (J) All of the students were in agreement right from the start.

21. A committee is like . . .

    (A) a team.
    (B) a monarchy.
    (C) a dictatorship.
    (D) an individual.

22. The author's purpose in writing this story was probably to . . .

    (F) create a fantasy about some students in a school situation.
    (G) present a mystery situation for the reader to solve.
    (H) tell an entertaining realistic story about some students.
    (J) give step-by-step instructions for planning a school dance.

23. In this story the word anonymous means . . .

    (A) by a well known author.
    (B) by an unknown author.
    (C) well thought out.
    (D) really original.

24. In this story the word <u>perimeter</u> means . . .

    (F) the elevated stage in an auditorium.
    (G) the outer edge of a room.
    (H) the tallest walls of a room.
    (J) the hanging light fixtures.

Answers:

17 (A) (B) (C) (D)   20 (F) (G) (H) (J)   23 (A) (B) (C) (D)
18 (F) (G) (H) (J)   21 (A) (B) (C) (D)   24 (F) (G) (H) (J)
19 (A) (B) (C) (D)   22 (F) (G) (H) (J)

Comprehension/Passages: Section 2/Page 1

Directions: Read the passage and the questions that follow it. Choose the best answer to each question and fill in the circle for your answer choice.

A marsupial is a kind of mammal that carries its young in an external pouch. The kangaroo is probably the first marsupial that comes to mind, but there are a number of others. Most marsupials live in the Americas and Australia. The opossum is the only marsupial that lives in the United States.

The opossum ranges from Canada in the north all the way to Patagonia in South America. Opossums are interesting animals with long scaly tails by which they can hang from tree branches. The young are born before they are fully developed and are about the size of a honeybee at birth. An opossum stays in its mother's pouch for about two months and then clings to her back for several more weeks.

Other marsupials include the bandicoot, the cuscus, and the dasyure. The bandicoot lives in Australia and New Guinea, and the cuscus lives in New Guinea, Indonesia, and the northern tip of Australia. The dasyure lives in Australia. Bandicoots vary in size, but none of them are very large. The largest bandicoots are about the size of a rabbit, while the smallest are no larger than a mouse. Bandicoots have pouches that open at the bottom rather than at the top like other marsupials. The cuscus is about as big as a house cat. It is nocturnal and makes its home in trees. It has woolly fur everywhere except for the tip of its tail which is covered with coarse scales. The dasyure is a small, catlike marsupial. It has short legs and a long, bushy tail.

Two marsupials are native to Tasmania, an island south of Australia. These are the wombat and the Tasmanian devil. Wombats are compact little burrowing animals about three feet in length. They are vegetarians, leaving their burrows at night to feed on leaves, roots, and vegetables. Wombats are said to make good pets. Tasmanian devils, on the other hand, do not make good pets. They are savage animals that look something like small bears. They kill and eat other animals and have been made famous by the whirling, ferocious character in animated cartoons.

All of these animals are marsupials, but none of them is as well known as the kangaroo. Kangaroos are the animals people think of first when they think of animals with pouches. Kangaroos are native to Australia and come in all sizes. The smallest are called wallabies and are about the size of a rabbit. The largest, the great kangaroos, may grow to be seven feet tall and weigh 200 pounds. Fossils have been found that show that there were once kangaroos that were twice as big as any of the kinds that are living today.

A baby kangaroo is called a "joey." It is only about an inch long when it is born. It finds its own way into the mother's pouch where it stays and grows, sometimes for as long as six months.

Kangaroos are timid creatures. They live in groups called "mobs." They escape their enemies by bounding along on their powerful hind legs. Kangaroos are vegetarians. They have very sharp teeth and clip off and eat the grasses and herbs very close to the ground. This makes them a problem to stock raisers who have killed many of them.

All in all, marsupials are some of the most interesting animals that live on earth.

GO→

Comprehension/Passages: Section 2/Page 2

1. In general, this passage presents information about . . .

 (A) animals known as mammals.
 (B) different kinds of marsupials.
 (C) the animals of Australia.
 (D) different types of kangaroos.

2. Bandicoots are different from other marsupials in that . . .

 (F) they live only in Australia.
 (G) they are nocturnal animals.
 (H) their pouches open at the bottom.
 (J) their tails are tipped with scales.

3. The only marsupial native to the United States is the . . .

 (A) kangaroo.
 (B) koala.
 (C) wombat.
 (D) opossum.

4. Which of these statements from the passage is an opinion?

 (F) The young are born before they are fully developed and are about the size of a honeybee at birth.
 (G) The bandicoot lives in Australia and New Guinea, and the cuscus lives in New Guinea, Indonesia, and the northern tip of Australia.
 (H) All in all, marsupials are some of the most interesting animals that live on earth.
 (J) Fossils have been found that show that there were once kangaroos that were twice as big as any of the kinds that are living today.

5. This passage was written to . . .

 (A) explain why there are so few kinds of marsupials on the earth.
 (B) describe in brief the kinds of marsupials that are alive today.
 (C) persuade people to protect and preserve the remaining marsupials.
 (D) entertain the reader with descriptions of odd and interesting animals.

6. Why have stock raisers killed many of the kangaroos in Australia?

 (F) Kangaroos clip off the grasses and herbs very close to the ground which destroys the vegetation for other grazing animals.
 (G) Stock raisers around the world have always done whatever they could to exterminate wild animals.
 (H) Kangaroos are dangerous animals, and they use their powerful hind legs to destroy the animals belonging to the stock raisers.
 (J) Australia is a very small country, and the stock raisers must protect every bit of the range for their herds.

7. The word nocturnal means . . .

 (A) a tree dweller.
 (B) covered with fur.
 (C) active during the day.
 (D) active during the night.

8. The word ferocious means . . .

 (F) meat-eating.
 (G) fierce.
 (H) likable.
 (J) comical.

GO→

Answers:

1 (A) (B) (C) (D)   4 (F) (G) (H) (J)   7 (A) (B) (C) (D)

2 (F) (G) (H) (J)   5 (A) (B) (C) (D)   8 (F) (G) (H) (J)

3 (A) (B) (C) (D)   6 (F) (G) (H) (J)

Comprehension/Passages: Section 2/Page 3

Directions: Read the passage and the questions that follow it. Choose the best answer to each question and fill in the circle for your answer choice.

"I'm not so sure I like this," Tricia gasped as she stuck her head out of the tent flap and looked into the darkness that had settled down on the plain like a thick blanket. "Why did we enter that contest anyway!"

"Because we didn't think we would win?" ventured a timid voice just behind her. "I certainly have never won anything before." Myra, the owner of the timid voice, sank back on her sleeping bag and literally shook with fear.

"Oh, come on now, girls," said Caitlyn briskly. "It will all look different tomorrow in the daylight." She was brushing her hair in preparation for crawling under her own blankets. She shivered too, but only because the African night was as cold as it was dark.

Just then there was a loud roar outside of the tent—and then another and yet another. Andrew, the guide, called softly through the tent flap, waited for the shy invitation to enter, and stuck his head in. "Just lions, ladies," he said. "And not nearly as close as they sound. If they get a kill tonight, maybe tomorrow you will be able to see them as well as hear them. They will sleep all day in the sun."

"Oh goody!" said Tricia as Andrew's head disappeared. "I hate this. Whatever made me think I wanted to explore Africa? I wonder how Miss Dramble likes it. At least we aren't each in a tent by ourselves!"

The girls had entered a contest through their photography club at school. The first prize was an all-expenses-paid, completely chaperoned and equipped African photo safari for the winning team and their teacher. They had written an essay describing their desire to capture African wildlife on film, and they had won!

Their own pictures had appeared in the school newspaper, their hometown newspaper, and even the weekend edition of the newspaper published in the big city near their town. Their parents had been proud and not a little *apprehensive*. Their friends had been green with envy. Their teacher had been wild with excitement. And the girls themselves had been in shock and a little scared. Now they were not in shock anymore, but they were more than a little scared.

"Relax, everyone," said Caitlyn. "I'll admit I'm a little frightened too, but it really is like something right out of a movie. First, the long plane flight, and then that crazy airport, and our guides, and all the equipment, and then the long drive in the dark. Why, back home we would have given anything just to have all this great stuff. Just look at these new cameras they gave us, and now we aren't even thinking about them!"

Hearing that, Myra stopped shaking and sat up on her camp cot with her sleeping bag draped around her shoulders. "You are right, of course, Caitlyn. Hand me my camera, please. Maybe we should read about them and load them with film so we will be ready for the morning. The film and a lot of other stuff is in that box in the corner."

Myra and Caitlyn began to read about their new cameras and, after giving a long dramatic sigh, Tricia decided to join them. It was not long before the three girls, who all knew a lot about cameras and film, had loaded their cameras and felt comfortable with the gadgets and accessories that came with them. They had each been given a vest, too, with little pockets and handy clips. They filled these with extra film, light meters, and various kinds of lenses and laid them across the ends of their cots, ready for the morning. They also discussed what they would wear for their first day on safari, and, finally, they were almost ready to drop off to sleep.

GO→

Comprehension/Passages: Section 2/Page 4

"I'm not scared anymore," Myra announced before she closed her eyes. But soft breathing from the other cots was her only answer.

The girls awoke to the sound of a spoon banging on a pot. "Rise and shine, ladies," said Andrew outside of their tent. "Hot water and towels are on a tray right outside." The smell of coffee drifted in through the flap when the girls opened it to pull in the tray. They had a quick wash, slipped into their clothes, and rushed out into the morning.

"Welcome to the real Africa," said Andrew, pointing out across the valley. The sun had not been up for very long. Everything looked as if it had been dipped in gold. The land was covered with grasses of all colors from the palest yellow to the darkest green. Here and there were trees in bunches, rising from the morning mist along the wandering river. All around them in the distance there was a circular rim of purple mountain peaks. The valley where they stood had once been the enormous crater of an extinct volcano which had become a refuge for wild game and finally a *preserve*. It was the favorite *destination* in all of Africa for photo safaris.

Miss Dramble was already busy taking pictures. The girls joined her and took shot after shot as the sun rose higher and the colors changed before their eyes. Then, just pausing long enough to stuff themselves with a delicious breakfast, everyone piled into all-terrain vehicles and they set off across the grassland toward the distant river.

They stopped when they were still some distance from the river. While the safari crew set up a new campsite, Andrew prepared to take the girls and their teacher nearer to the water.

"Now, remember," he warned, "the car windows must stay rolled up. If the animals found out that these vehicles contained a free lunch, they could rip them open as easily as you take the wrapper off of a candy bar!"

"How incredibly graphic!" muttered Miss Dramble, checking all of the windows.

With each passenger assigned a personal, closed window, Andrew headed the vehicle toward the river. They were almost there when Tricia whispered hoarsely, "Lion on the right."

Andrew eased the vehicle to a stop. A huge lion lay only a few feet off of the faint trail that they were following. His mane was enormous. His tail flipped. He stared at the vehicle and then he . . . yawned. Miss Dramble and the girls all tried to smother their giggles long enough to get pictures of the lion with his mouth wide open. Then they collapsed with laughter.

When everyone, including Andrew, had stopped laughing, he started the vehicle but immediately stopped it again. A regular parade of elephants came out of the brush just beyond the lion and crossed right in front of them. There were seven adults with long tusks and, most exciting of all, there were two babies. The only sound in the vehicle was of the cameras clicking and film being wound. When the last elephant disappeared, Andrew started up the vehicle again.

"If we could just see a giraffe, I would be completely happy," said Myra. "They are definitely my favorite animals."

"Well, make sure your cameras are loaded, ladies," said Andrew. "We'll pull up by the river as near as we can get to the water hole where the animals drink. Maybe you'll get to see your giraffe."

"If not today, then tomorrow," said Caitlyn. "Today is just the first of five days and we haven't even had lunch yet, but we have seen a lion close up and a whole parade of elephants." Myra and Tricia nodded in agreement.

"You girls are great traveling companions," said Miss Dramble. "I don't think I'll ever again be satisfied to travel with adults."

GO→

Comprehension/Passages: Section 2/Page 5

9. A good title for this story might be . . .

   (A) The Elephant Parade.
   (B) Breakfast in the Bush.
   (C) Scared and Shaking.
   (D) On Photo Safari.

10. The girls in this story are apparently . . .

    (F) newly acquainted.
    (G) very good friends.
    (H) complete strangers.
    (J) unable to make friends.

11. The last thing that the girls did before going to sleep on their first night in Africa was . . .

    (A) read about their new cameras and all of the accessories.
    (B) load film into their cameras and look at all the gadgets.
    (C) discuss what they would wear the next day.
    (D) fill the handy pockets of their new vests.

12. Which is the best summary of this story?

    (F) Three girls win a photo safari to Africa for themselves and their teacher and begin their adventure by taking pictures of some wild animals.
    (G) Caitlyn tries to get her companions to stop feeling scared and to begin to enjoy their adventure in Africa with their guide, Andrew.
    (H) In the morning the sun turns every part of the African landscape to gold, and Miss Dramble and the girls try to capture it on film.
    (J) A parade of elephants comes out of the tall grass on one side of the road and crosses the faint trail right in front of their vehicle.

13. Caitlyn is willing to wait to see more animals because . . .

    (A) Myra and Tricia are still scared and waiting will give them time to adjust.
    (B) Miss Dramble has turned out to be a great traveling companion.
    (C) so many things have already happened before lunch on the first day.
    (D) she is finding the whole safari experience boring and dull.

14. The lion they saw was yawning because . . .

    (F) he had been up all night hunting and had eaten plenty.
    (G) he was hungry and did not have enough energy to get up.
    (H) it was still too early in the morning for him to be active.
    (J) he was bored with all of the photo safaris that wanted to take his picture.

15. What is the literal meaning of this sentence: "Everything looked as if it had been dipped in gold"?

    (A) The scenery was covered in gold paint that shone in the sun.
    (B) The light from the newly risen sun gave everything a yellow glow.
    (C) Thick yellowish dew dripped from all of the vegetation.
    (D) The entire landscape was a dull, heavy yellow color.

16. Which traveler is the most positive about the experience?

    (F) Miss Dramble
    (G) Myra
    (H) Tricia
    (J) Caitlyn

GO→

Answers: 9 Ⓐ Ⓑ Ⓒ Ⓓ   12 Ⓕ Ⓖ Ⓗ Ⓙ   15 Ⓐ Ⓑ Ⓒ Ⓓ
10 Ⓕ Ⓖ Ⓗ Ⓙ   13 Ⓐ Ⓑ Ⓒ Ⓓ   16 Ⓕ Ⓖ Ⓗ Ⓙ
11 Ⓐ Ⓑ Ⓒ Ⓓ   14 Ⓕ Ⓖ Ⓗ Ⓙ

Comprehension/Passages: Section 2/Page 6

17. The entire story takes place . . .

  (A) at a meeting of the photography club at the girls' school.

  (B) at night inside a tent pitched in an African valley.

  (C) in an African valley formed from the crater of an extinct volcano.

  (D) at a water hole where the local animals come to drink.

18. At the end of the story, Miss Dramble has decided that the girls are really great traveling companions because . . .

  (F) they sleep in their own tent and leave her alone.

  (G) they have such positive attitudes about their adventure.

  (H) it was their essay that won the trip for all of them.

  (J) they keep their cameras loaded and are always ready to take pictures.

19. A photo safari is most like . . .

  (A) a long hike.

  (B) a vacation.

  (C) a shopping excursion.

  (D) a field trip.

20. In the first few paragraphs of the story, the girls are feeling . . .

  (F) a little scared.

  (G) extremely excited.

  (H) very homesick.

  (J) tired and hungry.

21. This story is an example of . . .

  (A) science fiction.

  (B) historical fact.

  (C) realistic fiction.

  (D) pure fantasy.

22. What will probably happen next?

  (F) The girls and their teacher will take more pictures and then cut their trip short and go home early.

  (G) The girls and their teacher will continue to enjoy their adventure, see more animals, and take more pictures.

  (H) The lion lying near the trail will wake up, jump on the vehicle, and scare everyone.

  (J) The weather will get even hotter, causing the animals to become less active and go into hiding.

23. The word apprehensive means . . .

  (A) worried.

  (B) jealous.

  (C) enthusiastic.

  (D) sympathetic.

24. In this selection, the word preserve means . . .

  (F) a spread made from fruit cooked with sugar.

  (G) to save in a way that prevents change from taking place.

  (H) land set aside for the protection of endangered animals.

  (J) to set aside for later use in some emergency situation.

Answers:

17 Ⓐ Ⓑ Ⓒ Ⓓ	20 Ⓕ Ⓖ Ⓗ Ⓙ	23 Ⓐ Ⓑ Ⓒ Ⓓ
18 Ⓕ Ⓖ Ⓗ Ⓙ	21 Ⓐ Ⓑ Ⓒ Ⓓ	24 Ⓕ Ⓖ Ⓗ Ⓙ
19 Ⓐ Ⓑ Ⓒ Ⓓ	22 Ⓕ Ⓖ Ⓗ Ⓙ	

Comprehension/Passages: Section 3/Page 1

Directions: Read the passage and the questions that follow it. Choose the best answer to each question and fill in the circle for your answer choice.

The Maya are one of the most interesting of the advanced civilizations that had developed in the Americas before the Spanish conquerors arrived in the early 1500s. They lived in what are now the countries of Guatemala, Honduras, El Salvador, and parts of Mexico. Most of their territory was only 200 to 600 feet above sea level and was covered with dense tropical forest. At the height of the Mayan civilization, from the 300s to the 800s A.D., they may have reached a population of about 2,000,000 people.

Today many Mayan ruins still lie buried in the dense growth of the tropical jungles. Not many of their ruins have been excavated and studied, but what we have learned about them tells us a lot about how these people lived. We have learned, for example, that they knew a great deal about astronomy and had developed a complicated calendar based on their study of heavenly bodies. They had also developed an advanced form of writing and a system of arithmetic. Their architecture and art are known and admired around the world.

The Maya were short and stocky with round heads, black hair, and brown skin. The men wore long loincloths and the women wore long straight skirts. In cold weather they added blankets to their costumes for warmth. The clothes were often painted with designs and decorated with feathers. The common people lived in log huts that were scattered throughout the countryside and came to the cities when they had business there or to attend religious festivals. They grew and ate corn, beans, squash, sweet potatoes, and chili peppers. Their only domestic animal seems to have been the turkey. They kept bees for their honey.

The Maya built cities that were centers for religious festivals, markets, and government business, but as far as we know, no one lived there on a permanent basis. The temples, built on top of high stone pyramids, were the focus of <u>urban</u> activities. Only the priests mounted the steep stone steps to the tops of these pyramids; the people watched from below. The Maya practiced human sacrifice in these temples but not to the same extent as the Aztecs who lived near what is now Mexico City.

Government, science, and art were all in the hands of the Mayan priesthood. It is thought that each large city governed the region around it, somewhat in the manner of the Ancient Greek city-states. A group of priests governed each city-state and these city-states may have banded together in loose federations. The priests were mainly interested in time. They predicted eclipses and decided which days were favorable for everything from starting a war to planting crops. The arts were also connected to the Mayan religion, and elaborate carvings decorated everything. Painters extended their art to common objects such as pottery. It is interesting to note that there was no attempt to include shadow or <u>perspective</u> in art.

Almost every city had a ball court. These courts were rectangular, made of stone, and had a hoop on at least one end. The hoops were circles made of stone and were vertical rather than horizontal. We do not know much about the game that was played there, but it is likely that there was a religious significance.

During the 800s, the Maya abandoned their great cities one by one, letting them fall into ruin. No one knows why. In the 900s, a new civilization began to develop. It was heavily influenced by the Toltecs who lived north of Mexico City. This was the civilization that was discovered by the Spanish conquerors who invaded the territory in the 1500s.

GO→

Student Practice Page —————————————— | TS 157 |

Comprehension/Passages: Section 3/Page 2

1. This passage is mainly about . . .
   (A) the Mayan civilization from 300 to 800 A.D.
   (B) the Mayan civilization after the Spanish invasion in the 1500s A.D.
   (C) the Mayan civilization before 300 A.D.
   (D) the Mayan civilization after 900 A.D.

2. The Ancient Mayan civilization was governed by . . .
   (F) a group of common people.
   (G) the priesthood.
   (H) the Toltecs.
   (J) the Spanish.

3. Which of these sentences is an opinion?
   (A) The Mayan are one of the most interesting of the advanced civilizations that had developed in the Americas before the Spanish conquerors arrived in the early 1500s.
   (B) They lived in what are now the countries of Guatemala, Honduras, El Salvador, and parts of Mexico.
   (C) Most of their territory was only 200 to 600 feet above sea level and was covered with dense tropical forest.
   (D) At the height of the Mayan civilization, from the 300s to the 800s A.D., they may have reached a population of about 2,000,000 people.

4. This story was written to . . .
   (F) describe the Spanish conquest of the Maya.
   (G) explore the reasons that made the Maya abandon their cities.
   (H) give interesting facts about the Maya.
   (J) provide a description of the Mayan calendar.

5. Why do you suppose the common people lived outside of the large cities?
   (A) Living in the city was too expensive.
   (B) They were not interested in either science or art.
   (C) The priests found control easier when the people were outside of the cities.
   (D) The people were afraid that they might be sacrificed in the temple.

6. Which word best describes the part played by the common people during religious ceremonies in the temples?
   (F) participant
   (G) audience
   (H) celebrant
   (J) assistant

7. The word urban means . . .
   (A) having to do with religion.
   (B) having to do with government.
   (C) characteristic of the country.
   (D) characteristic of the city.

8. In this selection the word perspective refers to . . .
   (F) a specific point of view in understanding or judging things or events.
   (G) the ability to see things in a true relationship to one another.
   (H) the art of picturing things in a way that shows their relative distance or depth.
   (J) the relationship or proportion of the parts of a whole.

GO→

Answers: 1 (A) (B) (C) (D)   4 (F) (G) (H) (J)   7 (A) (B) (C) (D)
           2 (F) (G) (H) (J)   5 (A) (B) (C) (D)   8 (F) (G) (H) (J)
           3 (A) (B) (C) (D)   6 (F) (G) (H) (J)

Comprehension/Passages: Section 3/Page 3

Directions: Read the passage and the questions that follow it. Choose the best answer to each question and fill in the circle for your answer choice.

"I just can't take care of Jeffie again, Mom! I have to go to practice. They'll throw me off of the team if I keep missing so many practices." Joella brushed away some hot tears and looked at her mother, sitting slumped at the kitchen table, her head resting in her hands.

"I can't help it, Jo," her mother sighed. "I have to go to work, and I can't afford to pay for a sitter this week. Could you take him with you?"

"Take him with me! Take a baby to practice? Wheel him into the gym in his stroller? Change his diapers in the huddle? Burp him on the bench? They'd throw me off of the team for sure!" Joella glared at Jeffie who blew a bubble and grinned at her toothlessly.

"Please, Jo," said her mother. "Just try it. You're afraid they'll drop you anyway if you don't go. At least, if you took him, you'd be there."

"All right, all right, all right!" Joella groaned through clenched teeth. "I'll try it but, if they laugh at me, I'm staying home from school tomorrow." She picked up Jeffie, buckled him into his stroller, grabbed a bottle from the refrigerator, checked the diaper bag for supplies as she stuffed the bottle in, patted her mother on top of the head, and raced out the door.

The school was just a few blocks away. Joella ran most of the way, steering the stroller expertly. She slowed down once she reached the school grounds and almost turned around at the door of the gym. It was too late, however. The boys were just leaving their practice, and the gym door burst open.

"Look what Joella's got, " said Rick Glover, the captain of the boys' team. "Hey, Joella, is he your secret weapon? Are you girls going to finally win a game this week?" He laughed, but he reached over her head and held the heavy door open until both Joella and the stroller were safely inside.

"Joella, you are crazy!" said her best friend, Francie. "Coach Cramer, look what Joella brought to practice!"

"Good decision, Joella," Coach Cramer yelled from the other end of the floor. "We need you! Put the stroller between the bleachers so that the baby won't get hit with a ball."

Jeffie gurgled and waved his arms as the girls gathered around to smile and make faces at him. Then, as the balls flew up and down the gym and the girl's feet pounded, Jeffie fell asleep. He woke up during the team meeting at the end of practice. Joella scooped him up and gave him his bottle while the coach outlined the plays she planned to try at the next day's practice.

"Bring Jeffie again tomorrow if you can, Joella," said Coach Cramer finally. "He can be our <u>mascot</u>. Maybe he will bring us good luck. We certainly had a good practice today. Can I give you a ride home? It's dark out."

"No need, Coach," said a voice by the gym door. "I'll walk them home. I had to come back to get something I left in my locker." The voice belonged to Rick Glover. "Okay, Joella?" he asked. "You're on my way."

"Thanks, Rick," said Joella. "That will be easier than trying to fit the stroller in Coach Cramer's car." Joella tucked Jeffie's blankets around him, and they started to leave the gym. "See you tomorrow, everybody," she called back to the team. "Thanks for letting me bring Jeffie to practice."

GO→

Comprehension/Passages: Section 3/Page 4

Jeffie came to practice every day for the rest of the week. Joella's mother relaxed. Joella relaxed. And Jeffie seemed to actually sparkle. Every afternoon Rick "forgot" something in his locker so that he was there when it was time for Joella and Jeffie to walk home after dark.

The game they had been practicing for was scheduled for Friday evening. Joella's mother did not have to work so Joella was not responsible for Jeffie. But, when she arrived at the gym alone, everyone panicked. "Where's Jeffie?" they chorused. "We can't play without Jeffie! The coach saved two seats on the aisle right in back of the bench."

Joella panicked too. "I'll call my mother," she said and dashed for the pay phone in the lobby of the gym. The phone rang and rang. Her mother wasn't answering. Joella dragged herself back into the gym. The game started. Joella's team played hard, but they were down by two at the half.

Then, from out of the blue, Rick appeared with Joella's mother and Jeffie. "They were by the door," he said. "They didn't want to disturb anyone, and Joella's mother wasn't sure where to sit." He helped them get settled in the two seats that had been saved for them. Then he changed his mind and sat in one of the seats himself so that he could hold Jeffie up to see the action.

Joella and the other girls on the team were ecstatic. They gave a big cheer.

Two! Four! Six! Eight!

Who do we appreciate?

Jeffie! Jeffie!

RAY-AY-AY!

Jeffie waved his hands in the air and beamed. He bounced and wiggled. He liked this place with all the noise and the people who obviously loved him.

The second half began. Joella's team played like tigers. They passed, they faked, they shot, and they scored! Feet thudded up and down the floor. People yelled and cheered. Jeffie loved every minute of it. He waved his hands in the air and made baby noises along with the crowd. And then, in the last period with just a few seconds left to play, Joella sank a jump shot that won the game.

Joella's mother grabbed Jeffie so that Rick could jump up and down and yell, but Jeffie started to cry so Rick held him and they jumped up and down together.

After all of the yells and the handshakes were over, the girls came back to the bench. They patted Jeffie and cooed over him. The coach thanked Joella's mother for bringing him. "Can he keep coming to practices?" she asked. "He is our good luck charm, you know."

"And look at this," said Rick reaching into his pocket. "I got him a trophy." Rick produced a rattle shaped like a basketball. Jeffie took it and gurgled. Then he bopped Rick on the head with it and laughed. "He likes it," said Rick. "That must be a good sign!"

Joella's mother waited with Jeffie and Rick until the girls' team meeting was over. When Joella was ready to leave, Rick said, "Tonight I can walk all three of you home. Okay?"

Rick lifted Jeffie's stroller up the steps and saw them safely inside their door before he left. "What a nice boy he is," Joella's mother commented as she picked up Jeffie.

"I know," smiled Joella.

"And what a nice girl you are," her mother went on. "I'm so proud of you."

"I know," laughed Joella, giving her mother a hug. Jeffie just waved his new rattle.

GO→

Comprehension/Passages: Section 3/Page 5

9. Which one of these things happened last?

   (A) Joella called her mother from the gym.
   (B) Rick found Joella's mother and Jeffie.
   (C) Rick gave Jeffie a basketball rattle.
   (D) Joella's team won the basketball game.

10. The girls on Joella's basketball team panicked because . . .

    (F) Joella's mother did not answer the phone.
    (G) Joella's mother was not sure where to sit.
    (H) They were down by two points at the half.
    (J) Joella arrived at the game without Jeffie.

11. Which word best describes the relationship between Joella and her mother?

    (A) one-sided
    (B) loving
    (C) cold
    (D) demanding

12. Which is the best summary of this story?

    (F) Joella's baby-sitting responsibilities turn into good luck when Jeffie is adopted as the team mascot and Rick decides to befriend both of them.
    (G) Joella tells her mother that she is afraid that the team will drop her because of her baby-sitting responsibilities.
    (H) Joella loves Jeffie but she does not want to take him to basketball practice because she is afraid everyone will make fun of her.
    (J) Joella is embarrassed when members of the boys' basketball team see her enter the gym with Jeffie in a stroller.

13. "And Jeffie seemed to actually sparkle" means . . .

    (A) Jeffie looked as if he were covered with glitter.
    (B) Jeffie had a bright, cheerful expression.
    (C) Jeffie's face reflected the lights in the gym.
    (D) Jeffie's smile came and went rapidly.

14. A good description of Rick might be . . .

    (F) helpful and kind.
    (G) conceited and self-absorbed.
    (H) violent and angry.
    (J) nervous and upset.

15. At the beginning of this story, Joella's mother seems to be . . .

    (A) happy.
    (B) depressed.
    (C) angry.
    (D) frantic.

16. Why do you suppose Joella's mother stood by the door when she brought Jeffie to the game?

    (F) She thought Jeffie might not last through the whole game, and she wanted to be able to get him out quickly if he started to cry.
    (G) She was not sure where she and Jeffie should sit.
    (H) She wanted to see Joella play but was not sure if Joella wanted Jeffie to be there after she had taken care of him all week.
    (J) The gymnasium was crowded and it was hard to maneuver the stroller to get to the bleachers.

GO→

Answers: 9 Ⓐ Ⓑ Ⓒ Ⓓ   12 Ⓕ Ⓖ Ⓗ Ⓙ   15 Ⓐ Ⓑ Ⓒ Ⓓ
          10 Ⓕ Ⓖ Ⓗ Ⓙ   13 Ⓐ Ⓑ Ⓒ Ⓓ   16 Ⓕ Ⓖ Ⓗ Ⓙ
          11 Ⓐ Ⓑ Ⓒ Ⓓ   14 Ⓕ Ⓖ Ⓗ Ⓙ

Comprehension/Passages: Section 3/Page 6

17. At the end of this story, the setting is . . .

   (A) inside of the school gym.
   (B) outside of the school gym.
   (C) outside of Joella's house.
   (D) inside of Joella's house.

18. At the end of this story, the mood is . . .

   (F) sad.
   (G) happy.
   (H) anxious.
   (J) angry.

19. This story is an example of . . .

   (A) science fiction.
   (B) historical fact.
   (C) realistic fiction.
   (D) pure fantasy.

20. Because there is a goal at each end of the playing area, basketball is most like . . .

   (F) baseball.
   (G) football.
   (H) figure skating.
   (J) track.

21. When basketball season is over, Joella and Rick will probably . . .

   (A) remain good friends.
   (B) dislike each other.
   (C) ignore each other.
   (D) talk about each other.

22. A good title for this story would be . . .

   (F) Rick Glover, Basketball Star.
   (G) The Girl's Basketball Team.
   (H) How Jeffie Helped Joella.
   (J) Joella and her Mother.

23. The word *mascot* means . . .

   (A) something adopted as a good luck symbol for a team.
   (B) something used to distract the other team from winning.
   (C) cheerleader.
   (D) flag waver.

24. The word *ecstatic* means . . .

   (F) miserable.
   (G) delighted.
   (H) hysterical.
   (J) depressed.

Answers:

17 (A) (B) (C) (D)   20 (F) (G) (H) (J)   23 (A) (B) (C) (D)

18 (F) (G) (H) (J)   21 (A) (B) (C) (D)   24 (F) (G) (H) (J)

19 (A) (B) (C) (D)   22 (F) (G) (H) (J)

Comprehension/Passages: Section 4/Page 1

Directions: Read the passage and the questions that follow it. Choose the best answer to each question and fill in the circle for your answer choice.

"Gem" is the name given to all of the minerals and stones that are used for jewelry and other ornamental purposes. Several gems are not stones: the pearl is obtained from the oyster, amber is <u>fossilized</u> resin, coral consists of the skeletons of tiny sea animals, and jet is fossilized coal.

Gems are identified by characteristics such as the shape of the crystals before they are cut, the color, the index of refraction, the hardness, the specific gravity, and so on.

The shape of the crystals in any one kind of gem mineral is always the same. Diamonds, for example, have eight triangular sides, forming a double pyramid.

The color of a gem, besides helping to identify it, contributes greatly to its beauty. The color can be the result of the color of the mineral itself or the result of the impurity in the mineral.

The index of refraction measures the speed at which light travels through a substance. The higher the index of refraction, the greater the luster and brilliance of the stone. When a diamond is properly cut, the gem will display bright flashes of color.

The hardness of a gem is important to its quality because the harder it is, the longer it will last. The diamond is the hardest substance in nature.

The specific gravity of a mineral is its weight in comparison to an equal amount of pure water. Diamonds have a specific gravity of 3.52. They weigh a little more than $3\frac{1}{2}$ times an equal amount of water.

Different kinds of gems are found in different parts of the world. The underlying rock largely determines the gems that will be found in a particular place. Emeralds, for example, are found where ancient rocks have been exposed by erosion. Diamonds are found in more recently molten rocks. Climate, too, may be a factor. Opal and turquoise are found in Australia and the American Southwest, areas where there is very little rainfall.

The value of gems is determined by their hardness, color, brilliance, rarity, and the extent to which they are in demand. Diamonds are the most valuable of the gems because of their hardness and brilliance. Rubies and sapphires have about the same degree of hardness, but rubies are more valuable because they are more rare. Emeralds are almost as valuable as diamonds. Pearls are graded in value by size, color, and shape.

One of the most famous gems in the world is the *Koh-i-noor* diamond. It was presented to Queen Victoria of England in 1850 by the East India Company. Another famous diamond is the 530 carat *Star of Africa*. It is part of the crown jewels of England and is set in the royal scepter. At one time it was part of the *Cullinan* diamond which originally weighed $1\frac{1}{3}$ pounds but was then cut into stones of various sizes.

Because gems are rare, they are very expensive. Many people who would like to own and wear real gems cannot afford to buy them, so there is a great market for artificial gems. These are often made from a soft glass called paste which is very brilliant but scratches easily. *Synthetic* gems are also produced in the laboratory. None of these substitutes are as good or as valuable as the real thing, however. People who really love gems want the real thing!

GO→

Comprehension/Passages: Section 4/Page 2

1. This selection is mainly about . . .

  (A) the minerals and stones that are used for jewelry and other ornamental purposes.

  (B) the specific gravity of minerals as compared to the weight of water.

  (C) the different kinds of gems found in different parts of the world.

  (D) the 530 carat diamond known as the *Star of Africa*.

2. The hardness of a gem is important because . . .

  (F) hardness determines the color of the gem.

  (G) hardness determines the speed at which light travels through the gem.

  (H) the harder it is, the longer it will last.

  (J) the harder it is, the more it will weigh.

3. Coral consists of . . .

  (A) resin that has become fossilized.

  (B) the skeletons of tiny sea animals.

  (C) deposits that form inside of oysters.

  (D) minerals and stones used for jewelry.

4. If a huge deposit of large diamonds were found somewhere in the world . . .

  (F) the value of diamonds would remain the same.

  (G) the value of diamonds would increase because more people could own one.

  (H) the value of diamonds would decrease because they would not be as rare.

  (J) the value of diamonds would go up on the world market.

5. Which sentence from the selection is an opinion?

  (A) "Gem" is the name given to all of the minerals and stones that are used for jewelry and other ornamental purposes.

  (B) The color can be the result of the color of the mineral itself or the result of an impurity in the mineral.

  (C) The color of a gem, besides helping to identify it, contributes greatly to its beauty.

  (D) The index of refraction measures the speed at which light travels through a substance.

6. An artificial gem is most like . . .

  (F) an artificial leg.

  (G) an artificial flower.

  (H) artificial light.

  (J) artificial intelligence.

7. The word *fossilized* means . . .

  (A) something in which the living cells have been replaced by minerals.

  (B) something that died a long, long time ago.

  (C) a substance that has existed since the time of the dinosaurs.

  (D) something we know about because they left prints in old rocks.

8. The word *synthetic* means . . .

  (F) occurring naturally.

  (G) very rare.

  (H) very common.

  (J) man-made.

GO→

- -

Answers:

1 (A) (B) (C) (D) 4 (F) (G) (H) (J) 7 (A) (B) (C) (D)

2 (F) (G) (H) (J) 5 (A) (B) (C) (D) 8 (F) (G) (H) (J)

3 (A) (B) (C) (D) 6 (F) (G) (H) (J)

Comprehension/Passages: Section 4/Page 3

Directions: Read the passage and the questions that follow it. Choose the best answer to each question and fill in the circle for your answer choice.

The spaceships were flying in a huge formation that blocked out the stars as far as the eye could see. Vyan raced from port to port around the circumference of the ship and looked in all directions. Nothing but more ships. He leaned his head against the thick, transparent plastic and sighed. He had wanted just one more real glimpse of Earth, but since that seemed to be impossible, he gave in and went to the viewing theater that had been set up in the hub of the ship.

Vyan slipped into one of the few vacant seats. On the screen on the left side of the theater, he could see Earth becoming smaller and smaller. On the screen to the right, he would soon be able to watch Mars growing bigger and bigger. Many days had already passed, and many more would pass before they reached their destination.

"And then what?" Vyan wondered. He thought about all of the things that he had been taught while they had waited for the space fleet to be built.

After the landing, they would all stay in the ships while the cadre of construction workers and engineers built and inflated the domes that would hold their atmosphere.

The agricultural experts would deal with the oxygen-producing plants that they had brought with them. They would leave most of them in their space containers while they experimented with the growing conditions of the Martian soil.

Another group of engineers would drill for the water that scientists believed was hidden in deep natural wells beneath the surface of the planet.

If everything went according to this plan, then they would all walk out of the spaceships and begin their lives on Mars. If, by a certain date, the plants had not grown and no hidden reservoirs of water had been found, then the second plan would need to be inaugurated. The specialists would all get back into the ships, and they would go to their alternative destination, one of the moons of Jupiter.

Vyan took a deep breath and one more look at Earth up on the screen. He had almost decided to make this look his last. At this moment, he was fairly sure that he did not want to watch Earth being demolished by the enormous asteroid that was hurtling toward it on a collision course.

Since the scientists had seen this asteroid coming toward Earth before Vyan was born, he had known about it all of his life. He had been made aware of and taught about the scenario that would take place as the asteroid started to exert its gravitational pull on the Earth. He knew that mountain ranges would rise up and oceans would be pulled out of their ancient beds long before the asteroid actually collided with his home planet. He knew that there would be destruction and fire until Earth's atmosphere had been pulled away and fire could no longer burn because there would be no oxygen to feed it. Right now, he felt that he did not want to watch this happen.

A bell rang softly through the ship, and Vyan joined the others as they left the theater and walked toward the huge dining hall. He picked up his boxed dinner and carried it to the table where he usually sat with a few of his friends.

"Are you all right, Vyan?" asked Brianna. "We missed you in class this afternoon. We had a guest speaker from the main ship. She talked about the landing."

GO→

Comprehension/Passages: Section 4/Page 4

"I went to the theater to have another look at Earth," Vyan admitted. "I keep saying I'll never look again, and then I go right back."

"We all do," Rykk assured him. "I was there too. I saw you slip in."

"Soon more of our cameras will be turned on Mars, and we will watch it getting closer and closer," said Quin. "I prefer to take a more optimistic view of our lives. We are the new pioneers, you know."

Vyan, Brianna, and Rykk looked at their friend and laughed sheepishly. "Okay, Quin," said Vyan. "We'll try it your way. Let's all think positively for awhile and see if we feel better."

The ships had landed without any mishaps. They covered a huge area of the red Martian surface. The crews were out doing their specialized jobs. The people who were not involved in the setup of the domes, the planting of the oxygen-producing vegetation, and the drilling for water spent their time anxiously watching the video screens in the theater.

On one screen Earth, which looked just like a star to the naked eye, was brought close by the powerful telescopic lenses that were trained on it. Earth's moon had already been vaporized by the asteroid, and the planet now had a ring around it where the moon's orbit had been. Then during one viewing period, Earth seemed to explode and rock in its orbit. The next day it was still there, but it did not look blue anymore. Some people in the theater looked shaken and unhappy. With a finality that seemed symbolic, someone turned off the Earth screen.

"The atmosphere is gone," whispered Quin. "We can never go back now."

"But we can start over," said Vyan. "Remember your positive attitude."

Just then the other screen, the one showing the Martian surface, lit up. It showed a gusher of water bursting from the surface. People in helmets raced around, capping the geyser, attaching the pipes that were already in place. A reservoir was waiting to catch and store the water, and a system of sprinklers started to water the newly planted, oxygen-producing vegetation.

That night there was a party in every spaceship. Plans were made to send everyone out to visit the surface. The people who were in charge of building houses began to organize their equipment. People who had been living in dormitories began to reorganize themselves into family groups. Everyone was happy and excited.

Life on Mars had settled down to a routine. One evening there was a party for old friends from the different ships. Vyan, Brianna, Rykk, and Quin were at the same one, of course. They ate and sang and danced and talked over their adventures.

"Well," said Quin. "Was I right or what?"

"Yes, you were," said Vyan. "But it doesn't hurt to remember sometimes.

And they all looked up at the bright spark that had been their Earth.

GO→

Comprehension/Passages: Section 4/Page 5

9. This story is mainly about . . .

   (A) the destruction of the Earth.
   (B) leaving Earth to colonize Mars.
   (C) the discovery of a new asteroid.
   (D) the growth of a friendship.

10. This story is an example of . . .

   (F) science fiction.
   (G) historical fact.
   (H) realistic fiction.
   (J) pure fantasy.

11. Which one of these things happened <u>last</u>?

   (A) That night there was a party in every spaceship.
   (B) A gusher of water burst from the surface.
   (C) The screen showing the Martian surface lit up.
   (D) People in helmets raced around, capping the geyser.

12. Which word best describes Vyan's feelings in the first part of the story?

   (F) excited
   (G) happy
   (H) homesick
   (J) angry

13. What kind of relationship do the four friends have?

   (A) competitive
   (B) cooperative
   (C) critical
   (D) supportive

14. Why was the geyser of water so exciting?

   (F) It meant that Earth would not be destroyed.
   (G) It meant that they could all go home again.
   (H) It meant that Mars could support life.
   (J) It meant that they would have to find another planet.

15. Why did people begin to reorganize themselves into family groups after water was found?

   (A) They knew that families would get the best houses.
   (B) They were tired of the other people on the ship.
   (C) They felt that life might soon be almost normal again.
   (D) They were afraid that they might become separated.

16. The "naked eye" refers to . . .

   (F) people who did not wear glasses.
   (G) people who had lost their glasses.
   (H) vision unaided by a telescope.
   (J) vision unaided by sunglasses.

GO→

Answers: 9 (A)(B)(C)(D) 12 (F)(G)(H)(J) 15 (A)(B)(C)(D)
10 (F)(G)(H)(J) 13 (A)(B)(C)(D) 16 (F)(G)(H)(J)
11 (A)(B)(C)(D) 14 (F)(G)(H)(J)

Comprehension/Passages: Section 4/Page 6

17. The best word to describe Quin is . . .

   (A) pessimistic.
   (B) futuristic.
   (C) optimistic.
   (D) idealistic.

18. The setting for most of this story is . . .

   (F) Earth.
   (G) Mars.
   (H) a time capsule.
   (J) a large spaceship.

19. The author's purpose in writing this story was probably . . .

   (A) to instruct.
   (B) to entertain.
   (C) to persuade.
   (D) to inform.

20. The spaceship was most like . . .

   (F) a cruise ship.
   (G) a submarine.
   (H) a lifeboat.
   (J) a destroyer.

21. Which is the best summary of this story?

   (A) Knowing that Earth would be destroyed by a giant asteroid, a large part of the population sets out to settle on Mars.
   (B) Filled with a sense of excitement, explorers from Earth set out to colonize the solar system.
   (C) Because they are lonely, four people meet and make friends on a spaceship headed for Mars.
   (D) Because of their scientific knowledge, four young people are asked to explore Mars for deposits of water.

22. The mood at the end of this story could be described as . . .

   (F) completely happy.
   (G) totally sad.
   (H) bittersweet.
   (J) ecstatic.

23. The word *cadre* means . . .

   (A) a large group of general workers.
   (B) a key group of special personnel.
   (C) an apprentice group.
   (D) an expendable group.

24. The word *inaugurated* means . . .

   (F) begun.
   (G) concluded.
   (H) considered.
   (J) ended.

Answers: 17 (A) (B) (C) (D)   20 (F) (G) (H) (J)   23 (A) (B) (C) (D)
           18 (F) (G) (H) (J)   21 (A) (B) (C) (D)   24 (F) (G) (H) (J)
           19 (A) (B) (C) (D)   22 (F) (G) (H) (J)

Spelling Skills (CAT/CTBS)

Directions: Read the sentence. Look for the correct spelling of the word that belongs in the sentence. Mark the answer space for your choice.

Samples

A. We thought that the new situation comedy was___.
- (A) hillarious
- (B) hilarious
- (C) hilerious
- (D) hilareous

B. My mother wants the new issue of that___.
- (F) magezine
- (G) maggazine
- (H) magazine
- (J) magasine

1. Please excuse the___.
- (A) interruption
- (B) interuption
- (C) intteruption
- (D) interrupshun

5. They took a ride in a___.
- (A) hellicopter
- (B) helicopter
- (C) heliocopter
- (D) helikopter

2. We were bothered by___at summer camp.
- (F) musquitoes
- (G) mosquitows
- (H) mosquitoes
- (J) moscutioes

6. There was a lot of___when our school won the game.
- (F) excitement
- (G) exsitement
- (H) excitment
- (J) exitement

3. Valentine's Day is always in___.
- (A) february
- (B) February
- (C) Febuary
- (D) Febbuary

7. Their___was terrible to see.
- (A) dissapointment
- (B) dissappointment
- (C) disappointment
- (D) disappointmente

4. We could hear the cheers from the___.
- (F) jymanasium
- (G) jimnasium
- (H) gimnasium
- (J) gymnasium

8. Don't forget to go over and___the other team.
- (F) congratulate
- (G) congrachulate
- (H) congrachulate
- (J) congratulait

Answers:

A Ⓐ Ⓑ Ⓒ Ⓓ   2 Ⓕ Ⓖ Ⓗ Ⓙ   5 Ⓐ Ⓑ Ⓒ Ⓓ   8 Ⓕ Ⓖ Ⓗ Ⓙ

B Ⓕ Ⓖ Ⓗ Ⓙ   3 Ⓐ Ⓑ Ⓒ Ⓓ   6 Ⓕ Ⓖ Ⓗ Ⓙ

1 Ⓐ Ⓑ Ⓒ Ⓓ   4 Ⓕ Ⓖ Ⓗ Ⓙ   7 Ⓐ Ⓑ Ⓒ Ⓓ

Spelling Skills (CAT/CTBS)

Directions: Read the phrases. Look for the underlined word in each set that is spelled incorrectly. Mark the answer space for your choice.

Samples

A.
- (A) <u>humorous</u> story
- (B) long <u>journy</u>
- (C) <u>inconsiderate</u> act
- (D) state <u>legislature</u>

B.
- (F) interesting <u>labratory</u>
- (G) situation <u>comedy</u>
- (H) <u>enormous</u> elephant
- (J) <u>accurate</u> measurement

1.
- (A) stomach <u>ache</u>
- (B) <u>background</u> noise
- (C) <u>benificial</u> climate
- (D) strict <u>budget</u>

2.
- (F) <u>cactus</u> flower
- (G) <u>automatic</u> garage door
- (H) thorough <u>analisys</u>
- (J) great <u>sympathy</u>

3.
- (A) national <u>symbol</u>
- (B) <u>treacherous</u> trail
- (C) <u>tropical</u> climate
- (D) modern <u>tecnology</u>

4.
- (F) original <u>receipt</u>
- (G) <u>speach</u> impediment
- (H) <u>spicy</u> food
- (J) usual <u>route</u>

5.
- (A) new <u>neighborhood</u>
- (B) <u>prairie</u> dogs
- (C) <u>oppossite</u> side
- (D) regular <u>procedure</u>

6.
- (F) <u>multipal</u> injuries
- (G) <u>perpetual</u> worry
- (H) folded <u>napkin</u>
- (J) new <u>publication</u>

7.
- (A) correct <u>pronounciation</u>
- (B) thick <u>pamphlet</u>
- (C) <u>narrow</u> staircase
- (D) <u>numerous</u> accidents

8.
- (F) large <u>profit</u>
- (G) <u>possable</u> reward
- (H) important <u>occasion</u>
- (J) <u>parallel</u> lines

9.
- (A) good <u>landmark</u>
- (B) <u>metal</u> spoon
- (C) busy <u>interseccion</u>
- (D) <u>liquid</u> measurement

10.
- (F) held <u>hostage</u>
- (G) bad <u>grammar</u>
- (H) fall <u>folliage</u>
- (J) lost <u>civilization</u>

Answers:
A Ⓐ Ⓑ Ⓒ Ⓓ 2 Ⓕ Ⓖ Ⓗ Ⓙ 5 Ⓐ Ⓑ Ⓒ Ⓓ 8 Ⓕ Ⓖ Ⓗ Ⓙ
B Ⓕ Ⓖ Ⓗ Ⓙ 3 Ⓐ Ⓑ Ⓒ Ⓓ 6 Ⓕ Ⓖ Ⓗ Ⓙ 9 Ⓐ Ⓑ Ⓒ Ⓓ
1 Ⓐ Ⓑ Ⓒ Ⓓ 4 Ⓕ Ⓖ Ⓗ Ⓙ 7 Ⓐ Ⓑ Ⓒ Ⓓ 10 Ⓕ Ⓖ Ⓗ Ⓙ

Student Practice Page

Spelling Skills (ITBS)

Directions: Read the words in each item and look for a spelling mistake. Mark your answer choice below. If you do not find a mistake, mark answer space 5.

Samples

A.
(1) maximum
(2) meeger
(3) kindergarten
(4) kangaroo
(5) no mistake

B.
(1) foreign
(2) evaporate
(3) fascination
(4) frontier
(5) no mistake

1.
(1) celery
(2) courteous
(3) embarass
(4) editorial
(5) no mistake

6.
(1) diagnose
(2) development
(3) emblum
(4) emphatic
(5) no mistake

2.
(1) barbeque
(2) boulder
(3) bulletin
(4) biscuit
(5) no mistake

7.
(1) undecided
(2) underwater
(3) unexpected
(4) unfinished
(5) no mistake

3.
(1) tough
(2) trolley
(3) tomatoe
(4) torpedo
(5) no mistake

8.
(1) weight
(2) villain
(3) yacth
(4) useless
(5) no mistake

4.
(1) volcano
(2) referrence
(3) political
(4) quarrel
(5) no mistake

9.
(1) opportunitys
(2) possession
(3) orchard
(4) obscure
(5) no mistake

5.
(1) procession
(2) plentiful
(3) principle
(4) pleged
(5) no mistake

10.
(1) institution
(2) moisture
(3) inferno
(4) merchandise
(5) no mistake

Answers:
A ① ② ③ ④ ⑤   2 ① ② ③ ④ ⑤   5 ① ② ③ ④ ⑤   8 ① ② ③ ④ ⑤
B ① ② ③ ④ ⑤   3 ① ② ③ ④ ⑤   6 ① ② ③ ④ ⑤   9 ① ② ③ ④ ⑤
1 ① ② ③ ④ ⑤   4 ① ② ③ ④ ⑤   7 ① ② ③ ④ ⑤   10 ① ② ③ ④ ⑤

72

Spelling Skills (SAT)

Directions: Look at each set of four words. Fill in the answer circle for the word that is not spelled correctly.

Samples

A.
- (A) individual
- (B) lavendar
- (C) minute
- (D) horrified

B.
- (F) infirmary
- (G) equator
- (H) gravity
- (J) mellody

1.
- (A) fortell
- (B) formation
- (C) formerly
- (D) forfeits

6.
- (F) frequent
- (G) frontier
- (H) firey
- (J) fundamentally

2.
- (F) dependent
- (G) destruction
- (H) desended
- (J) detection

7.
- (A) continent
- (B) convinse
- (C) community
- (D) conspicuous

3.
- (A) competative
- (B) dissatisfied
- (C) encourage
- (D) focus

8.
- (F) greivance
- (G) fortress
- (H) exterior
- (J) decorate

4.
- (F) iilusion
- (G) imajination
- (H) difference
- (J) duplicate

9.
- (A) bargain
- (B) calendar
- (C) doornobb
- (D) employees

5.
- (A) editorial
- (B) customer
- (C) directer
- (D) boredom

10.
- (F) avalanch
- (G) borrower
- (H) sequence
- (J) soldiers

Answers:

A (A) (B) (C) (D)	2 (F) (G) (H) (J)	5 (A) (B) (C) (D)	8 (F) (G) (H) (J)
B (F) (G) (H) (J)	3 (A) (B) (C) (D)	6 (F) (G) (H) (J)	9 (A) (B) (C) (D)
1 (A) (B) (C) (D)	4 (F) (G) (H) (J)	7 (A) (B) (C) (D)	10 (F) (G) (H) (J)

Spelling Skills (SAT)

Directions: Read each set of phrases. Look at the word that is underlined in each phrase. One of the underlined words is spelled incorrectly for the way it is used in the phrase. Find the word that is spelled incorrectly. Fill in the circle for your answer choice.

Samples

A.
  - (A) the <u>hole</u> thing
  - (B) a pitiful <u>whine</u>
  - (C) <u>pale</u> as a ghost
  - (D) a beautiful <u>rose</u>

B.
  - (F) a <u>knew</u> teacher
  - (G) the shy <u>doe</u>
  - (H) the sun's <u>rays</u>
  - (J) a bushy <u>tail</u>

1.
  - (A) the tropical <u>isle</u>
  - (B) a two-for-a-dollar <u>sail</u>
  - (C) one <u>for</u> all
  - (D) <u>close</u> the door

6.
  - (F) turn <u>right</u> here
  - (G) <u>one</u> the game
  - (H) calm <u>seas</u>
  - (J) <u>whether</u> or not

2.
  - (F) don't <u>waste</u> paper
  - (G) a grassy <u>plain</u>
  - (H) down the <u>aisle</u>
  - (J) <u>wear</u> is he

7.
  - (A) the <u>meat</u> market
  - (B) birds <u>sore</u>
  - (C) <u>rode</u> a horse
  - (D) whether or <u>not</u>

3.
  - (A) <u>weigh</u> the oranges
  - (B) a <u>week</u> foundation
  - (C) put it <u>there</u>
  - (D) find the <u>sum</u>

8.
  - (F) it might <u>break</u>
  - (G) please <u>be</u> careful
  - (H) climb the <u>stares</u>
  - (J) a starry <u>night</u>

4.
  - (F) the wind <u>blue</u>
  - (G) a <u>pair</u> of socks
  - (H) the mountain <u>peak</u>
  - (J) <u>through</u> the door

9.
  - (A) did you <u>see</u>
  - (B) <u>heard</u> the bell
  - (C) a long thin <u>tail</u>
  - (D) <u>tide</u> the score

5.
  - (A) common <u>sense</u>
  - (B) the lead <u>roll</u>
  - (C) <u>too</u> much candy
  - (D) all <u>grown</u> up

10.
  - (F) <u>wood</u> help them
  - (G) <u>threw</u> the ball
  - (H) <u>rows</u> of houses
  - (J) a faulty <u>brake</u>

- -

Answers:

A Ⓐ Ⓑ Ⓒ Ⓓ   2 Ⓕ Ⓖ Ⓗ Ⓙ   5 Ⓐ Ⓑ Ⓒ Ⓓ   8 Ⓕ Ⓖ Ⓗ Ⓙ

B Ⓕ Ⓖ Ⓗ Ⓙ   3 Ⓐ Ⓑ Ⓒ Ⓓ   6 Ⓕ Ⓖ Ⓗ Ⓙ   9 Ⓐ Ⓑ Ⓒ Ⓓ

1 Ⓐ Ⓑ Ⓒ Ⓓ   4 Ⓕ Ⓖ Ⓗ Ⓙ   7 Ⓐ Ⓑ Ⓒ Ⓓ   10 Ⓕ Ⓖ Ⓗ Ⓙ

Spelling Skills (MAT)

Directions: Read the sentence carefully. Fill in the circle for any word that is misspelled. If all the words are correct, fill in the circle for no mistake.

Samples

A. The <u>assinment</u> <u>required</u> unfamiliar <u>strategies</u>. <u>no mistake</u>
      A   B   C   D

B. <u>Steaks</u> and <u>hamburgers</u> can both be <u>barbecued</u>. <u>no mistake</u>
    E   F   G   H

---

1. The <u>animation</u> in that <u>motion</u> picture was <u>briliant</u>. <u>no mistake</u>
    A   B   C   D

2. He gave a <u>breif</u> summary of the <u>materials</u> we <u>studied</u>. <u>no mistake</u>
    E   F   G   H

3. A large <u>audiance</u> <u>attended</u> the <u>lecture</u>. <u>no mistake</u>
    A   B   C   D

4. She <u>approached</u> the <u>experiment</u> with <u>curiosity</u>. <u>no mistake</u>
    E   F   G   H

5. The <u>surgeon</u> <u>explaned</u> the <u>operation</u> to our class. <u>no mistake</u>
    A   B   C   D

6. <u>Mysterious</u> things <u>offen</u> <u>occur</u> in fiction. <u>no mistake</u>
    E   F   G   H

7. He <u>apologized</u> for his <u>behavior</u> during the <u>discusion</u>. <u>no mistake</u>
    A   B   C   D

8. The <u>clinic</u> was his <u>introduction</u> to <u>medical</u> practice. <u>no mistake</u>
    E   F   G   H

Answers:
A Ⓐ Ⓑ Ⓒ Ⓓ 2 Ⓔ Ⓕ Ⓖ Ⓗ 5 Ⓐ Ⓑ Ⓒ Ⓓ 8 Ⓔ Ⓕ Ⓖ Ⓗ
B Ⓔ Ⓕ Ⓖ Ⓗ 3 Ⓐ Ⓑ Ⓒ Ⓓ 6 Ⓔ Ⓕ Ⓖ Ⓗ
1 Ⓐ Ⓑ Ⓒ Ⓓ 4 Ⓔ Ⓕ Ⓖ Ⓗ 7 Ⓐ Ⓑ Ⓒ Ⓓ

Language Mechanics: Capitalization (CAT/CTBS)

Directions: Read the sentence. Look for the sentence part that contains a word that should begin with a capital letter. Mark the answer space for your choice. Mark the answer space for "none" if no other capital letter is needed.

Samples

A. My uncle | recently moved to | Tampa bay in Florida | where he has a house. | none
   A | B | C | D | E

B. "Have you seen | that great new | Disney movie?" | Laurie asked Fred. | none
   F | G | H | J | K

1. If you can | help me on saturday | I will be glad to | help you on Sunday. | none
   A | B | C | D | E

2. The state | of washington shares | a border with | Canada. | none
   F | G | H | J | K

3. We visited | the state capital | with mr. Davis, | our history teacher. | none
   A | B | C | D | E

4. The last basket | in the championship game | was shot | by richard. | none
   F | G | H | J | K

5. Last semester | we selected | the little Mermaid for | our class play. | none
   A | B | C | D | E

6. My brother | Fred and i | like to play | football at the park. | none
   F | G | H | J | K

7. When I told Jane | we could be there, | she exclaimed, | "oh, good!" | none
   A | B | C | D | E

8. last month | we enjoyed | an interesting visit | to the observatory. | none
   F | G | H | J | K

Answers:
A (A)(B)(C)(D)(E) 2 (F)(G)(H)(J)(K) 5 (A)(B)(C)(D)(E) 8 (F)(G)(H)(J)(K)
B (F)(G)(H)(J)(K) 3 (A)(B)(C)(D)(E) 6 (F)(G)(H)(J)(K)
1 (A)(B)(C)(D)(E) 4 (F)(G)(H)(J)(K) 7 (A)(B)(C)(D)(E)

Language Mechanics: Capitalization (ITBS)

Directions: Read each item and look for a capitalization mistake. In the answer rows below, mark the answer space for the number of the line with the mistake. If you do not find a mistake, mark answer space 4.

Samples

A.
(1) My sister Ellen is practicing for
(2) a dance recital. she rehearses for
(3) two hours every evening.
(4) **no mistakes**

B.
(1) Mr. Jenkins teaches arts and
(2) crafts every summer at Camp Fun-
(3) in-the-Sun.
(4) **no mistakes**

1.
(1) My Aunt Betty and Uncle Edward
(2) raise cotton. They own many acres
(3) of farmland in georgia.
(4) **no mistakes**

6.
(1) The kangaroo is an animal
(2) which is often associated with
(3) the australian continent.
(4) **no mistakes**

2.
(1) Tip yelled to his brother, "look
(2) out for that car coming down the
(3) hill behind you!"
(4) **no mistakes**

7.
(1) John Wayne airport in Southern
(2) California was named after a well-
(3) known movie star.
(4) **no mistakes**

3.
(1) After a spring rain the deserts
(2) bloom with thousands of wildflowers,
3) such as buttercups and poppies.
4) **no mistakes**

8.
(1) The Civil war, which was fought
(2) in the 1860s, was a tragic event in our
(3) country's history.
(4) **no mistakes**

4.
1) Switzerland has three official
(2) languages. People speak German,
(3) French, and Italian.
(4) **no mistakes**

9.
(1) The fourth of July is my favorite
(2) holiday because we celebrate it by
(3) setting off fireworks.
(4) **no mistakes**

5.
(1) The statue of Liberty was a gift
(2) to this country from the people of
(3) France.
(4) **no mistakes**

10.
(1) My grandmother and grandfather live
(2) in Wisconsin, but they met in Arizona
(3) where grandpa Dave was working.
(4) **no mistakes**

- -

Answers:

A ① ② ③ ④   2 ① ② ③ ④   5 ① ② ③ ④   8 ① ② ③ ④
B ① ② ③ ④   3 ① ② ③ ④   6 ① ② ③ ④   9 ① ② ③ ④
1 ① ② ③ ④   4 ① ② ③ ④   7 ① ② ③ ④   10 ① ② ③ ④

Language Mechanics: Capitalization (SAT)

Directions: Read each sentence. Choose the correct way to capitalize the word or group of words that go in the blank. Fill in the answer space for your choice.

Samples

A. Our teacher is from_____.

- (A) south dakota
- (B) South Dakota
- (C) south Dakota
- (D) South dakota

B. My mother read a poem called ____.

- (F) "Yesterday's flowers."
- (G) "yesterday's Flowers."
- (H) "yesterday's flowers."
- (J) "Yesterday's Flowers."

1. The teacher said,_____

- (A) "Please line up, Students."
- (B) "please line up, students."
- (C) "please line up, Students."
- (D) "Please line up, students."

5. Treasure Island was written by_____.

- (A) R. L. Stevenson
- (B) R. l. Stevenson
- (C) r. l. Stevenson
- (D) r. l. stevenson

2. This letter is from_____Gore.

- (F) Vice president
- (G) vice President
- (H) vice president
- (J) Vice President

6. To reach Alaska she must go_____.

- (F) North, then West
- (G) north, then West
- (H) North, then west
- (J) north, then west

3. The country fair will open on_____.

- (A) Saturday, July 8
- (B) Saturday, july 8
- (C) saturday, July 8
- (D) saturday, july 8

7. Mario's family lives in_____.

- (A) South america
- (B) South America
- (C) south america
- (D) south America

4. We saw many fossils at the_____

- (F) County Museum
- (G) County museum
- (H) county museum
- (J) county Museum

8. There are millions of stars in the_____.

- (F) Milky Way
- (G) milky Way
- (H) Milky way
- (J) milky way

Answers:
A Ⓐ Ⓑ Ⓒ Ⓓ 2 Ⓕ Ⓖ Ⓗ Ⓙ 5 Ⓐ Ⓑ Ⓒ Ⓓ 8 Ⓕ Ⓖ Ⓗ Ⓙ
B Ⓕ Ⓖ Ⓗ Ⓙ 3 Ⓐ Ⓑ Ⓒ Ⓓ 6 Ⓕ Ⓖ Ⓗ Ⓙ
1 Ⓐ Ⓑ Ⓒ Ⓓ 4 Ⓕ Ⓖ Ⓗ Ⓙ 7 Ⓐ Ⓑ Ⓒ Ⓓ

Language Mechanics: Punctuation (CAT/CTBS)

Directions: Read the sentence. Look for the punctuation mark that belongs in the sentence. Mark the answer space for your choice. Mark the space for "none" if no other punctuation mark is needed.

Samples

A.   My mother served hamburgers potato salad, and corn on the cob for dinner.

   (A) .   (B) ,   (C) ;   (D) "   (E) none

B.   I felt like laughing when I saw the mess, but I managed to control myself.

   (F) ?   (G) :   (H) ,   (J) .   (K) none

---

1.   "Do you understand the play?" asked the coach

   (A) "   (B) .   (C) :   (D) ;   (E) none

2.   What are you going to do with all of the newspapers you collected?

   (F) ,   (G) !   (H) "   (J) .   (K) none

3.   Lillian likes to swim in the ocean but Kelly would rather swim in a pool.

   (A) .   (B) ,   (C) ;   (D) ?   (E) none

4.   "Get out of the street" yelled the crossing guard.

   (F) ;   (G) "   (H) .   (J) !   (K) none

5.   Madeline would you collect the homework for me, please?

   (A) .   (B) ,   (C) ;   (D) :   (E) none

6.   July 4 1997, fell on a Friday.

   (F) ,   (G) ;   (H) "   (J) :   (K) none

7.   "When the sun comes out, said Jill, "we can play in the park."

   (A) .   (B) ,   (C) "   (D) :   (E) none

8.   Did you remember to turn out the kitchen light

   (F) "   (G) .   (H) ,   (J) ?   (K) none

Answers: A (A)(B)(C)(D)(E) 2 (F)(G)(H)(J)(K) 5 (A)(B)(C)(D)(E) 8 (F)(G)(H)(J)(K)
   B (F)(G)(H)(J)(K) 3 (A)(B)(C)(D)(E) 6 (F)(G)(H)(J)(K)
   1 (A)(B)(C)(D)(E) 4 (F)(G)(H)(J)(K) 7 (A)(B)(C)(D)(E)

Language Mechanics: Punctuation (CAT/CTBS)

Directions: Read the sentence. Look for the correct punctuation for the underlined part. Mark the answer space for your choice. Mark the space for "correct as it is" if no other punctuation is needed.

Samples

A. <u>Mrs. Johnson, our favorite teacher will</u> go on the field trip with us.

  (A) Mrs. Johnson our favorite teacher will
  (B) Mrs. Johnson, our favorite teacher, will
  (C) Mrs. Johnson our favorite teacher, will
  (D) Mrs. Johnson, our favorite teacher will,
  (E) correct as it is

B. <u>"We're sold out," said</u> the clerk at the ticket window.

  (F) We're sold out, said
  (G) "We're sold out." said
  (H) "We're sold out" said
  (J) We're sold out: said
  (K) correct as it is

---

1. It was <u>Mr. Brown the football coach,</u> who said we played a good game.

  (A) Mr. Brown, the football coach
  (B) Mr. Brown: the football coach
  (C) Mr. Brown, the football coach,
  (D) Mr. Brown: the football coach!
  (E) correct as it is

4. "I need a piece of paper and a <u>pencil, said</u> Jo, "if I'm going to keep score."

  (F) pencil, "said
  (G) pencil," said
  (H) pencil! said
  (J) pencil" said
  (K) correct as it is

---

2. These are the things that you need to make a chalk <u>mural chalk</u>, water, and a wall.

  (F) mural, chalk,
  (G) mural: chalk,
  (H) mural, chalk:
  (J) mural, "chalks
  (K) correct as it is

5. The batter needs <u>to chill, so put</u> it in the refrigerator for an hour.

  (A) to chill so, put
  (B) to chill so put,
  (C) to chill! so, put
  (D) to chill, so put,
  (E) correct as it is

---

3. Bob will prepare the sandwiches for the <u>party and, Jerry</u> will make the punch.

  (A) party: and Jerry
  (B) party? and Jerry
  (C) party and, Jerry
  (D) party, and Jerry
  (E) correct as it is

6. "Which continent has the smallest area, Australia or <u>Europe" Ben</u> asked.

  (F) Europe?" Ben
  (G) Europe," Ben
  (H) Europe." Ben
  (J) Europe? Ben
  (K) correct as it is

Answers:
A (A)(B)(C)(D)(E) 1 (A)(B)(C)(D)(E) 3 (A)(B)(C)(D)(E) 5 (A)(B)(C)(D)(E)
B (F)(G)(H)(J)(K) 2 (F)(G)(H)(J)(K) 4 (F)(G)(H)(J)(K) 6 (F)(G)(H)(J)(K)

Language Mechanics: Punctuation (ITBS)

Directions: Read each item and look for a punctuation mistake. In the answer rows below, mark the answer space for the number of the line with the mistake. If you do not find a mistake, mark answer space 4.

Samples

A. (1) There seems to be a difference
(2) of opinion on this issue, so lets
(3) take a vote.
(4) **no mistakes**

B. (1) Orlando, Florida, has become one of
(2) the most popular recreation centers,
(3) in the United States.
(4) **no mistakes**

1. (1) Last week Robert and Jeff got
(2) perfect scores on their spelling
(3) tests. Can they do it again.
(4) **no mistakes**

6. (1) Ruth can you drive to the beach
(2) with me today? We will be home in
(3) time for dinner.
(4) **no mistakes**

2. (1) The column of men stopped when
(2) the drill sergeant yelled, "Halt"
(3) It was time to take a break.
(4) **no mistakes**

7. (1) The twin buildings of the World
(2) Trade Center in New York City have
(3) a commanding view of the harbor.
(4) **no mistakes**

3. (1) The 1996 Olympic Games were
(2) held in Atlanta, Georgia. Many
(3) new records were set.
(4) **no mistakes**

8. (1) When Martin returned from practice,
(2) he asked his mother and father to see
(3) "if anyone had found his basketball."
(4) **no mistakes**

4. (1) I enjoy Daylight Savings Time
(2) It makes the days seem longer and
(3) happier.
(4) **no mistakes**

9. (1) Did your mother read
(2) The Dangers of Spraying for Insects
(3) before she sprayed the garden?
(4) **no mistakes**

5. (1) My favorite subjects in school are
(2) social studies science and math. Do
(3) you have any favorites?
(4) **no mistakes**

10. (1) Kareem Abdul Jabar played for the
(2) Los Angeles Lakers. As a college
(3) student, he attended UCLA.
(4) **no mistakes**

Answers:
A ① ② ③ ④   2 ① ② ③ ④   5 ① ② ③ ④   8 ① ② ③ ④
B ① ② ③ ④   3 ① ② ③ ④   6 ① ② ③ ④   9 ① ② ③ ④
1 ① ② ③ ④   4 ① ② ③ ④   7 ① ② ③ ④   10 ① ② ③ ④

Language Mechanics: Punctuation (SAT)

Directions: Read each sentence or question. Find the word or group of words with the correct punctuation. Fill in the answer space for your choice.

Samples

A. ____we should know more tomorrow.

(A) Well
(B) Well:
(C) Well,
(D) "Well"

B. The teacher smiled and____

(F) said, "Good morning."
(G) said "Good morning."
(H) said, Good morning.
(J) said Good morning.

1. The three____eyes had just opened.

(A) kitten's
(B) kittens'
(C) kittens
(D) kittens'es

5. Ginnie wanted to____every berry she had grown.

(A) pick box and sell
(B) pick, box, and sell
(C) pick, box, and, sell
(D) pick, box and, sell

2. "Oh," said Marian,____

(F) what a terrible experience!
(G) what a terrible experience!"
(H) "what a terrible experience!"
(J) "what a terrible experience!

6. To win the____we must study hard.

(F) contest
(G) contest;
(H) contest:
(J) contest,

3. We saw ____on TV last night.

(A) Ms. Chang our coach
(B) Ms. Chang, our coach
(C) Ms. Chang our coach,
(D) Ms. Chang, our coach,

7. Which is the correct way to end a letter?

(A) Sincerely,
(B) Sincerely.
(C) Sincerely
(D) Sincerely;

4. Which is the correct way to begin a letter?

(F) Dear Aunt Alice,
(G) Dear Aunt Alice
(H) Dear Aunt Alice.
(J) Dear Aunt Alice;

8. Everyone was____we were ready at six.

(F) excited.
(G) excited
(H) excited,
(J) excited;

Answers:
A (A)(B)(C)(D)   2 (F)(G)(H)(J)   5 (A)(B)(C)(D)   8 (F)(G)(H)(J)
B (F)(G)(H)(J)   3 (A)(B)(C)(D)   6 (F)(G)(H)(J)
1 (A)(B)(C)(D)   4 (F)(G)(H)(J)   7 (A)(B)(C)(D)

Language Mechanics: Capitalization and Punctuation

Directions: Mark the space for the answer that shows the correct punctuation and capitalization. Fill in the space for "correct as it is" if the underlined part is already correct.

Samples

A.
- (A) A new movie is opening, at the theater; downtown.
- (B) It won an Academy Award, an Oscar, just last year.
- (C) Would you like to see it with Jodie and me this afternoon.
- (D) We can leave now, we will be home for dinner.

B. We will need <u>poster paint, brushes, and</u> a roll of paper for the banner.
- (F) poster paint, brushes, and,
- (G) poster paint brushes, and
- (H) poster paint, brushes and,
- (J) correct as it is

1.
- (A) The library book's are on my desk.
- (B) We should return them before the fine's get larger.
- (C) They were checked out on my sister's library card.
- (D) Shall we return your's at the same time.

4. John <u>shouted, "I</u> won't forget to stop at the store."
- (F) shouted I
- (G) shouted "I
- (H) shouted", I
- (J) correct as it is

2.
- (F) During our day at the beach we rented, an umbrella and a raft.
- (G) Although the day was cloudy, we had fun.
- (H) The waves were big; because of a storm.
- (J) We took turns riding the raft: because we couldn't afford to rent two.

5. The store was <u>open; but</u> she was busy.
- (A) open but
- (B) open, but,
- (C) open, but
- (D) correct as it is

3.
- (A) my relatives visited many interesting places on their summer vacation.
- (B) They spent time in montreal, canada.
- (C) New York City interested them too.
- (D) Their last stop was in Orlando, florida.

6. "Gather your reference books together before you start <u>your report said</u> Ms. Li.
- (F) your report, "said"
- (G) your report. Said
- (H) your report," said
- (J) correct as it is

Answers:
A (A) (B) (C) (D) 1 (A) (B) (C) (D) 3 (A) (B) (C) (D) 5 (A) (B) (C) (D)
B (F) (G) (H) (J) 2 (F) (G) (H) (J) 4 (F) (G) (H) (J) 6 (F) (G) (H) (J)

Language Mechanics: Applied Mechanics—Page 1

Directions: Read the letter and then answer the questions about the letter.
Benny is writing this letter to his sister, Ellen, who is away at summer camp. Benny wants you to check the letter for errors before he sends it. You may write in the text or use editing marks as you read and revise the letter.

1   Dear Ellen,

2   You wouldn't beleive the weather we are having! As soon as you left for camp, the
3   sun came out. My friend, James, and I have been to the beach every day.
4   Your friends have been calling often. They are planning a party for this Friday, but
5   I told them you would still be away.
6   Mother said, "Remember to tell Ellen about the county fair." It was really great the three
7   times we went. It's too bad it will be over before you come home. Fortunately, it will close
8   before I go away to camp.
9   Your Loving Brother,
10   Randy

Sample

A. Which revision, if any, should Randy make in line 2?

(A) Insert a **comma** after *You*.
(B) Change the **exclamation point** at the end of the sentence to a **question mark**.
(C) Change **beleive** to **believe**.
(D) Make no change.

---

1. Which editing change, if any, is needed in line 4?

(A) Change **friends** to **friends'**.
(B) Change the **comma** after *Friday* to a **semicolon**.
(C) Change **Friday** to **Frieday**.
(D) Make no change.

---

2. Which editing change should be made in line 6?

(F) Mother said, "Remember to tell Ellen about the county fair."
(G) Mother said Remember to tell Ellen about the county fair.
(H) Mother said, Remember to tell Ellen about the county fair.
(I) Mother said, "remember to tell Ellen about the county fair."

---

3. Which editing change is needed in line 7?

(A) Change **It's** to **Its**.
(B) Insert a **comma** after *over*.
(C) Insert a **comma** after *bad*.
(D) Make no change.

4. Which editing change is needed in line 9?

(F) Your Loving Brother.
(G) Your loving brother,
(H) Your loving Brother.
(J) Your loving Brother,

Answers: A Ⓐ Ⓑ Ⓒ Ⓓ   1 Ⓐ Ⓑ Ⓒ Ⓓ   3 Ⓐ Ⓑ Ⓒ Ⓓ
                                    2 Ⓕ Ⓖ Ⓗ Ⓙ   4 Ⓕ Ⓖ Ⓗ Ⓙ

Language Mechanics: Applied Mechanics—Page 2

Directions: Read the passage. Decide which type of mistake is in the underlined part. If it is correct, mark "no error."

Sample

Finally, Marylee had finished her homework and

could go to the mall. She called her best

<u>friend Trudi,</u> grabbed her purse, and rushed out
    A
of the house. The two girls met at the bus stop.

Once settled on the <u>bus, Marylee and Trudi</u>
                  B

discussed what they would do first.

A.
- (A) spelling error
- (B) capitalization error
- (C) punctuation error
- (D) no error

B.
- (F) spelling error
- (G) capitalization error
- (H) punctuation error
- (J) no error

Pham lowered his voice and <u>said "Don't make any noises.</u> Maybe they won't see us. They don't have
                       (1)

any more right to be here than we do."

His friend, Pat, stood quietly behind one of the outside lockers near the gym. He and Pham had come

back to school to get the practice uniforms they had forgotten to take at the end of

<u>practise. They needed</u> to wash them before the next day's practice.
    (2)

1.
- (A) spelling error
- (B) capitalization error
- (C) punctuation error
- (D) no error

2.
- (F) spelling error
- (G) capitalization error
- (H) punctuation error
- (J) no error

GO→

Answers: **A** Ⓐ Ⓑ Ⓒ Ⓓ   **B** Ⓕ Ⓖ Ⓗ Ⓙ   **1** Ⓐ Ⓑ Ⓒ Ⓓ   **2** Ⓕ Ⓖ Ⓗ Ⓙ

Student Practice Page

Language Mechanics: Applied Mechanics—Page 3

Directions: Read the passage. Decide which type of mistake is in the underlined part. If it is correct, mark "no error."

Sample

<u>Dear Javier;</u>
   (3)

   You will never guess what happened <u>to us. Kari and I are going</u> to be on the radio on May 31.
                  (4)

Our song won first place in the music contest. We are not only going to be on <u>the radio we are</u> going to
              (5)

sing the song. Be sure to listen to KWIN at seven o'clock P.M. on the thirty-first.

          <u>Your Friend,</u>
            (6)

          Rob

3.
(A) spelling error
(B) capitalization error
(C) punctuation error
(D) no error

4.
(F) spelling error
(G) capitalization error
(H) punctuation error
(J) no error

5.
(A) spelling error
(B) capitalization error
(C) punctuation error
(D) no error

6.
(F) spelling error
(G) capitalization error
(H) punctuation error
(J) no error

Jancy MacGregor decided to try out for the Olympics when she was only seven years old. She

practiced for five hours each day <u>while she continue</u> her studies at school. Now that she is
            (7)

<u>older her family</u> provides a tutor for her while she trains.
  (8)

7.
(A) spelling error
(B) capitalization error
(C) punctuation error
(D) no error

8.
(F) spelling error
(G) capitalization error
(H) punctuation error
(J) no error

Answers:
3 (A) (B) (C) (D)   5 (A) (B) (C) (D)   7 (A) (B) (C) (D)
4 (F) (G) (H) (J)   6 (F) (G) (H) (J)   8 (F) (G) (H) (J)

Student Practice Page

Language Expression: Usage

Directions: Read each sentence. Look for the word or words that correctly complete the sentence. Mark the answer for your choice.

Samples

A. She helped____to food from the buffet table.

   (A) her
   (B) hers
   (C) herself
   (D) herselves

B. Jodie wanted to know what was in the package so she____it.

   (F) shook
   (G) shake
   (H) shaken
   (J) are shaking

---

1. The drama class____during today's assembly.

   (A) perform
   (B) will perform
   (C) have performed
   (D) performing

5. Soccer is____played than American football.

   (A) wider
   (B) widely
   (C) most widely
   (D) more widely

2. An____trunk is used almost like a hand.

   (F) elephants
   (G) elephant's
   (H) elephants'
   (J) elephant

6. Asia is the____continent.

   (F) large
   (G) larger
   (H) largest
   (J) most large

3. All of the neighborhood dogs____.

   (A) barking
   (B) is barking
   (C) was barking
   (D) were barking

7. Mary and____went to the show.

   (A) me
   (B) I
   (C) myself
   (D) us

4. A telescope____objects seem closer.

   (F) make
   (G) makes
   (H) making
   (J) have made

8. We huddled under the umbrella____the rain was pouring down.

   (F) because
   (G) unless
   (H) besides
   (J) until

Answers:

A (A) (B) (C) (D)   2 (F) (G) (H) (J)   5 (A) (B) (C) (D)   8 (F) (G) (H) (J)

B (F) (G) (H) (J)   3 (A) (B) (C) (D)   6 (F) (G) (H) (J)

1 (A) (B) (C) (D)   4 (F) (G) (H) (J)   7 (A) (B) (C) (D)

Language Expression: Usage

Directions: Read each item and look for a usage mistake. In the answer rows below, mark the answer space for the number of the line with the mistake. If you do not find a mistake, mark answer space 4.

Samples

A.
(A) I didn't know that my shirt was
(B) tore until I got back home. I wish
(C) someone had told me.
(D) **no mistakes**

B.
(J) The mall is having its fall sale
(K) next week. I think I will get some
(L) new school clothes.
(M) **no mistakes**

1.
(A) Most every day I take my lunch to
(B) school. Today, however, I will buy
(C) lunch in the cafeteria.
(D) **no mistakes**

6.
(J) Yesterday Mrs. Roberts' cat came
(K) into our house. He must have gained
(L) entry through a open door.
(M) **no mistakes**

2.
(J) Our new truck can pull our travel
(K) trailer easily. It is much powerfuller
(L) than our old one.
(M) **no mistakes**

7.
(A) Mel and his brother was surprised to
(B) learn that their parents planned to
(C) take them to Disney World.
(D) **no mistakes**

3.
(A) It rained on the first day of our
(B) vacation. We were bored and couldn't
(C) find nothing to do.
(D) **no mistakes**

8.
(J) The game was fun, and I maked three
(K) baskets. Next time I'll try to do even
(L) better.
(M) **no mistakes**

4.
(J) Maria and Jose saved their money
(K) and bought theirselves a microscope.
(L) Science is their favorite subject.
(M) **no mistakes**

9.
(A) Terri gave the tickets to Robert
(B) and I because her family has other plans
(C) for that evening.
(D) **no mistakes**

5.
(A) The mail had came when no one
(B) was home so the package was left on
(C) the doorstep.
(D) **no mistakes**

10.
(J) The bag of potatoes were on sale
(K) for a dollar. Last week we paid twice
(L) that much.
(M) **no mistakes**

- -

Answers:

A Ⓐ Ⓑ Ⓒ Ⓓ   2 Ⓙ Ⓚ Ⓛ Ⓜ   5 Ⓐ Ⓑ Ⓒ Ⓓ   8 Ⓙ Ⓚ Ⓛ Ⓜ
B Ⓙ Ⓚ Ⓛ Ⓜ   3 Ⓐ Ⓑ Ⓒ Ⓓ   6 Ⓙ Ⓚ Ⓛ Ⓜ   9 Ⓐ Ⓑ Ⓒ Ⓓ
1 Ⓐ Ⓑ Ⓒ Ⓓ   4 Ⓙ Ⓚ Ⓛ Ⓜ   7 Ⓐ Ⓑ Ⓒ Ⓓ   10 Ⓙ Ⓚ Ⓛ Ⓜ

Language Expression: Applied Usage

Directions: Read the selection and then answer the questions below it.
This selection is the rough draft of an essay that you wrote about a field trip. Read it over to catch any errors in usage that you might have made.

1 Our trip to the museum was a comedy of errors. First of all, the bus was an hour late to pick

2 us up at school. Because of this, we missed our appointment with the museum's tour guide and had

3 to go around on our own. Mrs. Brown, our teacher, forgets to notify the museum that we would

4 be eating lunch in the on-site restaurant, so we had to walk several blocks to find fast food. To

5 make matters worse, it was at least 100°. The hottest day of the year.

6 In spite of everything, however, our group have managed to have fun and learn a lot. One of

7 the things that we learned was how to plan a trip.

Sample

A. Which revision is needed in the first sentence?

(A) Our trip to the museum, was a comedy of errors.
(B) Our trip, to the museum, was a comedy of errors.
(C) Our trip to the museum was a comedy of error.
(D) Make no change.

---

1. Which revision, if any, is needed in lines 3 and 4? (*"Mrs. Brown . . . fast food."*)

(A) Change **forgets** to **forgot**.
(B) Change **be eating** to **be eaten**.
(C) Change **had to walk** to **had walked**.
(D) Make no change.

---

2. Which is the best way to revise the two sentences in lines 4 and 5 into one sentence? (*"To make . . . the year."*)

(A) It was the hottest day of the year, at least 100°, to make matters worse.
(B) To make matters worse, the hottest day of the year was at least 100°.
(C) To make matters worse, it was at least 100°, the hottest day of the year.
(D) It was 100° and to make matters worse the hottest day of the year.

---

3. Which revision, if any, is needed in line 6? (*"In spite . . . a lot."*)

(A) Change **everything** to **anything**.
(B) Change **have managed** to **managed**.
(C) Delete the words **a lot**.
(D) Make no change.

4. Which change, if any, is needed in the last sentence?

(A) Change **things** to **thing**.
(B) Change **learned** to **learn**.
(C) Insert a *comma* after **how**.
(D) Make no change.

Answers: A Ⓐ Ⓑ Ⓒ Ⓓ 1 Ⓐ Ⓑ Ⓒ Ⓓ 3 Ⓐ Ⓑ Ⓒ Ⓓ
2 Ⓐ Ⓑ Ⓒ Ⓓ 4 Ⓐ Ⓑ Ⓒ Ⓓ

Language Expression: Correct Words

Directions: Read the sentence in each exercise. Find the correct way to say the part that is underlined. In the answer rows, mark the space for the number of your choice. If no changes are needed, mark answer space 4.

Samples

A. Gary thinks that playing a guitar is more fun than <u>to practice</u> the piano.
(1) practicing
(2) the practice of
(3) having practiced
(4) **no change**

B. When my aunt <u>is</u> married, her new husband will be my uncle.
(1) was
(2) had been
(3) will have been
(4) **no change**

1. Mr. Jones decided <u>make</u> a cake for dessert and surprise his family.
(1) making
(2) to make
(3) to have made
(4) **no change**

5. Pham <u>will study</u> two hours a day for the past six months to pass the test.
(1) studying
(2) will be studying
(3) has been studying
(4) **no change**

2. <u>As</u> the telephone became common, people sent urgent messages by telegraph.
(1) After
(2) Until
(3) When
(4) **no change**

6. Please write your name, grade, and <u>homeroom teacher</u> at the top of your paper.
(1) homeroom
(2) your homeroom teacher
(3) the name of your teacher
(4) **no change**

3. Most of the students in our drama club like <u>to dance</u> but not singing.
(1) a dance
(2) dancing
(3) the dancing
(4) **no change**

7. When the emergency drill buzzer sounded, we <u>get</u> up and walked quickly to the playground.
(1) got
(2) have gotten
(3) are getting
(4) **no change**

4. The weather was stormy yesterday, but today it is cool, clear, and <u>with sunshine</u>.
(1) sunny
(2) is sunny
(3) has sunshine
(4) **no change**

8. Water freezes <u>until</u> it reaches a temperature of 0° C.
(1) but
(2) unless
(3) when
(4) **no change**

- -

Answers:
A ① ② ③ ④   2 ① ② ③ ④   5 ① ② ③ ④   8 ① ② ③ ④
B ① ② ③ ④   3 ① ② ③ ④   6 ① ② ③ ④
1 ① ② ③ ④   4 ① ② ③ ④   7 ① ② ③ ④

Language Expression: Grammar and Syntax

Directions: Read the words in each box. Then read each question below the box. Choose the best answers. Fill in the circles for your answer choices.

Samples

> I. Mr. Johnson is going to the football game.
> II. I am going to the football game.

A. Which of these words is used as an adjective in the sentences?
- (A) going
- (B) football
- (C) game
- (D) to

B. What is the subject of sentence I?
- (E) Mr. Johnson
- (F) is going
- (G) game
- (H) the football game

> I. Those bees have a hive in the maple tree.
> II. The bird has a nest in the maple tree.

1. Which word in these sentences is a preposition?
- (A) those
- (B) maple
- (C) in
- (D) the

2. What is the subject of sentence II?
- (E) a nest
- (F) bird has a nest
- (G) the maple tree
- (H) The bird

> I. The pencil is broken.
> II. The pencil was under your notebook.

3. Which of these words is used as a noun in the sentences?
- (A) notebook
- (B) under
- (C) the
- (D) broken

4. Which word in these sentences is a past tense verb?
- (E) was
- (F) is
- (G) under
- (H) broken

> I. The boys are at practice now.
> II. The boys were at practice on Friday.

5. Which word in these sentences is a present tense form of be?
- (A) were
- (B) at
- (C) are
- (D) on

6. Which of these words is used as an adverb in the sentences?
- (E) practice
- (F) were
- (G) now
- (H) Friday

GO→

- -

Answers:

A Ⓐ Ⓑ ⓒ Ⓓ   1 Ⓐ Ⓑ ⓒ Ⓓ   3 Ⓐ Ⓑ ⓒ Ⓓ   5 Ⓐ Ⓑ ⓒ Ⓓ
B Ⓔ Ⓕ Ⓖ Ⓗ   2 Ⓔ Ⓕ Ⓖ Ⓗ   4 Ⓔ Ⓕ Ⓖ Ⓗ   6 Ⓔ Ⓕ Ⓖ Ⓗ

Language Expression: Grammar and Syntax *(cont.)*

Directions: Read the words in each box. Then read each question below the box. Choose the best answers. Fill in the circles for your answer choices.

> I. The fire alarm sounded.
> II. Everyone left the building.

7. How can sentences I and II be written to form a compound sentence?

(A) After the fire alarm sounded, everyone left the building.
(B) The fire alarm sounded, and everyone left the building.
(C) Everyone left the building when the fire alarm sounded.
(D) Because the fire alarm sounded, everyone left the building.

8. What is the complete predicate of sentence II?

(E) left
(F) Everyone left
(G) left the building
(H) the building

> I. Her costume was red, white, and blue.
> II. The colors of our flag are red, white, and blue.

9. Which word in these sentences is a present tense form of be?
(A) are
(B) of
(C) was
(D) and

10. Which word in these sentences is a preposition?
(E) Her
(F) The
(G) of
(H) our

> I. The train is carrying freight.
> II. The train was going to New York City.

11. Which of these words is used as a preposition in the sentences?
(A) to
(B) train
(C) was
(D) freight

12. Which word in these sentences is a past tense verb?
(E) train
(F) freight
(G) was
(H) New York City

> I. My sister plays on the soccer team.
> II. Her team just won the championship.

13. Which one of these words is used as a noun in the sentences?
(A) My
(B) plays
(C) soccer
(D) championship

14. What is the complete predicate of sentence I?
(E) My sister plays
(F) sister plays no
(G) plays on the soccer team
(H) the soccer team

STOP

Answers:

A (A) (B) (C) (D) 1 (A) (B) (C) (D) 3 (A) (B) (C) (D) 5 (A) (B) (C) (D)
B (E) (F) (G) (H) 2 (E) (F) (G) (H) 4 (E) (F) (G) (H) 6 (E) (F) (G) (H)

Student Practice Page

Language Expression: Sentences

Directions: Read the sentence or sentences. Look for the simple subject, simple predicate, or complete sentence. Mark the answer space for your choice.

Samples

A. The <u>new</u> <u>streetlights</u> <u>came</u> on at <u>dusk</u>.

    (A)   (B)   (C)   (D)

B. The <u>train</u> <u>never</u> <u>arrives</u> on that <u>track</u>.

    F   G   H   J

C.
(A) A very interesting story just heard.
(B) I just heard a very interesting story.
(C) I just heard a story it was interesting.
(D) A story I just hear, being very interesting.

Look for the simple subject.

1. The <u>local</u> <u>bus</u> <u>runs</u> frequently on <u>Saturday</u>.
    A   B   C   D

2. The <u>tiny</u> <u>kitten</u> <u>was stuck</u> in the tall <u>tree</u>.
    F   G   H   J

3. <u>Javier</u> <u>forgot</u> his <u>books</u> on the <u>playground</u>.
    A   B   C   D

Look for the simple predicate.

4. In the <u>oven</u>, <u>delicious</u> <u>cookies</u> <u>were baking</u>.
    F   G   H   J

5. That <u>new</u> <u>movie</u> <u>looks</u> <u>interesting</u> to me.
    A   B   C   D

6. <u>Dad</u> <u>waxed</u> his new <u>car</u> twice last <u>week</u>
    F   G   H   J

Look for the complete sentence.

7.
(A) It snowed we went to the mountains.
(B) Going to the mountains when it snows.
(C) When the snowy weather began.
(D) We went to the mountains when it snowed.

8.
(F) Jo likes to play cards Meg does too.
(G) Jo and Meg like to play cards.
(H) Jo and Meg play they play cards.
(J) Joe and Meg playing cards.

9.
(A) The nest built in the tall oak tree.
(B) Birds building a nest in the tall oak tree.
(C) The birds built a nest in the tall oak tree.
(D) The birds built a nest it is in the tall oak tree.

10.
(F) Potato salad was served with the broiled hamburgers.
(G) Potato salad served along with hamburgers.
(H) Serving potato salad and hamburgers.
(J) We had potato salad we had broiled hamburgers.

Answers:
A (A) (B) (C) (D)
B (F) (G) (H) (J)
C (A) (B) (C) (D)
1 (A) (B) (C) (D)
2 (F) (G) (H) (J)
3 (A) (B) (C) (D)
4 (F) (G) (H) (J)
5 (A) (B) (C) (D)
6 (F) (G) (H) (J)
7 (A) (B) (C) (D)
8 (F) (G) (H) (J)
9 (A) (B) (C) (D)
10 (F) (G) (H) (J)

Language Expression: Sentence Combining

Directions: Read the underlined sentences. Look for the single sentence that is the best combination for the underlined sentences. Mark the answer space for your choice.

Sample

A. People live in family groups.

Animals live in family groups.

(A) People live with animals in family groups.

(B) People and animals live in family groups.

(C) People live in family groups and animals live in family groups too.

(D) In family groups, both people and animals live.

---

1. We went to the mountains last weekend.

We hiked on the trails all day and swam in the pool in the evening.

(A) We went to the mountains last weekend and we hiked on the trails all day and swam in the pool in the evening.

(B) When we went to the mountains last weekend, we hiked on the trails all day and swam in the pool in the evening.

(C) We went to the mountains and last weekend we hiked all day but we swam in the evening.

(D) We hiked and swam on the trails and in the pool last weekend in the mountains.

2. His family went to see a movie last night.

The movie was long.

The movie was scary.

(F) The movie was long and scary when his family went to see it last night.

(G) His family went to see a movie last night, it was long and scary.

(H) His family went to see a long, scary movie last night.

(J) Last night his family went to see a long movie and a scary movie.

3. Betsy got ready for the field trip.

Roger got ready for the field trip.

(A) Betsy got ready for the field trip with Roger.

(B) Betsy and Roger both got ready for the field trip.

(C) Betsy got ready for the field trip and so did Roger get ready.

(D) Betsy got ready for the field trip but Roger got ready for the field trip too.

Answers: A Ⓐ Ⓑ Ⓒ Ⓓ   1 Ⓐ Ⓑ Ⓒ Ⓓ   2 Ⓕ Ⓖ Ⓗ Ⓙ   3 Ⓐ Ⓑ Ⓒ Ⓓ

Language Expression: Sentence Completion

Directions: Read the passage and answer the questions that follow it.

Help your friend edit the story she wrote about a lost cat.

1   When Kitty Kat ran away, she was white and fluffy and had a blue bow tied around her neck.

2   When Marcie spotted her two days later high up in a tree, she was gray and matted and not wearing

3   a ribbon. It was hard to believe that she was the beautiful cat.

4   Kitty Kat paced up and down her branch. She cried mournfully. Marcie felt like

5   crying too. It was awful to see her panic.

6   The neighborhood children began to gather under the tree. They stared up at Kitty Kat and she

7   paced and cried.

8   "Why do you want that dirty cat, Marcie?" one of the children asked. "You have such a pretty

9   white cat." He couldn't believe that she wanted a cat.

10   "That _is_ my beautiful white cat," said Marcie. "And now she is too scared."

11   "I'll call the fire department, Marcie," said Mrs. Brown who lived next door. "They will

12   know."

Sample

A. Which word should be added in line 3 after *she was the* to clarify the meaning of the paragraph?

    (A)   less   (C)   new

    (B)   very   (D)   same

---

1. Which words should be added after *panic* in line 5 to clarify the meaning of the paragraph?

    (A)   so terribly.   (C)   and not know what was the matter.

    (B)   and not be able to help.   (D)   last time.

2. Which words should be added at the end of line 9 to clarify the meaning of the paragraph?

    (A)   that was so dirty.   (B)   that was so scared.

    (C)   that was up in a tree.   (D)   that was crying.

3. Which revision in line 10 after *too scared* would clarify the meaning of the paragraph?

    (A)   to cry.   (B)   of me.

    (C)   to come down.   (D)   to get clean.

4. Which words should be added after *know* in the last line to clarify the meaning of the paragraph?

    (A)   what to do.   (B)   what to say.

    (C)   about it.   (D)   how it is.

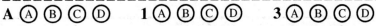

Answers: A Ⓐ Ⓑ Ⓒ Ⓓ   1 Ⓐ Ⓑ Ⓒ Ⓓ   3 Ⓐ Ⓑ Ⓒ Ⓓ

                                      2 Ⓐ Ⓑ Ⓒ Ⓓ   4 Ⓐ Ⓑ Ⓒ Ⓓ

Language Expression: Paragraphs and Topic Sentences

Directions: Read each paragraph. Then look for the best topic sentence for each paragraph.

Sample

A. _____. It gives us the energy to work and play. It makes us grow and keeps our bodies healthy and strong. Without food, we die. All living things, including animals and people, need food to live and grow.

    (A) But only plants make their own food.

    (B) They also provide food for animals and people.

    (C) Food is one of our most important daily needs.

    (D) All foods that we eat come from plants and animals.

Look for the best topic sentence.

1. _____. There are several types of fractures. In a simple fracture, there is no connecting wound between the broken bone and the skin. A compound fracture has such a wound. A multiple fracture has more than one break. In a greenstick fracture, the bone does not break all the way through.

    (A) Bones can break at any age, but the bones of the elderly are most fragile.

    (B) Fracture is a term that generally means the breaking of a bone.

    (C) In some cases, only an X-ray examination can reveal the fracture.

    (D) There may be pain, often accompanied by swelling.

2. _____. It was sometimes called "the war hatchet." The original tomahawks had hatchet heads made of flint or bronze. They were tied to wooden handles with cords made of animal skin. Later, tomahawks were fitted with iron heads.

    (A) The tomahawk was one of the handiest weapons and tools of the North American Indians.

    (B) The Indians also used tomahawks for ceremonies.

    (C) They were often decorated with feathers or porcupine quills.

    (D) Some tomahawks were fitted with bowls so that they could be used for pipes.

3. _____. He had been Vice President for only 83 days when President Franklin Roosevelt died. World War II had not yet been won. The organization to be known as the United Nations was still in the planning stages.

    (A) Before becoming vice president, he had been known for his work in the Senate.

    (B) Truman faced other great problems during his years in the White House.

    (C) When North Korea invaded South Korea in 1950, Truman faced a grave challenge.

    (D) Harry S Truman became president at one of the most crucial times in American history.

Answers: A Ⓐ Ⓑ Ⓒ Ⓓ   1 Ⓐ Ⓑ Ⓒ Ⓓ   2 Ⓐ Ⓑ Ⓒ Ⓓ   3 Ⓐ Ⓑ Ⓒ Ⓓ

Language Expression: Paragraphs and Sentence Sequence

Directions: Read each paragraph. Look for the correct order for the sentences. Mark the answer space for your choice.

Sample

A. 1   By the time we left for home, we were all skiing pretty well.

    2   We started out by buying skis and clothes for each of us.

    3   Last winter my whole family learned to ski.

    4   Then we all took a plane to a ski resort in Colorado.

        (A) 1 - 2 - 3 - 4
        (B) 1 - 3 - 2 - 4
        (C) 3 - 2 - 4 - 1
        (D) 4 - 3 - 1 - 2

---

1. 1   The first thing we learned was how to fall down without getting hurt.

    2   Today I took my very first ice skating lesson at the rink.

    3   I can hardly wait to take my second lesson next week.

    4   Then we practiced gliding with one foot at a time.

        (A) 1 - 3 - 4 - 2
        (B) 2 - 1 - 4 - 3
        (C) 2 - 4 - 1 - 3
        (D) 4 - 3 - 2 - 1

2. 1   After the car was parked, an individual speaker was hooked over the window.

    2   Families dressed children in pajamas and everybody got into their cars.

    3   Today, however, people rent movies and play them at home on their VCRs.

    4   Drive-in movies used to be very popular, especially in the summer.

        (F) 1 - 3 - 2 - 4
        (G) 2 - 1 - 4 - 3
        (H) 3 - 4 - 1 - 2
        (J) 4 - 2 - 1 - 3

Answers: **A** Ⓐ Ⓑ Ⓒ Ⓓ   **1** Ⓐ Ⓑ Ⓒ Ⓓ   **2** Ⓕ Ⓖ Ⓗ Ⓙ

Language Expression: Transitions

Directions: Read the passage and then answer the questions that follow it.

Help Max edit his story before he turns it in to his teacher, Mrs. Henderson. He is particularly interested in improving his transitions because that is what Mrs. Henderson stressed in class this week.

1   Mr. Duncan was packing the car for the vacation trip he and his family would be taking. Mrs.
2   Duncan was washing and drying the last load of clothes they would need. Mike and Laura mowed the lawn
3   and tidied up the yard.
4   Mr. Duncan wanted to hike. Mrs. Duncan wanted to lie in a hammock and read. Mike and
5   Laura wanted to swim and water ski.
6   They all jumped into the car and set off. It was a long trip, but they had driven it before and
7   they were prepared. They had brought a supply of games, tapes, and magazines.
8   They arrived at their destination, a resort situated on a beautiful mountain lake. Before they
9   unpacked the car, they all took time to walk to the edge of the lake and take a deep breath of the
10 fresh, crisp air.
11 "Well," said Mr. Duncan, "here we are!"

Sample

A. Which word should be added at the beginning of the sentence on lines 2 and 3 to make the sentence more logical? ("Mike and . . . the yard.")

    (A) Moreover   (C) Although

    (B) Therefore   (D) Meanwhile

---

1. Max is thinking about adding a transition sentence at the beginning of the second paragraph. Which one would be the **best** choice?

    (A) The family had planned for this vacation all year.
    (B) They would board their pets in the kennel.
    (C) Mr. Duncan was an electrical engineer.
    (D) Mr. and Mrs. Duncan liked their regular jobs.

2. Which addition would improve the beginning of the third paragraph in line 6?

    (A) The yard looked very nice so . . .
    (B) All the clothes were packed and . . .
    (C) Once everything was done . . .
    (D) They worked and worked until . . .

3. Which word would improve the paragraph beginning in line 8?

    (A) Until   (B) Therefore
    (C) Although   (D) Finally

Answers: A Ⓐ Ⓑ Ⓒ Ⓓ   1 Ⓐ Ⓑ Ⓒ Ⓓ   2 Ⓐ Ⓑ Ⓒ Ⓓ   3 Ⓐ Ⓑ Ⓒ Ⓓ

Language Expression: Descriptive Writing (TAAS)
Student Prewriting Page

Directions: Write a composition for your classmates, describing the most interesting place that you have ever visited. Describe in detail where the place is, how you got there, what you saw, and how you felt.

On this page you will organize your ideas.
- Read the directions carefully.
- Use this page to brainstorm your ideas and make notes in any form that will help you.
- Do not include anything that does not refer to the topic.

Language Expression: Descriptive Writing (TAAS)
Student Draft Page

Directions: Write a composition for your classmates, describing the most interesting place that you have ever visited. Describe in detail where the place is, how you got there, what you saw, and how you felt.

On this page you will write your composition.
- Review your notes.
- Organize your composition.
- Consider your audience.
- Use adjectives and adverbs to enhance your description.
- Use your best English skills, but do not worry about making mistakes.
- Add more pages if necessary.

_____

_____

_____

_____

_____

_____

_____

_____

_____

_____

_____

_____

_____

_____

Language Expression: Informative Writing (TAAS)
Student Prewriting Page

Directions: Imagine that you have been asked to explain to a group of students from a foreign country how to prepare a hot dog for lunch. They have never eaten hot dogs before and do not know anything about them. Tell them each step that you take in preparing a hot dog.

On this page you will organize your ideas.
- Read the directions carefully.
- Use this page to list the steps that you must follow to prepare a hot dog.
- Do not include anything that does not refer to the topic.

Language Expression: Informative Writing (TAAS)
Student Draft Page

Directions: Imagine that you have been asked to explain to a group of students from a foreign country how to prepare a hot dog for lunch. They have never eaten hot dogs before and do not know anything about them. Tell them each step that you take in preparing a hot dog.

On this page you will write your composition.
- Review your notes.
- Organize your composition.
- Consider your audience.
- List the steps in order, one after the other.
- Use your best English skills, but do not worry about making mistakes.
- Add more pages if necessary.

_____

_____

_____

_____

_____

_____

_____

_____

_____

_____

_____

_____

_____

_____

_____

_____

_____

Student Practice Page

Language Expression: Classificatory Writing (TAAS)
Student Prewriting Page

Directions: You have been chosen to represent your school at an international convention for students. This convention will take place during your family's scheduled summer vacation, and it is being held in Paris, France. You will be traveling alone. Write a composition as if you were explaining this situation to a friend. Write about the good and bad aspects of attending this convention. Explain each of your points completely.

On this page you will organize your ideas.
- Read the directions carefully.
- Use this page to list the good things and the bad things about going to this convention.
- Do not write about anything else, just the good and bad points. What would be good about your experience? What would be a problem? How would you feel? How would your family feel?

Language Expression: Classificatory Writing (TAAS)
Student Draft Page

Directions: You have been chosen to represent your school at an international convention for students. This convention will take place during your family's scheduled summer vacation, and it is being held in Paris, France. You will be traveling alone. Write a composition as if you were explaining this situation to a friend. Write about the good and bad aspects of attending this convention. Explain each of your points completely.

> On this page you will write your composition.
> - Review your notes.
> - Organize your composition.
> - Consider your audience.
> - Discuss the good and bad points about your situation in separate paragraphs.
> - Use your best English skills, but do not worry about making mistakes.
> - Add more pages if necessary.

_____

_____

_____

_____

_____

_____

_____

_____

_____

_____

_____

_____

_____

_____

_____

_____

_____

Language Expression: Persuasive Writing (TAAS)
Student Prewriting Page

Directions: Suppose that you learned that your neighborhood might be condemned so that the property could be used for a new freeway. Your family would be paid for your house and land, but you would have to relocate to somewhere else. What is your position on this issue? Write a letter to your local newspaper, explaining your position. Be sure to give good reasons for your point of view and explain them completely.

On this page you will organize your ideas.

- Read the directions carefully.
- Use this page to get organized. Choose a position that is either "for" or "against."
- Do not write about anything else except your thoughts and feelings about this issue.

Language Expression: Persuasive Writing (TAAS)
Student Draft Page

Directions: Suppose that you learned that your neighborhood might be condemned so that the property could be used for a new freeway. Your family would be paid for your house and land, but you would have to relocate to somewhere else. What is your position on this issue? Write a letter to your local newspaper, explaining your position. Be sure to give good reasons for your point of view and explain them completely.

On this page you will write your composition.

- • Review your notes.
- • Organize your composition.
- • Consider your audience.
- • Try to convince your reader that your position on the issue is sensible.
- • Use your best English skills, but do not worry about making mistakes.
- • Add more pages if necessary.

Language Expression: Comparative Writing (TAAS)
Student Prewriting Page

Directions: Because of budget cuts, your school will have to drop either shop or chorus classes. You are not involved in either program, but you have friends in both. Write a letter to your local newspaper discussing both options. State your position on the issue and give good reasons for your position.

On this page you will organize your ideas.

- Read the directions carefully.

- Use this page to get organized. List the advantages and disadvantages of both options.

- Do not write about anything else except the two options and the reasons that you favor one of them.

Language Expression: Comparative Writing (TAAS)
Student Draft Page

Directions: Because of budget cuts, your school will have to drop either shop or chorus classes. You are not involved in either program, but you have friends in both. Write a letter to your local newspaper discussing both options. State your position on the issue and give good reasons for your position.

On this page you will write your composition.

- Review your notes.
- Organize your composition.
- Consider your audience.
- Try to convince your reader that your position on the issue is sensible.
- Use your best English skills, but do not worry about making mistakes.
- Add more pages if necessary.

_____

_____

_____

_____

_____

_____

_____

_____

_____

_____

_____

_____

_____

_____

_____

_____

Language Expression: Solving a Problem (NJ EWT)

General Directions

In this lesson you will show how well you can explain your solution to a problem. The Writing Situation and Directions for Writing below will tell you what to do. You will have 60 minutes to complete this writing exercise.

Begin by thinking about the writing task and how you will organize your thoughts. Use scratch paper for your prewriting. You may use one side of the paper you have been given for the prewriting and up to four sides for your composition. Take your time. Use your best English skills, and write carefully so that the reader will understand what you are saying.

Writing Situation

Many young people your age often go to their neighborhood theaters. They sometimes buy snacks during the movies and leave popcorn containers, drink cups, and candy wrappers all over the floor where they were sitting. This makes the area unpleasant for other patrons, and some adults want young people to be restricted to a special section of the theater or even be prevented from buying snacks altogether. You want to do something about this problem.

You have decided to write a letter to the manager of the theater suggesting a solution to the problem. Think about how the theater employees and the young people could work together to solve the problem of littering. Your solution should make sense to the theater management, the concerned adults, and the young people involved.

Directions for Writing

Write a letter to the manager of the theater explaining your solution to the problem. Your solution should be simple and not expensive. Think of a solution that will prevent the problem of littering in the theater and will show both the theater manager and the concerned adults that young people can be responsible.

Language Expression: Cause and Effect (NJ EWT)

General Directions

In this lesson you will show how well you can explain why a change in society is taking place. The Writing Situation and Directions for Writing below will tell you what to do. You will have 60 minutes to complete this writing exercise.

Begin by thinking about the writing task and how you will organize your thoughts. Use scratch paper for your prewriting. You may use one side of the paper you have been given for the prewriting and up to four sides for your composition. Take your time. Use your best English skills, and write carefully so that the reader will understand what you are saying.

Writing Situation

Many young people your age read very little. They get their news and entertainment from television and the movies. They would rather read a magazine than a novel. No one is quite sure why this is true, but many people are concerned about the situation.

Your teacher has asked you and your classmates to write essays which explain your thoughts about the causes of this situation. Your essays will be shared with other students in your school. Your teacher hopes that these essays will help the school develop a program to increase the popularity of reading for pleasure.

Directions for Writing

Write an essay in which you give an explanation for the fact that students read very little. Use your own experiences and what you know about other people your age to support your position. Write in a way that shows that you have given serious thought to the situation.

Language Expression: Opinion (NJ EWT)

General Directions

In this lesson you will show how well you can express your opinion. The Writing Situation and Directions for Writing below will tell you what to do. You will have 60 minutes to compete this writing exercise.

Begin by thinking about the writing task and how you will organize your thoughts. Use scratch paper for your prewriting. You may use one side of the paper you have been given for the prewriting and up to four sides for your composition. Take your time. Use your best English skills, and write carefully so that the reader will understand what you are saying.

Writing Situation

Some states are considering changing the legal age for getting a driver's license from sixteen to eighteen. The people who are in favor of this change base their views on the number of accidents that claim the lives of teenagers as well as the number of accidents that they feel are caused by the reckless driving habits of young people.

Your teacher has asked you and the other students in your class to write essays in which you explain your thoughts about this change in the legal driving age. Your essays will be sent to a state commission that is considering the proposal to raise the legal age for driving.

Directions for Writing

Write an essay explaining your position on this topic. Be sure to give good reasons for your point of view and support them completely. Try to be convincing when you write so that the state commission will take your opinions seriously.

Work-Study Skills: Library and Dictionary Skills

Directions: Read the questions. Look for the best answer for each question. Mark the answer space for your choice.

Samples

A. If a dictionary page has kipper and kitten as guide words, which one of the following words would be on the same page?

(A) kip
(B) Kipling
(C) kitchen
(D) kitty

B. Where should you look for information about the government of France?

(F) an atlas
(G) an encyclopedia
(H) an almanac
(J) a travel guidebook

1. "Document" would be found on a dictionary page with which of these guide words?

(A) divider - dobbin
(B) docent - docket
(C) doctrine - dogfight
(D) doable - docent

2. To find the most information about the battles of the Boer War, you should look in . . .

(F) a newspaper.
(G) a magazine.
(H) an almanac.
(J) an encyclopedia.

3. Where should you look to find the best way to get to Disneyland in Anaheim, California?

(A) an atlas
(B) a globe
(C) a road map
(D) a world map

4. Which probably best shows the geography of the states along the Mississippi?

(F) a road map
(G) a travel guide
(H) an atlas
(J) a globe

For items 5 and 6, find the answers by using this library catalog card.

> 629.1 **Interplanetary Flight**
>
> C597
>
> Interplanetary Flight, by Arthur Clarke; illus. with photographs and diagrams by Maury Hendrickson and Alice Bentley; New York: Jay Harper and Brothers, 1953
>
> 224 pages; illustrated
>
>   1. Space exploration   2. Science

5. The book is about . . .

(A) space exploration.
(B) Arthur Clarke.
(C) New York.
(D) Jay Harper and Brothers.

6. Who is the author of the book?

(F) Maury Hendrickson
(G) Alice Bentley
(H) Jay Harper
(J) Arthur Clarke

Answers:

A (A) (B) (C) (D)   1 (A) (B) (C) (D)   3 (A) (B) (C) (D)   5 (A) (B) (C) (D)

B (F) (G) (H) (J)   2 (F) (G) (H) (J)   4 (F) (G) (H) (J)   6 (F) (G) (H) (J)

Work-Study Skills: Alphabetizing

Directions: Read the directions for each section. Choose the best answer for each item. Mark the answer space for your choice.

Samples

A.
- (A) campus
- (B) beach
- (C) steeple
- (D) leopard

B.
- (F) welcome
- (G) yard
- (H) zero
- (J) zephyr

Which word or name comes first in alphabetical order?

1.
- (A) flock
- (B) dumpling
- (C) bridge
- (D) elephant

2.
- (F) grape
- (G) jungle
- (H) hungry
- (J) knight

3.
- (A) somewhere
- (B) safety
- (C) stairway
- (D) scramble

4.
- (F) trundle
- (G) tree house
- (H) truffle
- (J) triangle

5.
- (A) Johnson, Paula
- (B) Johnson, Jim
- (C) Johnson, Phil
- (D) Johnson, Hazel

Which word would come last in the dictionary?

6.
- (F) dolphin
- (G) upset
- (H) peninsula
- (J) magnet

7.
- (A) elegant
- (B) violet
- (C) question
- (D) wiggle

8.
- (F) yesterday
- (G) fantastic
- (H) laughter
- (J) breakable

9.
- (A) floor
- (B) freezer
- (C) fiddle
- (D) fourth

10.
- (F) know
- (G) kneel
- (H) knife
- (J) knight

Answers:

A (A) (B) (C) (D)   2 (F) (G) (H) (J)   5 (A) (B) (C) (D)   8 (F) (G) (H) (J)

B (F) (G) (H) (J)   3 (A) (B) (C) (D)   6 (F) (G) (H) (J)   9 (A) (B) (C) (D)

1 (A) (B) (C) (D)   4 (F) (G) (H) (J)   7 (A) (B) (C) (D)   10 (F) (G) (H) (J)

Word-Study Skills: Table of Contents

Directions: Read the question in each item. Then look at the table of contents and find the best answer. Mark the answer space for your choice.

Samples

This is the table of contents from the book *Celebrations Around the World.*

Table of Contents	
Chapter	**Page**
1 Christmas Feasts in France	4
2 New Year's Day in Brazil	15
3 ANZAC Day in Australia	26
4 Carnival Dances in Brazil	38
5 Guy Fawkes Day in England	47
6 Sukkot in Israel	60

A. For information about Brazilian folk dances you should look in which chapter?

(1) 1   (2) 2   (3) 3   (4) 4

B. In Chapter 3 you might find out . . .

(1) what holidays are celebrated in England.
(2) when Carnival takes place.
(3) who Guy Fawkes was.
(4) what ANZAC means.

This is the table of contents from the book *Up in the Attic.*

Table of Contents	
Chapter	**Page**
1 A Rainy Saturday	3
2 Meg and Barb Explore	12
3 A Mysterious Shadow	20
4 The Locked Chest	29
5 The Key in the Corner	40
6 Grandmother's Treasure	52

1. In which chapter might this sentence appear?

"Oh, it's just the tree outside the attic window," Meg gasped in relief.

(1) Chapter 1
(2) Chapter 2
(3) Chapter 3
(4) Chapter 4

2. In which chapter might you find this sentence?

"I had planned to spend the day hiking in the woods," said Meg.

(1) Chapter 1   (3) Chapter 4
(2) Chapter 2   (4) Chapter 6

3. In which chapter might these sentences appear?

"Look, Meg" Barb whispered. "What is that shiny thing over there?"

(1) Chapter 3   (3) Chapter 5
(2) Chapter 4   (4) Chapter 6

4. In which chapter might you read this?

"I think Grandmother would be happy that we found it," said Meg.

(1) Chapter 1   (3) Chapter 4
(2) Chapter 3   (4) Chapter 6

Answers:
A ① ② ③ ④   1 ① ② ③ ④   3 ① ② ③ ④
B ① ② ③ ④   2 ① ② ③ ④   4 ① ② ③ ④

Work-Study Skills: Index

Directions: Read the question in each item. Then look at the index and find the best answer. Fill in the answer circle for your choice.

Samples

This is part of the index from the book *Science in Action*.

Index

Astronomy, 14–20 (see also Telescopes);
comets, 45; planets, 95–106; stars, 130–140;
sun, 155–157
Biology, 25–36
Geology, 60–75
Geography, physical, 76–80
Rocks (see Geology)
Telescopes, 160–165

A. To learn about the sun you would start on which page?

(1) 14   (2) 95   (3) 130   (4) 155

B. On which page should you begin reading to find out about physical geography?

(1) 14
(2) 25
(3) 76
(4) 160

This is part of the Index from the book *How Things Work*.

Index

Accordion, 139
Airplane, 168, 269
Air pressure, 30, 268, 269, 318
Atom, 183–193, 289
Automobile (see Car)
Ax, 224, 241
Axle, 250, 251, 260, 261
  car, 301
  electric motor, 283
Bell, 91–95
  clock, 97
  door-, 5, 18, 19
Boat, 257, 265–267, 292, 293, 301
Bulb
  electric, 201, 205, 208–213
  flashlight, 185
Car battery, 189
Car horn, 102, 103
Car motor, 189, 280

1. To learn about flashlight bulbs you should look at which page?

(1) 185   (2) 201   (3) 283   (4) 208

2. On which page would you find information about the axle of a car?

(1) 250   (2) 251   (3) 261   (4) 301

3. On which page should you start reading to get the most information about atoms?

(1) 183   (2) 185   (3) 193   (4) 289

4. What page might have information about gasoline engines?

(1) 301   (2) 283   (3) 280   (4) 103

Answers:
A ① ② ③ ④   1 ① ② ③ ④   3 ① ② ③ ④
B ① ② ③ ④   2 ① ② ③ ④   4 ① ② ③ ④

Work-Study Skills: Dictionary Skills

Directions: Read each question. Find the best answer. Fill in the answer circle for your choice.

Sample

novice (nov´is) noun 1. a person who enters a religious group on probation: He became a novice in the monastery. 2. a person new to an activity: She is a novice when it comes to mountain climbing.

A. What part of speech is the word <u>novice</u>?

(A) verb
(B) noun
(C) adverb
(D) adjective

Use the dictionary entry below to answer questions 1 through 5.

gallery (gal´ər ē) noun 1. a covered walk open on one side: The gallery was a shady place. 2. the highest seats in a theater: The cheapest seats are in the gallery. 3. a place for exhibiting artworks: Her paintings hang in that gallery. 4. the spectators at a sporting event: He always plays to the gallery.

1. Which answer shows how to pronounce the <u>y</u> in <u>gallery</u>?

(A) y
(B) e
(C) i
(D) a

2. What part of speech is the word <u>gallery</u>?

(F) noun
(G) verb
(H) adjective
(J) adverb

3. Which definition of <u>gallery</u> is used in the sentence "Our tickets won't cost too much if we sit in the gallery"?

(A) 1
(B) 2
(C) 3
(D) 4

4. The word <u>gallery</u> would be found on a dictionary page with which of these guide words?

(F) gallop—gallows
(G) galleon—galling
(H) gall—galleria
(J) Gallic—gamble

5. When someone talks about the rowdy <u>gallery</u> at a soccer match, which definition of <u>gallery</u> is she using?

(A) 1
(B) 2
(C) 3
(D) 4

Answers: A Ⓐ Ⓑ Ⓒ Ⓓ   2 Ⓕ Ⓖ Ⓗ Ⓙ   4 Ⓕ Ⓖ Ⓗ Ⓙ
          1 Ⓐ Ⓑ Ⓒ Ⓓ   3 Ⓐ Ⓑ Ⓒ Ⓓ   5 Ⓐ Ⓑ Ⓒ Ⓓ

Work-Study Skills: Outlines

Directions: Look at the information and read each question. Find the best answer to each question and mark your answer choice.

Sample

Geography

I._____

   A. Mountains
   B. Bodies of Water
   C. Plains and Plateaus
   D. Deserts

A. Which heading best fits into I. in the outline titled "Geography"?

   (A) Political Divisions
   (B) Physical Features
   (C) Continents
   (D) Rivers

Study this outline for a research paper about communication. Then do items 1 through 3.

Communication Through the Ages

I. Early ways of sending messages

   A. Drums
   B. Smoke signals
   C. _____

II. The beginning of writing

   A. Pictures
   B. Symbols
   C. _____

III._____

   A. Fiber Optics
   B. Telephone
   C. Satellites
   D. Computers

1. Which one of these topics would fit best in space II, C?

   (A) Word of mouth
   (B) Numbers
   (C) Alphabets
   (D) Electronic mail

2. What is a good title for section III?

   (F) Prehistoric communication
   (G) Communication today
   (H) Person to person
   (J) Cellular phones

3. Which one of these would be a good section to add to the outline?

   (A) The future of communication
   (B) The history of communication
   (C) Communication and transportation
   (D) Communication and entertainment

Answers: **A** Ⓐ Ⓑ Ⓒ Ⓓ   **1** Ⓐ Ⓑ Ⓒ Ⓓ   **2** Ⓕ Ⓖ Ⓗ Ⓙ   **3** Ⓐ Ⓑ Ⓒ Ⓓ

Work-Study Skills: Key Terms

Directions: Read the question in each item. Choose the answer that you consider to be the best. Mark the answer space for your choice.

Samples

A. Which key term would you use to find the diameter of the planet Mercury, the nearest planet to the sun in our solar system?

(A) Diameter   (B) Mercury

(C) Planet   (D) Size

B. Which key term would you use to learn about Bastille Day, one of France's national holidays?

(J) France   (K) National

(L) Holiday   (M) Bastille Day

---

1. Which key term would you use to find out about both Los Angeles and San Francisco, California's two largest cities?

(A) Cities   (B) San Francisco

(C) Los Angeles   (D) California

2. Which key term would you use to find out about the first meetings of the United Nations which took place in San Francisco in 1945?

(J) United Nations   (K) San Francisco

(L) Meetings   (M) 1945

3. Which key term would you use to learn about the Allied invasion of Europe during World War II?

(A) Allies   (B) Invasion

(C) Europe   (D) World War II

4. Which key term would you use to find out about the Adelie penguin which lives inside the Antarctic Circle near Australia?

(J) Adelie   (K) Penguins

(L) Australia   (M) Antarctica

5. Which key term would you use to find out about Cinco de Mayo, one of Mexico's national holidays?

(A) Mexico   (B) National

(C) Holiday   (D) Cinco de Mayo

6. Which key term would you use to find out about Guy Fawkes Day, one of England's national holidays?

(J) Guy Fawkes Day   (K) National

(L) Holiday   (M) England

7. Which key term would you use to find out about the "Iron Curtain" which separated Eastern and Western Europe?

(A) Europe   (B) Iron Curtain

(C) Eastern Europe (D) Western Europe

8. Which key term would you use to learn about the origin of Halloween, one of our most popular fall holidays?

(J) Fall   (K) Holidays

(L) Popular   (M) Halloween

Answers:
A (A) (B) (C) (D)   2 (J) (K) (L) (M)   5 (A) (B) (C) (D)   8 (J) (K) (L) (M)

B (J) (K) (L) (M)   3 (A) (B) (C) (D)   6 (J) (K) (L) (M)

1 (A) (B) (C) (D)   4 (J) (K) (L) (M)   7 (A) (B) (C) (D)

Work-Study Skills: Bibliography

Directions: Read the question in each item. Choose the answer that you consider to be the best. Mark the answer space for your choice.

Sample

Study this entry taken from a bibliography. Then answer the question.

Yolen, Jane. <u>All Those Secrets of the World</u>. New York: Little, Brown, and Co., 1992.

A. Who published this book?
  - (A) Jane Yolen
  - (B) Little, Brown, and Co.
  - (C) The World
  - (D) New York

Study this bibliography. Then answer questions 1 through 5.

Fowler, Susi Gregg. <u>When Summer Ends</u>. New York: Greenwillow Books, 1989.

Frank, Anne. <u>The Diary of a Young Girl</u>. New York: Pocket Books, 1952.

Lowry, Lois. <u>Number the Stars</u>. New York: Dell, 1989.

McSwigen, Marie. <u>Snow Treasure</u>. New York: Scholastic, 1986.

Reiss, Johanna. <u>The Upstairs Room</u>. New York: Harper Trophy, 1972.

Turner, Ann. <u>Grasshopper Summer</u>. New York: Macmillan, 1989.

1. Which entry in the bibliography has the earliest publication date?
  - (A) *Number the Stars*
  - (B) *The Upstairs Room*
  - (C) *The Diary of a Young Girl*
  - (D) *Grasshopper Summer*

2. Who is the author of <u>When Summer Ends</u>?
  - (F) Gregg Fowler
  - (G) Susi Gregg Fowler
  - (H) New York
  - (J) Greenwillow Books

3. Which book was published by Scholastic?
  - (A) <u>When Summer Ends</u>
  - (B) <u>Number the Stars</u>
  - (C) <u>Grasshopper Summer</u>
  - (D) <u>Snow Treasure</u>

4. Which book was written by Marie McSwigen?
  - (F) <u>Snow Treasure</u>
  - (G) <u>When Summer Ends</u>
  - (H) <u>The Upstairs Room</u>
  - (J) <u>Number the Stars</u>

5. Who published <u>Grasshopper Summer</u>?
  - (A) Greenwillow Books
  - (B) Scholastic
  - (C) Macmillan
  - (D) Pocket Books

Answers:
A (A) (B) (C) (D)   2 (F) (G) (H) (J)   4 (F) (G) (H) (J)
1 (A) (B) (C) (D)   3 (A) (B) (C) (D)   5 (A) (B) (C) (D)

Work-Study Skills: Maps

Directions: Read the question in each item. Then look at the map and find the best answer. Fill in the answer circle for your choice.

Samples

This map shows the state routes, streets, and some buildings in downtown Piedmont.

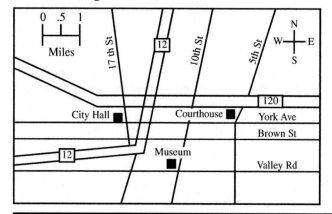

A. Every weekday Mr. Weeks walks from City Hall to the courthouse. About how far does he walk each day?

(1) 1 mile   (2) 2.5 miles

(3) 3 miles   (4) 3.5 miles

B. If you drive into Piedmont on Route 120 from the east and turn north at the first exit, on which street would you leave the downtown area?

(1) York Avenue   (2) Brown Street

(3) 5th Street   (4) 10th Street

This map shows a continent and some of the major cities on the continent.

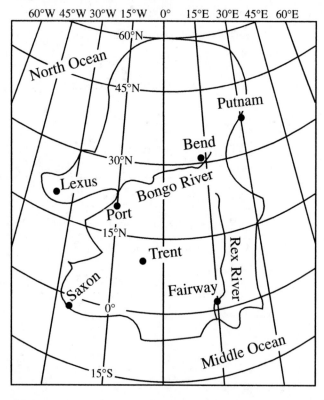

1. Which place is the farthest away from the city of Putnam?

(1) Saxon   (2) Fairway

(3) Port   (4) Trent

2. What would you be near if you were at longitude 10° east and the equator?

(1) Saxon   (2) Trent

(3) the Rex River   (4) the Bongo River

3. What would you be near if you were at longitude 15° east and latitude 30° north?

(1) Fairway   (2) Bend

(3) Port   (4) Saxon

4. The city that would be least likely to have a shipping industry is . . .

(1) Fairway   (2) Putnam

(3) Saxon   (4) Trent

Answers: A ① ② ③ ④ 1 ① ② ③ ④ 3 ① ② ③ ④

B ① ② ③ ④ 2 ① ② ③ ④ 4 ① ② ③ ④

Work-Study Skills: Graphs and Tables

Directions: Read each question. Then look at the graph and find the best answer. Mark the answer space for your choice.

Samples

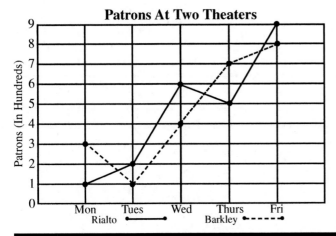

Patrons At Two Theaters

A. How many more patrons were at the Rialto than at the Barkley on Wednesday?

   (1) 100   (2) 200

   (3) 300   (4) 400

B. The graph indicates that the greatest theater attendance was on . . .

   (1) Tuesday   (2) Wednesday

   (1) Thursday   (4) Friday

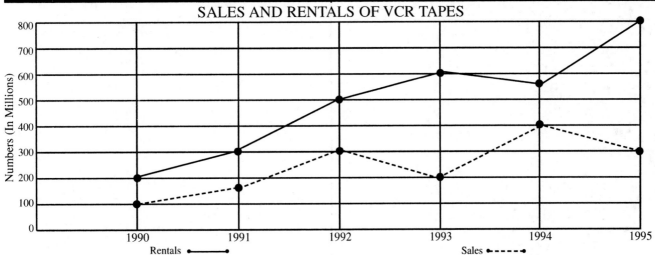

SALES AND RENTALS OF VCR TAPES

1. During which year did the rental of VCR tapes fall?

   (1) 1991   (2) 1992

   (3) 1994   (4) 1995

2. In which year were the fewest VCR tapes sold?

   (1) 1990   (2) 1991

   (3) 1992   (4) 1993

3. In which year was the difference between sales and rentals the least?

   (1) 1990   (2) 1991

   (3) 1992   (4) 1994

4. In which year was the difference between sales and rentals the greatest?

   (1) 1990   (2) 1992

   (3) 1993   (4) 1995

Answers:

A ① ② ③ ④   1 ① ② ③ ④   3 ① ② ③ ④

B ① ② ③ ④   2 ① ② ③ ④   4 ① ② ③ ④

Math Computation: Addition

Directions: Mark the answer space for the correct answer to each addition problem. Choose "none of these" if the right answer is not given.

Samples

A.

$216.01 + 2.37 =$

- (A) 21.838
- (B) 218.38
- (C) 218.48
- (D) 449.01
- (E) none of these

B.

$7\frac{5}{9}$
$+2\frac{2}{9}$

- (F) 9 2/9
- (G) 9 5/18
- (H) 9 7/18
- (J) 9 4/9
- (K) none of these

1.

$\frac{1}{7} + \frac{5}{7} =$

- (A) 1/7
- (B) 4/7
- (C) 6/7
- (D) 1
- (E) none of these

5.

$4\frac{5}{8}$
$+2\frac{1}{3}$

- (A) 6 6/11
- (B) 6 4/5
- (C) 6 23/24
- (D) 7 23/24
- (E) none of these

2.

7.81
+ 2.04

- (F) 0.985
- (G) 9.85
- (H) 9.95
- (J) 99.5
- (K) none of these

6.

$-6 + 7 =$

- (F) 13
- (G) 1
- (H) -1
- (J) -13
- (K) none of these

3.

$0.746 + 0.69 =$

- (A) .0815
- (B) 0.815
- (C) 7.69
- (D) 14.36
- (E) none of these

7.

$0.02 + 0.002 =$

- (A) 0.0004
- (B) 0.0002
- (C) 0.022
- (D) 0.22
- (E) none of these

4.

265, 413
1, 480
889
+ 8, 533

- (F) 264,105
- (G) 275,315
- (H) 276,212
- (J) 276,315
- (K) none of these

8.

$ 104.59
+ 73.67

- (F) $30.92
- (G) $177.16
- (H) $177.26
- (J) $178.26
- (K) none of these

GO→

Answers: A Ⓐ Ⓑ © Ⓓ Ⓔ   2 Ⓕ Ⓖ Ⓗ Ⓙ Ⓚ   5 Ⓐ Ⓑ © Ⓓ Ⓔ   8 Ⓕ Ⓖ Ⓗ Ⓙ Ⓚ

B Ⓕ Ⓖ Ⓗ Ⓙ Ⓚ   3 Ⓐ Ⓑ © Ⓓ Ⓔ   6 Ⓕ Ⓖ Ⓗ Ⓙ Ⓚ

1 Ⓐ Ⓑ © Ⓓ Ⓔ   4 Ⓕ Ⓖ Ⓗ Ⓙ Ⓚ   7 Ⓐ Ⓑ © Ⓓ Ⓔ

Math Computation: Addition *(cont.)*

9.

$$\frac{1}{2} + \frac{1}{3} =$$

(A) 1/6
(B) 2/5
(C) 3/4
(D) 5/6
(E) none of these

10.

476
+ 767
─────

(F) 1,133
(G) 1,243
(H) 1,311
(J) 1,343
(K) none of these

11.

$$2\frac{2}{3}$$
$$+5\frac{4}{5}$$
─────

(A) 7 7/15
(B) 7 2/3
(C) 8
(D) 8 7/15
(E) none of these

12.

$ 564.00
+ 281.95
─────

(F) $845.95
(G) $847.05
(H) $956.95
(J) $965.95
(K) none of these

13.

0.45 + 0.045 =

(A) 0.00495
(B) 0.0495
(C) 0.495
(D) 0.90
(E) none of these

14.

-10 + 5 =

(F) -15
(G) -5
(H) 5
(J) 15
(K) none of these

15.

63 + ☐ = 120

(A) 47
(B) 67
(C) 57
(D) 183
(E) none of these

16.

$$\frac{1}{12} + \frac{3}{8} =$$

(F) 7/24
(G) 11/24
(H) 3/20
(J) 1/5
(K) none of these

17.

29 + 0.4 =

(A) 2.94
(B) 3.3
(C) 33.0
(D) 330
(E) none of these

18.

56
8
25
401
+ 6
─────

(F) 476
(G) 496
(H) 596
(J) 622
(K) none of these

Answers:

9 (A)(B)(C)(D)(E)   12 (F)(G)(H)(J)(K)   15 (A)(B)(C)(D)(E)   18 (F)(G)(H)(J)(K)

10 (F)(G)(H)(J)(K)   13 (A)(B)(C)(D)(E)   16 (F)(G)(H)(J)(K)

11 (A)(B)(C)(D)(E)   14 (F)(G)(H)(J)(K)   17 (A)(B)(C)(D)(E)

Student Practice Page ——————————— TS 179

Math Computation: Subtraction

Directions: Mark the answer space for the correct answer to each subtraction problem. Choose "none of these" if the right answer is not given.

Samples

A.

$$36.08 - 5.90$$

(A) 0.18
(B) 3.018
(C) 30.18
(D) 31.18
(E) none of these

B.

$$15\frac{5}{6} - 6\frac{1}{12}$$

(F) 8 1/3
(G) 9
(H) 9 1/2
(J) 10 1/6
(K) none of these

1.

$$71,254 - 5,864$$

(A) 65,390
(B) 74,610
(C) 76,494
(D) 77,118
(E) none of these

5.

$$2.641 - 0.321 =$$

(A) 2.220
(B) 2.320
(C) 2.920
(D) 2.962
(E) none of these

2.

$$9.36 - 3.01$$

(F) 0.635
(G) 6.03
(H) 6.35
(J) 63.5
(K) none of these

6.

$$\$25.96 - 2.97$$

(F) $22.99
(G) $23.01
(H) $23.91
(J) $27.01
(K) none of these

3.

$$-36 - (-12) =$$

(A) 24
(B) 48
(C) -48
(D) -24
(E) none of these

7.

$$7\frac{26}{39} - 3\frac{15}{39}$$

(A) 4 1/39
(B) 4 3/13
(C) 4 11/39
(D) 4 1/3
(E) none of these

4.

$$\frac{7}{10} - \frac{2}{5} =$$

(F) 1/5
(G) 3/10
(H) 1/3
(J) 1
(K) none of these

8.

$$0.361 - 0.22 =$$

(F) 0.131
(G) 0.141
(H) 0.339
(J) 0.581
(K) none of these

Answers:
A Ⓐ Ⓑ Ⓒ Ⓓ Ⓔ   2 Ⓕ Ⓖ Ⓗ Ⓙ Ⓚ   5 Ⓐ Ⓑ Ⓒ Ⓓ Ⓔ   8 Ⓕ Ⓖ Ⓗ Ⓙ Ⓚ
B Ⓕ Ⓖ Ⓗ Ⓙ Ⓚ   3 Ⓐ Ⓑ Ⓒ Ⓓ Ⓔ   6 Ⓕ Ⓖ Ⓗ Ⓙ Ⓚ
1 Ⓐ Ⓑ Ⓒ Ⓓ Ⓔ   4 Ⓕ Ⓖ Ⓗ Ⓙ Ⓚ   7 Ⓐ Ⓑ Ⓒ Ⓓ Ⓔ

Math Computation: Subtraction *(cont.)*

9.

$$\begin{array}{r} 485 \\ -298 \\ \hline \end{array}$$

(A) 177
(B) 187
(C) 213
(D) 277
(E) none of these

14.

$$\begin{array}{r} \$9.98 \\ -9.97 \\ \hline \end{array}$$

(F) $.01
(G) $.10
(H) $1.00
(J) $1.01
(K) none of these

10.

$$3\frac{5}{7}$$
$$-1\frac{1}{2}$$

(F) 1 9/14
(G) 2 3/14
(H) 2 4/7
(J) 2 4/5
(K) none of these

15.

$1.066 - 0.278 =$

(A) 0.788
(B) 1.344
(C) 1.444
(D) 1.788
(E) none of these

11.

$\boxed{} - 14 = 56$

(A) 42
(B) 52
(C) 60
(D) 70
(E) none of these

16.

$\frac{4}{5} - \frac{1}{10} =$

(F) 7/10
(G) 9/10
(H) 3/15
(J) 3/5
(K) none of these

12.

$\frac{1}{2} - \frac{1}{3} =$

(F) 1/12
(G) 1/10
(H) 1/6
(J) 1/3
(K) none of these

17.

$$\begin{array}{r} 23,754 \\ -21,895 \\ \hline \end{array}$$

(A) 1,769
(B) 1,859
(C) 2,141
(D) 2,969
(E) none of these

13.

$$\begin{array}{r} 9,954 \\ -7,756 \\ \hline \end{array}$$

(A) 2,198
(B) 2,202
(C) 2,208
(D) 2,710
(E) none of these

18.

$98 - \boxed{} = 21$

(F) 67
(G) 77
(H) 78
(J) 87
(K) none of these

Answers:

9 (A)(B)(C)(D)(E) 12 (F)(G)(H)(J)(K) 15 (A)(B)(C)(D)(E) 18 (F)(G)(H)(J)(K)

10 (F)(G)(H)(J)(K) 13 (A)(B)(C)(D)(E) 16 (F)(G)(H)(J)(K)

11 (A)(B)(C)(D)(E) 14 (F)(G)(H)(J)(K) 17 (A)(B)(C)(D)(E)

Math Computation: Multiplication

Directions: Mark the answer space for the correct answer to each multiplication problem. Choose "none of these" if the right answer is not given.

Samples

A.

79
x 30

(A) 109
(B) 237
(C) 2,170
(D) 2,370
(E) none of these

B.

0.3 x 0.8 =

(F) .024
(G) .0024
(H) 2.40
(J) 24.0
(K) none of these

1.

78
x 11

(A) 156
(B) 789
(C) 858
(D) 7,811
(E) none of these

5.

0.41
x 0.5

(A) 0.0205
(B) 0.205
(C) 2.05
(D) 20.5
(E) none of these

2.

$\frac{1}{5}$ x $\frac{5}{8}$ =

(F) 1/8
(G) 5/8
(H) 8/25
(J) 1/40
(K) none of these

6.

$4\frac{1}{3}$ x 9 =

(F) 13 1/3
(G) 15
(H) 36 1/3
(J) 39
(K) none of these

3.

$ 41.98
x 4

(A) $167.01
(B) $167.92
(C) $168.95
(D) $177.92
(E) none of these

7.

$ 19.94
x 6

(A) $119.00
(B) $119.64
(C) $120.00
(D) $120.64
(E) none of these

4.

(-3) (-4) (2) =

(F) -9
(G) 9
(H) 24
(J) -24
(K) none of these

8.

674
x 3

(F) 2,021
(G) 2,022
(H) 2,122
(J) 2,132
(K) none of these

GO→

Answers:
A Ⓐ Ⓑ Ⓒ Ⓓ Ⓔ   2 Ⓕ Ⓖ Ⓗ Ⓙ Ⓚ   5 Ⓐ Ⓑ Ⓒ Ⓓ Ⓔ   8 Ⓕ Ⓖ Ⓗ Ⓙ Ⓚ
B Ⓕ Ⓖ Ⓗ Ⓙ Ⓚ   3 Ⓐ Ⓑ Ⓒ Ⓓ Ⓔ   6 Ⓕ Ⓖ Ⓗ Ⓙ Ⓚ
1 Ⓐ Ⓑ Ⓒ Ⓓ Ⓔ   4 Ⓕ Ⓖ Ⓗ Ⓙ Ⓚ   7 Ⓐ Ⓑ Ⓒ Ⓓ Ⓔ

Math Computation: Multiplication *(cont.)*

9.

$$\begin{array}{r} 72 \\ \times\,65 \\ \hline \end{array}$$

(A) 137
(B) 792
(C) 4,570
(D) 4,680
(E) none of these

14.

$$1\frac{2}{3} \times 3\frac{3}{4} =$$

(F) 6 1/4
(G) 6
(H) 5 1/4
(J) 5
(K) none of these

10.

$$\frac{3}{4} \times \frac{2}{3} =$$

(F) 1/3
(G) 1/2
(H) 8/9
(J) 1
(K) none of these

15.

$$\begin{array}{r} 764.5 \\ \times\,100 \\ \hline \end{array}$$

(A) 76,450
(B) 7645
(C) 764.5
(D) 76.45
(E) none of these

11.

$$\begin{array}{r} 413 \\ \times\,18 \\ \hline \end{array}$$

(A) 431
(B) 3,717
(C) 7,414
(D) 7,434
(E) none of these

16.

$$\begin{array}{r} 555 \\ \times\,424 \\ \hline \end{array}$$

(F) 979
(G) 25,530
(H) 35,552
(J) 235,320
(K) none of these

12.

$$\frac{4}{5} \times 20 =$$

(F) 4
(G) 5
(H) 15
(J) 16
(K) none of these

17.

$$\begin{array}{r} \$\,7.50 \\ \times\,4 \\ \hline \end{array}$$

(A) $3.00
(B) $30.00
(C) $30.30
(D) $300.00
(E) none of these

13.

$$\frac{5}{6} \times \frac{3}{4} =$$

(A) 3/4
(B) 5/8
(C) 1/2
(D) 9/10
(E) none of these

18.

$$7\frac{1}{8} \times 8 =$$

(F) 4
(G) 8
(H) 16
(J) 57
(K) none of these

Answers: 9 Ⓐ Ⓑ Ⓒ Ⓓ Ⓔ 12 Ⓕ Ⓖ Ⓗ Ⓙ Ⓚ 15 Ⓐ Ⓑ Ⓒ Ⓓ Ⓔ 18 Ⓕ Ⓖ Ⓗ Ⓙ Ⓚ
10 Ⓕ Ⓖ Ⓗ Ⓙ Ⓚ 13 Ⓐ Ⓑ Ⓒ Ⓓ Ⓔ 16 Ⓕ Ⓖ Ⓗ Ⓙ Ⓚ
11 Ⓐ Ⓑ Ⓒ Ⓓ Ⓔ 14 Ⓕ Ⓖ Ⓗ Ⓙ Ⓚ 17 Ⓐ Ⓑ Ⓒ Ⓓ Ⓔ

Math Computation: Division

Directions: Mark the answer space for the correct answer to each division problem. Choose "none of these" if the right answer is not given.

Samples

A.

$3\overline{)603}$

(A) 201 R1
(B) 201
(C) 204
(D) 204 R3
(E) none of these

B.

$6\overline{)0.36}$

(F) 0.006
(G) 0.6
(H) 6.0
(J) 60.0
(K) none of these

1.

$14\overline{)53}$

(A) 3
(B) 3 R1
(C) 3 R11
(D) 4 R11
(E) none of these

5.

$\dfrac{3}{8} \div \dfrac{1}{8} =$

(A) 3/8
(B) 1 1/4
(C) 1 3/8
(D) 3
(E) none of these

2.

$1\dfrac{5}{8} \div \dfrac{1}{8} =$

(F) 7
(G) 11
(H) 13
(J) 15
(K) none of these

6.

$6\overline{)0.54}$

(F) 0.09
(G) 0.9
(H) 9.0
(J) 90.0
(K) none of these

3.

$16,092 \div 6 =$

(A) 268
(B) 2682
(C) 2862
(D) 26,082
(E) none of these

7.

$30.6 \div 3 =$

(A) 0.102
(B) 1.02
(C) 102.0
(D) 10.2
(E) none of these

4.

$0.15\overline{)0.090}$

(F) 6.0
(G) 0.006
(H) 0.06
(J) 0.6
(K) none of these

8.

$8\overline{)312}$

(F) 30
(G) 38
(H) 39
(J) 49
(K) none of these

GO→

Answers:
A (A)(B)(C)(D)(E)   2 (F)(G)(H)(J)(K)   5 (A)(B)(C)(D)(E)   8 (F)(G)(H)(J)(K)
B (F)(G)(H)(J)(K)   3 (A)(B)(C)(D)(E)   6 (F)(G)(H)(J)(K)
1 (A)(B)(C)(D)(E)   4 (F)(G)(H)(J)(K)   7 (A)(B)(C)(D)(E)

Math Computation: Division *(cont.)*

9.

$164\overline{)8300}$

(A) 51
(B) 50 R10
(C) 50 R100
(D) 49
(E) none of these

14.

$1\frac{5}{8} \div \frac{3}{8} =$

(F) 4
(G) 4 1/3
(H) 4 2/3
(J) 4 5/8
(K) none of these

10.

$\$ 69.65 \div 7 =$

(F) $9.95
(G) 99.50
(H) $995.00
(J) $9950.00
(K) none of these

15.

$.007\overline{).49}$

(A) 0.07
(B) 0.7
(C) 7.0
(D) 70
(E) none of these

11.

$9.4 \div 4.7 =$

(A) 20
(B) 2.0
(C) 0.2
(D) 00.2
(E) none of these

16.

$29\overline{)3640}$

(F) 125 R5
(G) 125 R15
(H) 126 R6
(J) 126 R16
(K) none of these

12.

$\frac{7}{8} \div \frac{3}{4} =$

(F) 1
(G) 1 1/6
(H) 2
(J) 2 1/3
(K) none of these

17.

$50.5 \div .5 =$

(A) 101
(B) 10.1
(C) 1.01
(D) 0.101
(E) none of these

13.

$36\overline{)1502}$

(A) 41
(B) 41 R26
(C) 42
(D) 42 R10
(E) none of these

18.

$19\overline{)8588}$

(F) 453 R1
(G) 452
(H) 451 R31
(J) 450
(K) none of these

Answers:

9 Ⓐ Ⓑ Ⓒ Ⓓ Ⓔ   12 Ⓕ Ⓖ Ⓗ Ⓙ Ⓚ   15 Ⓐ Ⓑ Ⓒ Ⓓ Ⓔ   18 Ⓕ Ⓖ Ⓗ Ⓙ Ⓚ

10 Ⓕ Ⓖ Ⓗ Ⓙ Ⓚ   13 Ⓐ Ⓑ Ⓒ Ⓓ Ⓔ   16 Ⓕ Ⓖ Ⓗ Ⓙ Ⓚ

11 Ⓐ Ⓑ Ⓒ Ⓓ Ⓔ   14 Ⓕ Ⓖ Ⓗ Ⓙ Ⓚ   17 Ⓐ Ⓑ Ⓒ Ⓓ Ⓔ

Math Computation: Ratios and Percents

Directions: Mark the answer space for the correct answer to each problem. Choose "none of these" if the right answer is not given.

Samples

A.

$$\frac{1}{5} = \frac{\square}{10}$$

(A) 1
(B) 2
(C) 3
(D) 10
(E) none of these

B.

$5 = \square$ % of 10

(F) 5
(G) 10
(H) 25
(J) 50
(K) none of these

1.

$$\frac{1}{8} = \frac{\square}{24}$$

(A) 1
(B) 2
(C) 3
(D) 6
(E) none of these

5.

25 % of 160 = $\square$

(A) 25
(B) 40
(C) 50
(D) 100
(E) none of these

2.

$$\frac{\square}{3} = \frac{4}{6}$$

(F) 1
(G) 2
(H) 3
(J) 4
(K) none of these

6.

$\square$ % of 70 = 35

(F) 25
(G) 30
(H) 35
(J) 40
(K) none of these

3.

$$\frac{4}{\square} = \frac{12}{15}$$

(A) 1
(B) 3
(C) 5
(D) 7
(E) none of these

7.

40 % of $\square$ = 200

(A) 300
(B) 400
(C) 500
(D) 600
(E) none of these

4.

$$\frac{3}{8} = \frac{15}{\square}$$

(F) 24
(G) 32
(H) 40
(J) 48
(K) none of these

8.

12 % of 25 = $\square$

(F) 3
(G) 5
(H) 7
(J) 10
(K) none of these

GO→

Answers:
A Ⓐ Ⓑ Ⓒ Ⓓ Ⓔ   2 Ⓕ Ⓖ Ⓗ Ⓙ Ⓚ   5 Ⓐ Ⓑ Ⓒ Ⓓ Ⓔ   8 Ⓕ Ⓖ Ⓗ Ⓙ Ⓚ
B Ⓕ Ⓖ Ⓗ Ⓙ Ⓚ   3 Ⓐ Ⓑ Ⓒ Ⓓ Ⓔ   6 Ⓕ Ⓖ Ⓗ Ⓙ Ⓚ
1 Ⓐ Ⓑ Ⓒ Ⓓ Ⓔ   4 Ⓕ Ⓖ Ⓗ Ⓙ Ⓚ   7 Ⓐ Ⓑ Ⓒ Ⓓ Ⓔ

Math Computation: Ratios and Percents *(cont.)*

9.

$$\frac{1}{20} = \frac{\boxed{}}{100}$$

(A) 2
(B) 5
(C) 10
(D) 20
(E) none of these

14.

$$6 = \boxed{} \text{ \% of } 24$$

(F) 5
(G) 10
(H) 25
(J) 50
(K) none of these

10.

$$\frac{2}{5} = \frac{\boxed{}}{10}$$

(F) 2
(G) 4
(H) 5
(J) 10
(K) none of these

15.

$$30 \text{ \% of } 120 = \boxed{}$$

(A) 36
(B) 40
(C) 50
(D) 60
(E) none of these

11.

$$\frac{\boxed{}}{8} = \frac{5}{40}$$

(A) 1
(B) 2
(C) 3
(D) 4
(E) none of these

16.

$$\boxed{} \text{ \% of } 80 = 20$$

(F) 20
(G) 25
(H) 40
(J) 50
(K) none of these

12.

$$\frac{5}{\boxed{}} = \frac{20}{32}$$

(F) 4
(G) 5
(H) 6
(J) 7
(K) none of these

17.

$$30 \text{ \% of } \boxed{} = 30$$

(A) 60
(B) 80
(C) 100
(D) 120
(E) none of these

13.

$$\frac{3}{11} = \frac{9}{\boxed{}}$$

(A) 11
(B) 22
(C) 33
(D) 44
(E) none of these

18.

$$15 \text{ \% of } 60 = \boxed{}$$

(F) 6
(G) 9
(H) 12
(J) 15
(K) none of these

Answers:

9 (A) (B) (C) (D) (E)   12 (F) (G) (H) (J) (K)   15 (A) (B) (C) (D) (E)   18 (F) (G) (H) (J) (K)

10 (F) (G) (H) (J) (K)   13 (A) (B) (C) (D) (E)   16 (F) (G) (H) (J) (K)

11 (A) (B) (C) (D) (E)   14 (F) (G) (H) (J) (K)   17 (A) (B) (C) (D) (E)

Math Concepts/Applications: Numeration

Directions: Read and work each problem. Look for the answer. Mark the answer space for your choice.

Samples

A. What does the 8 in 198,234 stand for?

    (A) 8

    (B) 800

    (C) 8000

    (D) 80,000

B. What is 68,231 rounded to the nearest hundred?

    (F) 68,000

    (G) 68,100

    (H) 68,200

    (J) 68,300

1. What fractional part of the figures is not colored in?

    (A) 2/3   (C) 1 1/4

    (B) 3/4   (D) 1 1/3

2. On Friday 61 books were checked out of the school library. On Monday 27 books were checked out. Which answer shows how to estimate the number of books that were checked out to the nearest 10?

    (F) 60 + 20

    (G) 60 + 30

    (H) 70 + 20

    (J) 70 + 30

3. Which has the same meaning as 5^5 ?

    (A) 5 – 5

    (B) 5 x 5

    (C) 5 + 5 + 5 + 5 + 5

    (D) 5 x 5 x 5 x 5 x 5

4. What is 48.61 rounded to the nearest one?

    (F) 48.0

    (G) 49.0

    (H) 50.0

    (J) 51.0

5. Which figure is colored in to indicate 0.37?

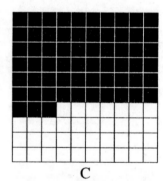

A

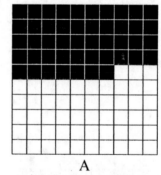

C

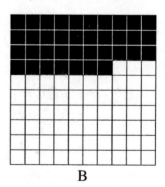

B

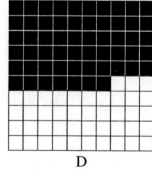

D

Answers:

A Ⓐ Ⓑ Ⓒ Ⓓ   1 Ⓐ Ⓑ Ⓒ Ⓓ   3 Ⓐ Ⓑ Ⓒ Ⓓ   5 Ⓐ Ⓑ Ⓒ Ⓓ

B Ⓕ Ⓖ Ⓗ Ⓙ   2 Ⓕ Ⓖ Ⓗ Ⓙ   4 Ⓕ Ⓖ Ⓗ Ⓙ

Math Concepts/Applications: Number Sentences

Directions: Read and work each problem. Look for the right answer. Mark the answer space for your choice.

Samples

A. $5n - 10 = 25$.   So *n* equals . . .

(A) 5

(B) 7

(C) 8

(D) 45

B. Which number will make the number sentence true?

$$8 \times 7 = \square \times 28$$

(F) 1

(G) 2

(H) 15

(J) 56

1. Which sign will make the number sentence true?

$$180 \div 9 < 14 \; \square \; 4$$

(A) +

(B) −

(C) x

(D) ÷

4. Which number sentence is true when w = 9?

(F) 3w = 24

(G) 3w < 24

(H) 3w > 24

(J) ÷ w 3 = 24

2. Jenny uses 6 lemons to make 2 quarts of lemonade. To make 8 quarts of lemonade, how many lemons will Jenny need?

(F) 12

(G) 18

(H) 24

(J) 48

5. Which sign will make the number sentence true?

$$8 \; \square \; 6 = 8 + 40$$

(A) +

(B) −

(C) x

(D) ÷

3. $8 + y = 14$. So *y* =

(A) 4

(B) 6

(C) 8

(D) 22

6. $2n = 26$. So *n* equals . . .

(F) 3

(G) 8

(H) 13

(J) 14

Answers:

A Ⓐ Ⓑ Ⓒ Ⓓ   1 Ⓐ Ⓑ Ⓒ Ⓓ   3 Ⓐ Ⓑ Ⓒ Ⓓ   5 Ⓐ Ⓑ Ⓒ Ⓓ

B Ⓕ Ⓖ Ⓗ Ⓙ   2 Ⓕ Ⓖ Ⓗ Ⓙ   4 Ⓕ Ⓖ Ⓗ Ⓙ   6 Ⓕ Ⓖ Ⓗ Ⓙ

Math Concepts/Applications: Number Theory

Directions: Read and work each problem. Look for the right answer. Mark the answer space for your choice.

Samples

A. Which is another name for 6.7?

    (A) 6/7

    (B) 6 1/7

    (C) 6 7/10

    (D) 67

B. Another way of writing 1/5 is . . .

    (F) 2/15

    (G) 3/20

    (H) 4/25

    (J) $1 \div 5$

1. What number makes the number sentence true?

$$94 + \square = 94$$

    (A) 0

    (B) 1

    (C) 94

    (D) 188

4. Which is another name for 4.9?

    (F) 49/100

    (G) 1 2/3

    (H) 4 9/10

    (J) 4 1/9

2. The number that can be evenly divided by 4 is . . .

    (F) 10

    (G) 12

    (H) 26

    (J) 41

5. Which number has 2, 3, and 7 as prime factors?

    (A) 12

    (B) 42

    (C) 46

    (D) 56

3. A common factor of 5 and 25 is 5. Another way of writing 5/25 is . . .

    (A) 1/3

    (B) 1/4

    (C) 1/5

    (D) 1/8

6. The least common multiple of 2, 3, and 7 is . . .

    (F) 6

    (G) 12

    (H) 30

    (J) 42

Answers:
A Ⓐ Ⓑ Ⓒ Ⓓ   1 Ⓐ Ⓑ Ⓒ Ⓓ   3 Ⓐ Ⓑ Ⓒ Ⓓ   5 Ⓐ Ⓑ Ⓒ Ⓓ
B Ⓕ Ⓖ Ⓗ Ⓙ   2 Ⓕ Ⓖ Ⓗ Ⓙ   4 Ⓕ Ⓖ Ⓗ Ⓙ   6 Ⓕ Ⓖ Ⓗ Ⓙ

Student Practice Page

Math Concepts/Applications: Whole Numbers and Integers

Directions: Read the question in each item and find the best answer. Mark the answer space for your choice.

Samples

A. Which is the best estimate for 47 times 51?

(A) 40 x 60
(B) 45 x 60
(C) 50 x 50
(D) 50 x 70

B. Find the value of *p*.

$$8 - (-5) = p$$

(F) -13   (H) 3
(G) -3   (J) 13

1. Which of the following is true?

(A) 319 rounded to the nearest ten is 300.
(B) 574 rounded to the nearest hundred is 600.
(C) 8672 rounded to the nearest thousand is 8000.
(D) 57,064 rounded to the nearest thousand is 60,000.

2. Which of these numbers is **not** a multiple of 9?

(F) 27   (G) 38
(H) 45   (J) 54

3. Sandy added 15 to the result of dividing 8 by 4. Which number sentence shows how Sandy found the answer?

(A) $(8 \div 4) + 15 = r$
(B) $(15 \div 8) + 3 = r$
(C) $8 + (15 \div 4) = r$
(D) $4 + (15 \div 8) = r$

4. Which number makes this number sentence true?

$$-9 > \square$$

(F) -10   (H) 0
(G) -5   (J) 4

5. Find the greatest common factor of 25 and 40.

(A) 5   (B) 10
(C) 20   (D) 25

6. If $2192 + 2847 = a$, which of the following is true?

(F) *a* is less than 4000.
(G) *a* is between 2000 and 4000.
(H) *a* is close in value to 4000.
(J) *a* is close in value to 5000.

7. Last Fourth of July, 28 families bought fireworks on July 3rd, and 93 families bought fireworks on July 4th. Which answer shows how to estimate how many more families bought fireworks on July 4th?

(A) 30 + 90
(B) 90 − 20
(C) 90 − 30
(D) 95 − 30

8. Which of these numbers is a factor of 48?

(F) 7   (G) 10
(H) 14   (J) 16

Answers:
A Ⓐ Ⓑ Ⓒ Ⓓ   2 Ⓕ Ⓖ Ⓗ Ⓙ   5 Ⓐ Ⓑ Ⓒ Ⓓ   8 Ⓕ Ⓖ Ⓗ Ⓙ
B Ⓕ Ⓖ Ⓗ Ⓙ   3 Ⓐ Ⓑ Ⓒ Ⓓ   6 Ⓕ Ⓖ Ⓗ Ⓙ
1 Ⓐ Ⓑ Ⓒ Ⓓ   4 Ⓕ Ⓖ Ⓗ Ⓙ   7 Ⓐ Ⓑ Ⓒ Ⓓ

Math Concepts/Applications: Geometry and Measurement

Directions: Read each question and find the correct answer. Fill in the answer circle for your choice.

Samples

A. Which two lines appear to be parallel?

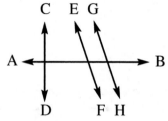

(A) AB and CD

(B) EF and GH

(C) CD and EF

(D) AB and GH

B. A living room is 6 meters wide and 8 meters long. What is the area of the room?

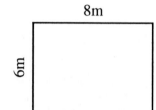

(F) 14 m

(G) 28 m

(H) 48 m

(J) 50 m

---

1. Which two figures are congruent?

  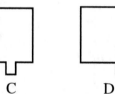

A   B   C   D

(A) A and C

(B) A and D

(C) B and C

(D) B and D

---

2. What is the volume of this cube?

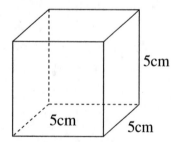

(F) 15m³

(G) 30m³

(H) 90m³

(J) 125m³

---

3. How long is the diameter of this circle?

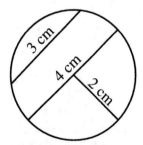

(A) 2 cm

(B) 3 cm

(C) 4 cm

(D) 9 cm

GO→

Answers: A Ⓐ Ⓑ Ⓒ Ⓓ   1 Ⓐ Ⓑ Ⓒ Ⓓ   2 Ⓕ Ⓖ Ⓗ Ⓙ   3 Ⓐ Ⓑ Ⓒ Ⓓ

B Ⓕ Ⓖ Ⓗ Ⓙ

Math Concepts/Applications: Geometry and Measurement *(cont.)*

4. Find the perimeter of this figure.

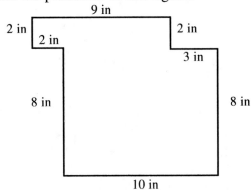

(F) 34 inches

(G) 35 inches

(H) 44 inches

(J) 80 inches

5. What are the coordinates of point A?

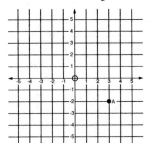

(A) (3, -3)

(B) (-2, 3)

(C) (-3, -2)

(D) (3, -2)

6. Which two lines intersect with line c?

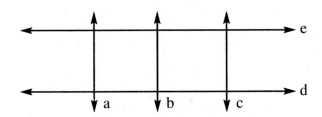

(F) line d and line e

(G) line a and line b

(H) line b and line d

(J) line a and line d

7. How many sides are there in this figure?

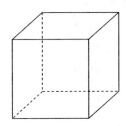

(A) 4   (C) 6

(B) 5   (D) 8

8. How many corners are there in this figure?

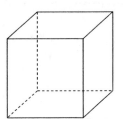

(F) 2   (H) 6

(G) 4   (J) 8   **GO→**

Answers:
4 Ⓕ Ⓖ Ⓗ Ⓙ   6 Ⓕ Ⓖ Ⓗ Ⓙ   8 Ⓕ Ⓖ Ⓗ Ⓙ
5 Ⓐ Ⓑ Ⓒ Ⓓ   7 Ⓐ Ⓑ Ⓒ Ⓓ

Math Concepts/Applications: Geometry and Measurement *(cont.)*

9. The area of this circle is . . .

(Remember π = 3.14.)

(A) 25.12 in²

(B) 50.24 in²

(C) 75.36 in²

(D) 166.89 in²

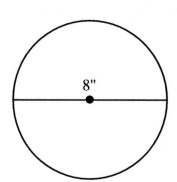

10. To form a line segment parallel to line segment ZU, which two points should you connect?

(F) T and X

(G) X and W

(H) Y and V

(J) Y and W

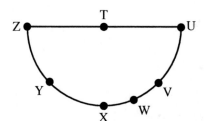

11. To form a line segment perpendicular to line segment ZU, which two points should you connect?

(A) T and X

(B) X and W

(C) Y and V

(D) Y and W

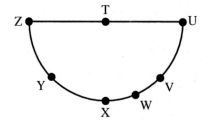

12. Which one of these angles is obtuse?

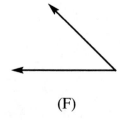   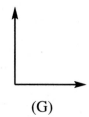   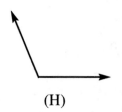   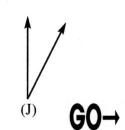

(F)   (G)   (H)   (J)   **GO→**

Answers:
    9 (A) (B) (C) (D)   **11** (A) (B) (C) (D)

    10 (F) (G) (H) (J)   **12** (F) (G) (H) (J)

Math Concepts/Applications: Geometry and Measurement *(cont.)*

13. What is the length of BC?

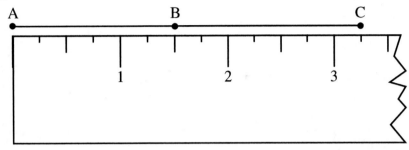

(A) 3 inches

(B) 2 3/4 inches

(C) 2 1/2 inches

(D) 1 3/4 inches

---

14. There are four time zones in the continental United States. When it is 10:00 AM in New York, it is 7:00 AM in California. If your plane leaves New York at 7:00 AM and lands in California at 10:00 AM, how long was the flight?

(F) 2 hours
(G) 6 hours
(H) 7 hours
(J) 8 hours

15. Beth has basketball practice at 4:30 p.m. and an awards banquet at 7:00 p.m. If practice takes an hour, how much time does Beth have to get ready for the dinner?

(A) 30 minutes
(B) 45 minutes
(C) 1 hour 30 minutes
(D) 1 hour 45 minutes

---

16. Which figure has the most corners?

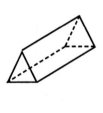   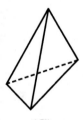   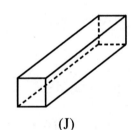

(F)   (G)   (H)   (J)

---

17. What is the volume of this figure?

(A) 8 in³

(B) 10 in³

(C) 15 in³

(D) 30 in³

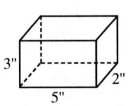

18. Which figure has the greatest area?

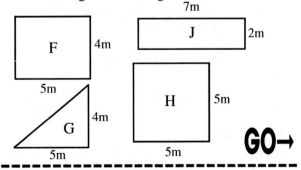

GO→

Answers: **13** Ⓐ Ⓑ Ⓒ Ⓓ   **15** Ⓐ Ⓑ Ⓒ Ⓓ   **17** Ⓐ Ⓑ Ⓒ Ⓓ
           14 Ⓕ Ⓖ Ⓗ Ⓙ   **16** Ⓕ Ⓖ Ⓗ Ⓙ   **18** Ⓕ Ⓖ Ⓗ Ⓙ

Math Concepts/Applications: Geometry and Measurement *(cont.)*

19. This figure is an example of . . .

(A) rotation

(B) reflection

(C) symmetry

(D) translation

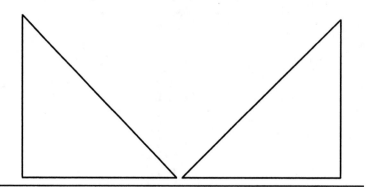

20. What is the area of △ ABC?

(F) 70 sq ft

(G) 35 sq ft

(H) 34 sq ft

(J) 17 sq ft

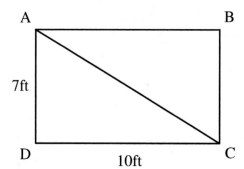

21. What is the volume of this ice chest?

(A) 9.5 ft³

(B) 14 ft³

(C) 24 ft³

(D) 40.5 ft³

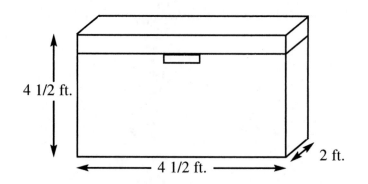

22. What is the perimeter of this square?

(F) 18 ft

(G) 36 ft

(H) 81 ft

(J) 90 ft

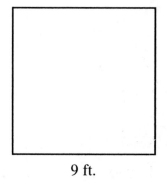

9 ft.

Answers: **19** Ⓐ Ⓑ Ⓒ Ⓓ   **21** Ⓐ Ⓑ Ⓒ Ⓓ
              20 Ⓕ Ⓖ Ⓗ Ⓙ   **22** Ⓕ Ⓖ Ⓗ Ⓙ

Math Concepts/Applications: Temperature

Directions: Read each question and find the correct answer. Mark the answer space for your choice.

Sample

_____

A. What temperature does this thermometer show?

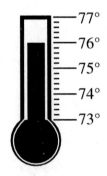

(A) 73°

(B) 74°

(C) 75°

(D) 76°

_____

1. What temperature does this thermometer show?

(A) 30°

(B) 31°

(C) 32°

(D) 33°

_____

2. What temperature does this thermometer show?

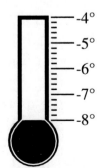

(F) -4°

(G) -8°

(H) -10°

(J) -12°

- -

Answers: **A** Ⓐ Ⓑ Ⓒ Ⓓ   **1** Ⓐ Ⓑ Ⓒ Ⓓ   **2** Ⓕ Ⓖ Ⓗ Ⓙ

Math Concepts/Applications: Probability and Statistics

Directions: Read each question and find the correct answer. Mark the answer space for your choice.

Sample

A. This graph shows the amount of rain that fell in an area over a six-year period. What was the average yearly rainfall during this period?

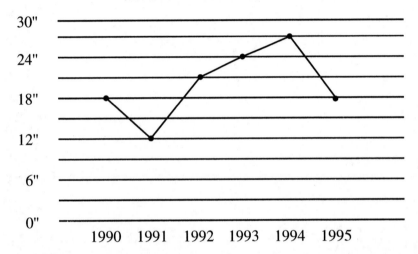

YEARLY RAINFALL IN INCHES

(A) 17 in

(B) 20 in

(C) 23 in

(D) 26 in

---

1. This chart shows the population of a small private school.

Position	Number
Administrators	2
Office Staff	3
Teachers	8
Students	62

If you were waiting outside the door of the school, what are the chances that the next person through the door would be one of the office staff?

(A) 3/63
(B) 1/25
(C) 1/5
(D) 1/3

Refer to the "Yearly Rainfall in Inches" chart at the top of the page to answer these questions.

2. In which year was there the least amount of rainfall?

(F) 1990   (H) 1992
(G) 1991   (J) 1994

3. In which year was there the greatest amount of rainfall?

(A) 1992   (C) 1994
(B) 1993   (D) 1995

4. In which two years did the same amount of rainfall occur?

(F) 1991 and 1995
(H) 1993 and 1994
(G) 1990 and 1995
(J) 1992 and 1995

Answers: A Ⓐ Ⓑ Ⓒ Ⓓ   1 Ⓐ Ⓑ Ⓒ Ⓓ   3 Ⓐ Ⓑ Ⓒ Ⓓ

                                                        2 Ⓕ Ⓖ Ⓗ Ⓙ   4 Ⓕ Ⓖ Ⓗ Ⓙ

Math Concepts/Applications: Estimation

Directions: Read each question and find the correct answer. Mark the answer space for your choice.

Samples

A. The number of days in a month range from a low of 28 in February to a high of 31 in several others. If you spend $3.00 a day on lunch, about how much will you spend each month?

    (A) $100.00
    (B) $93.00
    (C) $90.00
    (D) $84.00

B. What is the best estimate of the area of this triangle?

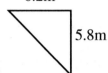
6.2m
5.8m

    (F) 62 square meters
    (G) 36 square meters
    (H) 18 square meters
    (J) 12 square meters

1. A school's PTA is raising money for college scholarships. They have set a goal of $5000, and they have already raised $4719. About how much more money must they raise before they reach their goal?

    (A) $100
    (B) $200
    (C) $300
    (D) $400

2. If you bought a card for $1.75 and a gift for $6.95, about how much change would you receive if you pay with a $10 bill?

    (F) $1.00
    (G) $3.00
    (H) $6.00
    (J) $9.00

3. A day on earth is 24 hours. A day on the moon is 7 hours, 43 minutes. One day on earth equals about how many days on the moon?

    (A) 2
    (B) 3
    (C) 4
    (D) 5

4. Jeff's mother and father walk about 1.9 miles each day. They walk 7 days a week regardless of the weather. About how far do they walk in a week?

    (F) 7 miles
    (G) 14 miles
    (H) 17 miles
    (J) 19 miles

5. Which of these could be used to estimate how to divide a 42-ounce bag of jelly beans among 5 people?

    (A) $5 \div 40$
    (B) $40 - 5$
    (C) $40 + 5$
    (D) $40 \div 5$

6. A car gets 30 miles per gallon of gas. About how much gas would a family use traveling to and from the ocean which is 58 miles away from their home?

    (F) 2 gallons
    (G) 3 gallons
    (H) 4 gallons
    (J) 5 gallons

Answers:
A ⒶⒷⒸⒹ 1 ⒶⒷⒸⒹ 3 ⒶⒷⒸⒹ 5 ⒶⒷⒸⒹ
B ⒡ⒼⒽⒿ 2 ⒡ⒼⒽⒿ 4 ⒡ⒼⒽⒿ 6 ⒡ⒼⒽⒿ

Math Concepts/Applications: Strategies

Directions: Read each question and find the correct answer. Mark the answer space for your choice.

Sample

A. Look at the cube drawn below. What do you need to know to find the surface area of this cube?

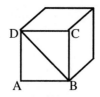

    (A) the perimeter of side ABCD
    (B) the perimeter of ABD
    (C) the length of DB
    (D) the length of AB

---

1. Joe often travels by plane from Los Angeles to St. Louis and back. For each mile he flies he receives two frequent flier credits. What else do you need to know to find the total number of credits that each round trip earns?

    (A) the distance from Los Angeles to St. Louis
    (B) the number of people on the plane
    (C) the number of credits Joe already has
    (D) the distance Joe travels from his home to the airport

2. What information do you need to find the average height of the students in a class?

    (F) the number of students and their grade level
    (G) the number of students and their heights
    (H) the total number of students
    (J) the height of each student

3. Bill's times for three races were 12.0 seconds, 10.8 seconds, and 11.2 seconds. How would you find his average time?

    (A) Add the times and subtract 3.
    (B) Add the times and multiply by 3.
    (C) Add the times and divide by 3.
    (D) Take the middle time.

4. How would you find the width of a door if you knew that it had a height of 7 feet and an area of 2,520 square inches?

    (F) Multiply 7 by 12 (which equals 84). Divide 2,520 by 84.
    (G) Divide 2,520 by 210 (which equals 12) and add 7.
    (H) Subtract 7 from 2,520.
    (J) Divide 2,520 by 12.

5. The county fair was open for 10 days during July. Last year it took in $540,000 in admissions. Each admission cost $6. How can you figure out the average number of people who attended the fair each day?

    (A) Divide $540,000 by 10. Divide again by $6.
    (B) Divide $540,000 by $6.
    (C) Multiply $540,000 by $6 and divide by 10.
    (D) Multiply $540,000 by $6. Multiply again by 10.

6. How would you find the difference in price between airline tickets costing $458.32 and $392.50?

    (F) ($458.32 + $392.50)
    (G) $485.32 - $392.50
    (H) ($458.32 + $392.50) – ($458.32 – $392.50)
    (J) $458.32 + $392.50

Answers: A Ⓐ Ⓑ Ⓒ Ⓓ   1 Ⓐ Ⓑ Ⓒ Ⓓ   3 Ⓐ Ⓑ Ⓒ Ⓓ   5 Ⓐ Ⓑ Ⓒ Ⓓ
                                  2 Ⓕ Ⓖ Ⓗ Ⓙ   4 Ⓕ Ⓖ Ⓗ Ⓙ   6 Ⓕ Ⓖ Ⓗ Ⓙ

Math Concepts/Applications: Problem Solving and Data Analysis

Directions: Read each question and find the correct answer. Mark the answer space for your choice.

Samples

A. A large estate contains many pools, both swimming pools and reflection pools. The total area of the estate is 10 acres. How can you find the land area of the estate?

    (A) pool area - 10

    (B) pool area + 10

    (C) 10 - pool area

    (D) 2(pool area) + 10

B. Mrs. Roberts bought four items at a store and received $6.17 in change from $20. She knew the prices of three of the items that she bought. How can she find out the price of the fourth item?

    (F) $20.00 - $6.17

    (G) $20.00 - $6.17 - cost of 4 items

    (H) $20.00 - $6.17 - cost of 3 items

    (J) $6.17 + cost of 4 items

This graph shows the electric bill of a family for one year. Use the graph to answer questions 1 and 2.

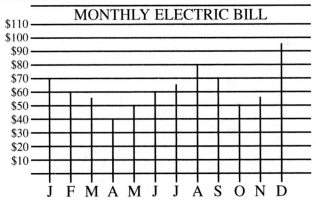

MONTHLY ELECTRIC BILL

The graph below shows the percentage of people who voted for different candidates in an election. The percentage who voted for Grant is missing.

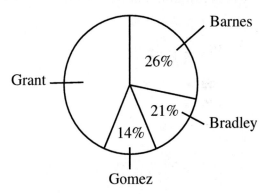

1. How much did the family spend on electricity in April and May?

    (A) $125   (C) 155

    (B) $90   (D) $110

2. In which two months did the family use the most electricity?

    (F) August and September

    (G) August and December

    (H) December and January

    (J) April and May

3. What percentage voted for Grant?

    (A) 14%   (C) 26%

    (B) 39%   (D) 21%

4. Bert paid back the $40 he owed his friend plus 2% interest. Which equation shows this?

    (F) $40 + 2 = □

    (G) ($40 x 0.02) + $40 = □

    (H) $40 x 20 = □

    (J) $40 - 0.2 = □

Answers: **A** (A) (B) (C) (D)   **1** (A) (B) (C) (D)   **3** (A) (B) (C) (D)

    B (F) (G) (H) (J)   **2** (F) (G) (H) (J)   **4** (F) (G) (H) (J)

Math Concepts/Applications: Reasonable Answers

Directions: Read each question and find the correct answer. Mark the answer space for your choice.

Samples

A. At noon, 198 students eat lunch in the school cafeteria. Each table can hold 10 students. About how many tables are there?

    (A) 10

    (B) 19

    (C) 20

    (D) 21

B. A school bus can hold 60 students. A group of 90 students is going on a field trip. How many buses will they need?

    (F) 1

    (G) 1 1/2

    (H) 2

    (J) 2 1/2

1. A half-gallon is 4 times larger than a pint, and a pint is twice as large as a cup. How would you find out how many cups there are in a half-gallon?

    (A) 4 x 4 x 4

    (B) 4 + 4 + 2

    (C) 4 x 2

    (D) 4 x 4

3. One dozen eggs fit into a regular egg carton. How many cartons would you need to store 40 eggs?

    (A) 2

    (B) 3

    (C) 4

    (D) 5

2. About how high is a regular door?

    (F) 12 inches

    (G) 36 inches

    (H) 7 feet

    (J) 15 feet

4. Suppose you are using a calculator to multiply 10 x 100. How many zeroes will be in the answer?

    (F) 1

    (G) 2

    (H) 3

    (J) 4

Answers: A Ⓐ Ⓑ Ⓒ Ⓓ   1 Ⓐ Ⓑ Ⓒ Ⓓ   3 Ⓐ Ⓑ Ⓒ Ⓓ

                       B Ⓕ Ⓖ Ⓗ Ⓙ   2 Ⓕ Ⓖ Ⓗ Ⓙ   4 Ⓕ Ⓖ Ⓗ Ⓙ

Math Concepts/Applications: Pre-Algebra

Directions: Read each question and find the correct answer. Mark the answer space for your choice.

Sample

A. Which point on this grid best shows the coordinates (1, 4)?

    (A) P

    (B) Q

    (C) R

    (D) S

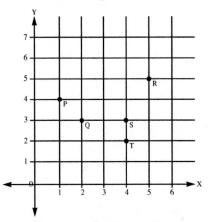

---

1. What is the value of x in this equation?

$$27 - x = 18$$

    (A) 7

    (B) 8

    (C) 9

    (D) 10

2. The table below shows how to convert from miles to kilometers. What number belongs in the box in the table?

Miles	Kilometers
6	10
9	15
12	20
	☐

    (F) 15   (H) 25

    (G) 18   (J) 30

Use the figure below to answer questions 3 and 4.

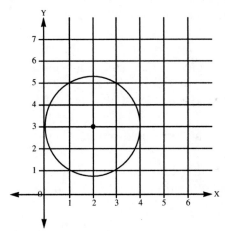

3. Which one of these points is on the circumference of the circle?

    (A) (4, 3)   (C) (2, 2)

    (B) (4, 4)   (D) (1, 5)

4. If you moved the circle two units to the right and one unit up, at which point would the center of the circle be?

    (F) (3, 5)

    (G) (4, 3)

    (H) (2, 5)

    (J) (4, 4)

Answers: A Ⓐ Ⓑ Ⓒ Ⓓ   1 Ⓐ Ⓑ Ⓒ Ⓓ   3 Ⓐ Ⓑ Ⓒ Ⓓ

                                                2 Ⓕ Ⓖ Ⓗ Ⓙ   4 Ⓕ Ⓖ Ⓗ Ⓙ

Teacher Scripts

NOTE: The boxed information for each skill on the following pages references the Student Practice Pages (SPP).

Word Analysis: Consonant and Vowel Sounds

SPP 32

- Open your book to page _____. (Check to make sure that everyone has found the right page.)

- On this page you will match consonant sounds with the beginning sounds of words. Look at the directions at the top of the page and read them to yourself as I read them aloud. (Read the directions to your students.)

- Look at sample A. Read the first word. What part is underlined in the word shape? (the letters sh) Now say the answer choices to yourself and listen for the same sound as the sh in shape. Which word does not have the same sound as the sh in shape? (answer B, descent) Find the answer spaces for sample A at the bottom of the page and mark answer choice B.

- Now look at sample B. Read the first word. What part is underlined in the word fortune? (the letters or) Now say the answer choices to yourself and listen for the same sound as the or in fortune. Which word does not have the same sound as the or in fortune? (answer H, worthy) Find the answer spaces for sample B at the bottom of the page and mark answer choice H.

- Work by yourself to do the rest of the page. Do items 1 through 8 the same way that we did the samples. Then mark your answer choices at the bottom of the page.

Word Analysis: Root Words and Affixes

SPP 33

- Open your book to page _____. (Check to make sure that everyone has found the right page.)

- On this page you will be searching for the root words, prefixes, and suffixes of words. Look at the directions at the top of the page and read them to yourself as I read them aloud. (Read the directions to your students.)

- Look at sample A. The first word, readable, is underlined. You are to find the root word of the underlined word. What is the root word of readable? (read) Now look for the word read among the answer choices. Which answer choice is correct? (C) Find the answer spaces for sample A at the bottom of the page and mark answer choice C.

- Now look at sample B. Read the underlined word. You are to find the prefix of submarine. What is the root word of submarine? (marine) What prefix was added to the beginning of the word marine? (sub) Now look at the answer choices. Which answer choice is correct? (F) Find the answer spaces for sample B at the bottom of the page and mark answer choice F.

- Work by yourself to do the rest of the page. Do items 1 through 6 the same way that we did the samples. Then mark your answer choices at the bottom of the page.

Teacher Scripts

Vocabulary: Synonyms

- Open your book to page _____. (Check to make sure that everyone has found the right page.)

- On this page you will find words that have the same or almost the same meanings. Look at the directions at the top of the page and read them to yourself as I read them aloud. (Read the directions to your students.)

- Look at sample A. Read the phrase. What is the underlined word? (somber) Now read the four words under the phrase. Each word makes sense in the phrase. You can have an angry look, a surprised look, a yearning look, or a melancholy look, so you will have to think about the meaning of the word somber in order to find the correct answer. Which word has the same or almost the same meaning as somber? (answer choice D, melancholy) Find the answer spaces for sample A at the bottom of the page and mark answer choice D.

- Now look at sample B. Read the phrase to yourself and think about the meaning of the underlined word. Then read the four answer choices. Which word in the phrase is underlined? (champion) Which word means the same or almost the same as the word champion as it is used in the phrase? (answer choice F, support) Find the answer spaces for sample B at the bottom of the page and mark answer choice F.

- Work by yourself to do the rest of the page. Do items 1 through 10 the same way that we did the samples. Then mark your answer choices at the bottom of the page.

Vocabulary: Antonyms

- Open your book to page _____. (Check to make sure that everyone has found the right page.)

- On this page you will find words that have the opposite meanings. Look at the directions at the top of the page and read them to yourself as I read them aloud. (Read the directions to your students.)

- Look at sample A. Read the phrase. What is the underlined word? (bashful) Now read the four words under the phrase. Each word makes sense in the phrase. You can have a modest attitude, a bold attitude, an unpleasant attitude, or a self-conscious attitude, so you will have to think about the meaning of the word bashful in order to find the word that means the opposite. Which answer choice word means the opposite of bashful? (answer choice B, bold) Find the answer spaces for sample A at the bottom of the page and mark answer choice B.

- Now look at sample B. Read the phrase to yourself and think about the meaning of the underlined word. Then read the four answer choices. Which word in the phrase is underlined? (ecstatic) Which answer choice means the opposite of ecstatic? (answer choice J, miserable) Find the answer spaces for sample B at the bottom of the page and mark answer choice J.

- Work by yourself to do the rest of the page. Do items 1 through 10 the same way that we did the samples. Then mark your answer choices at the bottom of the page.

Teacher Scripts

Vocabulary: Word Meanings

- Open your book to page_____. (Check to make sure that everyone has found the right page.)

- On this page you will be looking for the meanings of the words I say. Look at the directions at the top of the page and read them to yourself as I read them aloud. (Read the directions to your students.)

- Look at sample A. Listen as I read a sentence. Then read the answer choices to yourself as I read them aloud. This is the sentence: A pedestrian is a person who—A. rides . . . B. walks . . . C. drives . . . D. flies. Which word completes the sentence correctly? (answer choice B, walks) Yes, walks completes the sentence correctly because a pedestrian is a person who walks. Find the answer spaces for sample A at the bottom of the page and mark answer choice B.

- Now look at sample B. Here is the sentence: Something that is one of a kind is—F. valuable . . . G. typical . . . H. radical . . . J. unique. Which word completes the sentence correctly? (answer choice J, unique) Yes, unique is the correct answer because it means one of a kind. Find the answer spaces for sample B at the bottom of the page and mark answer choice J.

- Now we will do the rest of the page. Listen carefully as I read each sentence. Then follow along in your booklet as I read the answer choices. Choose the best answer for each question. Mark your answer choices in the answer spaces at the bottom of the page.

    1. Platinum is a kind of—A. vegetable . . . B. animal . . . C. tree . . . D. metal.
    2. A person who sticks to a job until it is done has—F. perseverance . . . G. ability . . . H. independence . . . J. personality.
    3. To diminish is to—A. increase . . . B. decrease . . . C. intensify . . . D. cooperate.
    4. A garnet is a kind of—F. attic . . . G. clothing . . . H. gem . . . J. flower.
    5. A courteous person is—A. intelligent . . . B. wealthy . . . C. stubborn . . . D. polite.
    6. To antagonize someone is to make him feel—F. special . . . G. irritated . . . H. calm . . . J. attractive.
    7. A person who is conscientious always does what is—A. right . . . B. easy . . . C. fun . . . D. safe.
    8. Something that is appropriate is—F. close . . . G. suitable . . . H. friendly . . . J. cherished.
    9. To expire is to—A. sweat . . . B. happen . . . C. end . . . D. breathe.
    10. A multitude of people is a—F. crowd . . . G. majority . . . H. crusade . . . J. few.

Teacher Scripts

Vocabulary: Affixes `SPP 37`

- Open your book to page _____. (Check to make sure that everyone has found the right page.)
- On this page you will be looking for the best meanings for the prefixes and suffixes of the words. Look at the directions at the top of the page and read them to yourself as I read them aloud. (Read the directions to your students.)
- Look at sample A. You will see two words with the prefix under underlined. Read the words. Now think about the meanings of the words undertow and underage. What does undertow mean? (a current of water moving below the surface) What does underage mean? (below the age required for something) So what does the prefix under mean in both words? (below) Now look at the four answer choices. Which answer choice gives the meaning of the prefix under? (choice B, below) Find the answer spaces for sample A at the bottom of the page and mark answer choice B.
- Now look at sample B. You will see two words with the suffix less underlined. Read the words. Now think about the meanings of the words sugarless and weightless. Then find the answer choice that best tells the meaning of the suffix less as it is used in the two words. Which answer choice best tells the meaning of the suffix less as it is used in sugarless and weightless? (choice H, without) Yes, sugarless means without sugar and weightless means without weight. Find the answer spaces for sample B at the bottom of the page and mark answer choice H.
- Work by yourself to do items 1 through 8 in the same way that we did the samples. Mark your answer choices at the bottom of the page.

Vocabulary: Multiple Meanings `SPP 38`

- Open your book to page _____. (Check to make sure that everyone has found the right page.)
- On this page you will find words that have two meanings. Look at the directions at the top of the page and read them to yourself as I read them aloud. (Read the directions to your students.)
- Look at sample A. You will see two underlined word meanings. Both meanings are for the same word. Read the two meanings. Now read each answer choice and check the words against both meanings. Which word means to jump and a place to keep valuables? (choice D, vault) Find the answer spaces for sample A at the bottom of the page and mark answer choice D.
- Now look at sample B. Read the two underlined word meanings. Next, read each answer choice and check the words against both meanings. Which word means to walk heavily and wood sawed into boards? (choice G, lumber) Find the answer spaces for sample B at the bottom of the page and mark answer choice G.
- Work by yourself to do items 1 through 8 in the same way that we did the samples. Mark your answer choices at the bottom of the page.

Vocabulary: Multiple Meanings `SPP 39`

- Open your book to page _____. (Check to make sure that everyone has found the right page.)
- On this page you will be looking for words that have two meanings. Look at the directions at the top of the page and read them to yourself as I read them aloud. (Read the directions to your students.)
- Look at sample A. There are two sentences and a blank in each sentence. The same word goes in both blanks. Read the sentences and the four words under the sentences. Which word best fits in both sentences? (note) Yes, a note is a short written message and also a musical sound. Find the answer spaces for sample A at the bottom of the page and mark answer choice D for note.
- Now look at sample B. Read the sentences and the four words under the sentences. Which word best fits in both sentences? (choice G, pass) Find the answer spaces for sample B at the bottom of the page and mark answer choice G.
- Work by yourself to do items 1 through 6 in the same way that we did the samples. Mark your answer choices at the bottom of the page.

Teacher Scripts

Vocabulary: In Context

- Open your book to page _____. (Check to make sure that everyone has found the right page.)

- On this page you will be looking for the meanings of words. Look at the directions at the top of the page and read them to yourself as I read them aloud. (Read the directions to your students.)

- Look at sample A. The sentence is: She looked so woebegone as she waved from the door that we had a hard time leaving. Woebegone means—(blank). What does the underlined word mean in this sentence? (sad) Yes, sad is the correct answer because woebegone means sad. Find the answer spaces for sample A at the bottom of the page and mark answer choice A for sad.

- Now look at sample B. The sentence is: As the roller coaster car strained to reach the top of the rise, Anne gasped in trepidation of the long plunge down. Trepidation means—(blank). What does the underlined word mean in this sentence? (fear) Yes, fear is the correct answer because trepidation means fear. Find the answer spaces for sample B at the bottom of the page and mark answer choice G for fear.

- Work by yourself to do items 1 through 6 in the same way that we did the samples. Mark your answer choices at the bottom of the page.

Vocabulary: In Context

- Open your book to page _____. (Check to make sure that everyone has found the right page.)

- On this page you will be looking for the best words to complete the sentences and paragraphs. Look at the directions at the top of the page and read them to yourself as I read them aloud. (Read the directions to your students.)

- Look at sample A. You will see a short paragraph. One sentence in the paragraph has a blank to show that a word is missing. Read the paragraph. The words in the paragraph will help you decide which answer choice is the missing word. Now read the four answer choices. If you need to, reread the paragraph to yourself, substituting each answer choice for the missing word. Which is the best word to use in place of the blank? (quivered) Read the completed paragraph. Which words helped you to decide that quivered was the missing word? (freezing . . . wet . . . cold) Find the answer spaces for sample A at the bottom of the page and mark answer choice C for quivered.

- Now look at sample B. Read the paragraph. The words in the paragraph will help you decide which answer choice is the missing word. Now read the four answer choices. If you need to, reread the paragraph to yourself, substituting each answer choice for the missing word. Which is the best word to use in place of the blank? (answer choice F, fortify) Find the answer spaces for sample B at the bottom of the page and mark answer choice F.

- Work by yourself to do items 1 through 8 in the same way that we did the samples. Mark your answer choices at the bottom of the page.

Teacher Scripts

Vocabulary: In Context

SPP 42

- Open your book to page _____. (Check to make sure that everyone has found the right page.)

- On this page you will be looking for the best words to complete the sentences in the passages. Look at the directions at the top of the page and read them to yourself as I read them aloud. (Read the directions to your students.)

- Look at sample A. Find the passage with blanks in it. A word in each of the sentences is missing. Read the passage and look at the four answer choices for sample A. Read the first sentence again with each of the answer choices in place of the blank. Which word makes the most sense in the sentence? (permission) What is the complete sentence? (After a great deal of discussion, Vivian's mother gave her permission to go to the movies with her friends.) Why are the other answer choices not as good? (They do not make sense with the other words in the sentence.) Find the answer spaces for sample A at the bottom of the page and mark answer choice A for permission.

- Now look at sample B. Read the four answer choices for sample B under the passage. Which word makes the most sense in blank B? (answer choice J, responsible) Find the answer spaces for sample B at the bottom of the page and mark answer choice J.

- Read the passage below the samples. Work by yourself to do items 1 through 6 in the same way that we did the samples. Mark your answer choices at the bottom of the page.

Vocabulary: Derivations

SPP 43

- Open your book to page _____. (Check to make sure that everyone has found the right page.)

- On this page you will be looking for the modern word that comes from an older word in another language. Look at the directions at the top of the page and read them to yourself as I read them aloud. (Read the directions to your students.)

- Look at sample A. Read the question and think about what you are supposed to do. Who can explain what the question means? (Our English words come to us from many other languages and are usually related in both sound and meaning.) Which answer probably comes from the Latin word imitari meaning copy? (imitate) Yes, imitate (answer choice A) is to copy. Find the answer spaces for sample A at the bottom of the page and mark answer choice A for imitation.

- Now look at sample B. Which answer probably comes from the Hindi word jangal meaning forest? (jungle) Yes, a jungle (answer choice J) is a place where trees grow like a forest. Find the answer spaces for sample B at the bottom of the page and mark answer choice J.

- Work by yourself to do items 1 through 6 in the same way that we did the samples. Mark your answer choices at the bottom of the page.

Teacher Scripts

Reading Comprehension: Listening

- Turn to page _____ in your test booklet. (Check to make sure that everyone has found the right page.)

- On this page you will be listening to stories and answering questions about them. Look at the directions at the top of the page and read them to yourself as I read them aloud. (Read the directions to your students.)

- Look at sample A. Listen to the story, the question, and the answer choices that I will read. Here is the story:

- Jeff pulled on his knee pads and elbow pads. Then he sat on the front steps to lace up his rollerblades. He stood up and put on his helmet. Then he set off down the street to meet his friends.

- Here is the question for sample A. Just before Jeff set off down the street, he—A. pulled on his knee pads . . . B. pulled on his elbow pads . . . C. laced up his rollerblades . . . D. put on his helmet. What is the answer? (answer choice D, put on his helmet) Find the answer choices for sample A at the bottom of the page and mark answer space D.

- Next, look at sample B. Here is the question. What is Jeff going to do? F. ride a bike . . . G. skate . . . H. visit a friend . . . J. play ball. What is the answer? (answer choice G, skate) Find the answer choices for sample B at the bottom of the page and mark answer space G.

- Now we will do the rest of the page together. Listen carefully as I read the stories and the answer choices. Mark your answer choices as you did in the samples.

- Find the boxes with questions 1 and 2 in them. Listen to this story.

> Ralph Bunche was the grandson of a slave. He was born in Detroit, Michigan, on August 7, 1904, and he grew up to become a famous diplomat and United Nations mediator. In 1950, he became the first African American to win the Nobel Peace Prize for his work in promoting peace throughout the world. He died on December 9, 1971.

- Item 1. What college did Ralph Bunche attend? A. Detroit City College . . . B. United Nations University . . . C. American University . . . D. The passage does not say.

- Item 2. The people most proud of Ralph Bunche's success were probably—F. citizens of Michigan . . . G. other diplomats . . . H. African Americans . . . J. people at the United Nations.

- Find the box with questions 3 through 5 in it. Listen to this story.

> Greta opened the front door, looked out, and grinned. Last month the seeds she had planted had poked through the soil. Then their leaves had begun to spread out. This morning the dew was glistening on the flower buds that had started to form. As Greta watched, a beautiful butterfly dropped down to look at the place where flowers would soon be blooming. Greta could hardly wait to enjoy the warm months ahead.

- Item 3. Most likely, what season is it in this story? A. spring . . . B. summer . . . C. fall . . . D. winter.

- Item 4. What was on the flower buds? F. soil . . . G. rain . . . H. leaves . . . J. dew.

- Item 5. What happened last? A. The seeds came up . . . B. The leaves spread out . . . C. The flower buds formed . . . D. A butterfly dropped down.

Teacher Scripts

Reading Comprehension: Listening *(cont.)*

- Find the boxes with questions 6 and 7 in them. Listen to this passage.

> We are writing to ask you to support the proposed recreation center which would be built near Anderson School. The students at Anderson School need this center to provide interesting and safe activities during the afternoon and evening hours. There are no playground or sports facilities near our school, and the streets are too dangerous for any organized games. We students have agreed to follow all of the rules of good sportsmanship and good citizenship at the recreation center. Now we need your help. Please vote to build the center.
> Sincerely,
> The seventh grade students of Anderson School

- Item 6. This passage was written as a—F. newspaper article . . . G. fictional story . . . H. letter . . . J. television news bulletin.

- Item 7. The authors' purpose in this passage is to—A. entertain . . . B. inform . . . C. describe . . . D. persuade.

- Find the boxes with questions 8 through 10 in them. Listen to this story.

> Juan inspected his surroundings carefully. Surely, there must be a clue here somewhere. There must be some way to figure out where he was and how he had gotten there. He shook his head and rubbed his eyes. Why couldn't he remember?
> All around him were flat green fields that looked smooth and freshly mowed. There were no mountains, no hills, not even any trees. And there were no people. Juan was entirely alone.

- Item 8. What is the mood of this passage? F. happy . . . G. eerie . . . H. triumphant . . . J. angry.

- Item 9. How does Juan feel? A. confused . . . B. confident . . . C. apathetic . . . D. patient.

- Item 10. The best title for this passage would be—F. Green Fields . . . G. Juan's Day in the Country . . . H. Alone at Last! . . . J. Where Am I?

Teacher Scripts

Reading Comprehension: Stories

Explanatory Notes

1. The sample for "Reading Comprehension: Passages" consists of one page. A short selection is followed by five questions. The skills tested are indicated by the numbers listed in the Table of Contents. In the sample these skills are the following:

   3 (Main Ideas)   13 (Author's Purpose)
   2 (Details)   1 (Word Meanings)
   5 (Cause/Effect)

   The sample will give students an idea of the story format.

2. The Student Practice Pages and Reading Comprehension: Passages consist of four sections, each of which is comprised of multiple pages. Each section contains one fiction passage and one non-fiction passage. Each passage is followed by a group of questions. Within each section, all of the reading comprehension skills are tested once. Skill 1, Word Meaning, is tested four times.

   In this way, each two-passage section tests a full range of comprehension skills. If you include all four sections in your Practice Test, you will assess each skill four times. Word meanings will be assessed sixteen times.

   The comprehension skills are listed by number in the "Table of Contents" and below for your convenience.

---

1. **Word Meanings**	12. **Relationships**
2. **Details**	13. **Author's Purpose**
3. **Main Idea**	14. **Figurative Language**
4. **Sequence**	15. **Interpreting Events**
5. **Cause and Effect**	16. **Plot**
6. **Inferring the Main Idea**	17. **Characters**
7. **Drawing Conclusions**	18. **Mood**
8. **Predicting Outcomes**	19. **Setting**
9. **Identifying Feelings**	20. **Making Comparisons**
10. **Reality and Fantasy**	21. **Analogies**
11. **Fact and Opinion**	

Note: The comprehension skill numbers are noted on the appropriate answer key pages at the back of this book.

Teacher Scripts

Reading Comprehension: Passages/Sample (Skills 3, 2, 5, 13, 1) SPP 45

- Turn to page _____ in your test booklet. (Check to make sure everyone has found the right place.)

- On this page you will answer questions about a reading passages. Listen as I read the directions to you.

- Read the selection in the first column to yourself. Look at the five questions that follow the selection. Each question has four answer choices. Check back in the selection to decide on your answers and then mark the answer spaces at the bottom of the page.

- Which answer did you choose for question number 1? (C, <u>anthropology in general</u>) Yes, this selection is about anthropology as a general topic. Which answer did you choose for question number 2? (G, <u>the history of human biology</u>) Physical anthropologists get much of their information from the bones of people who died long ago. Which answer did you choose for question number 3? (C, <u>human beings are so complex</u>) Human beings are so complex that physical and cultural anthropology overlap each other. Which answer did you choose for question number 4? (F, <u>establish a basis for considering both the physical and cultural branches of anthropology</u>) This is the best description of the author's purpose.

- Which answer did you choose for question number 5? (D, <u>a combination of the physical and cultural approaches to anthropology</u>) The word itself is a combination of <u>biological (physical) and cultural</u>.

- Now you are ready to read more selections and answer question about them.

Reading Comprehension: Passages/Sections 1–4 (All Skills) SPP 46–69

- Turn to page _____ in your test booklet. (Check to make sure everyone has found the right place.)

- On the next few pages you will answer questions about selections you will read. Find the directions at the top of the page and read them to yourself as I read them aloud.

- Read the first selection to yourself. Then answer the questions that follow it. Each question has four answer choices. Check back in the selection to decide on your answers and then mark the answer spaces at the bottom of the page.

- When you come to the arrows at the bottom of the pages, turn to the next page and continue to read and answer the questions. Keep going until you come to the stop sign.

Teacher Scripts

Spelling

Note:

- The formats for testing spelling skills differ widely among the tests, even from grade level to grade level. As often as possible, these testing formats are identified for you on the title line at the beginning of each script and practice page.

- You may want to give your students the benefit of trying all of these formats, or you may wish to use the Spelling List (starting on page 190) to create more practice pages of your own in the appropriate format(s). The Spelling List contains many words that are tested as well as those used as distracters in the various spelling items.

Spelling Skills (CAT/CTBS)   SPP 70

- Turn to page _____ in your test booklet. (Check to make sure that everyone has found the right page.)

- On this page you will be looking for the correct spellings of words that complete sentences. Look at the directions at the top of the page. Read them to yourself as I read them aloud. (Read the directions to students.)

- Look at the sentence in sample A. The blank shows that a word is missing. Read the sentence. Now look at the four words under the sentence. One word shows the right way to spell the missing word. Which answer choice shows the correct spelling of the word that belongs in the sentence? (choice B) Yes, h-i-l-a-r-i-o-u-s is the correct spelling of the word hilarious. Find the answer spaces for sample A at the bottom of the page and fill in answer choice B.

- Now look at sample B. Read the sentence. Examine the four answer choices and find the correct spelling of the missing word. Which answer choice shows the correct spelling of the word that belongs in the sentence? (choice H) Yes, m-a-g-a-z-i-n-e is the correct spelling of the word magazine. Find the answer spaces for sample B at the bottom of the page and fill in answer choice H.

- Work by yourself to finish the rest of the page in the same way that we did the samples. Mark your answer choices at the bottom of the page.

Spelling Skills (CAT/CTBS)   SPP 71

- Turn to page _____ in your test booklet. (Check to make sure that everyone has found the right page.)

- On this page you will show how well you can spell words. Look at the directions at the top of the page. Read them to yourself as I read them aloud. (Read the directions to your students.)

- Look at sample A. Read the four phrases. Find the underlined word that is spelled incorrectly. Which answer has an incorrectly spelled word? (choice B) The correct spelling of journey is j-o-u-r-n-e-y. Find the answer spaces for sample A at the bottom of the page and fill in answer choice B.

- Look at sample B. Read the four phrases. Find the underlined word that is spelled incorrectly. (choice F) The correct spelling of laboratory is l-a-b-o-r-a-t-o-r-y. Find the answer spaces for sample B at the bottom of the page and fill in answer choice F.

- Work by yourself to finish the rest of the page in the same way that we did the samples. Mark your answer choices at the bottom of the page.

Teacher Scripts

Spelling

Spelling Skills (ITBS)

SPP 72

- Turn to page _____ in your test booklet. (Check to make sure that everyone has found the right page.)

- On this page you will be looking for words with spelling mistakes. Look at the directions at the top of the page. Read them to yourself as I read them aloud. (Read the directions to your students.)

- Look at sample A. Read the last answer choice. (no mistake) You should choose this answer only if all of the words in an item are spelled correctly. Now read the words in sample A and look for one with a spelling mistake. Did you find a word with a mistake? (yes) Which answer should you choose? (choice 2, meeger) Find the answer spaces for sample A at the bottom of the page and fill in answer choice 2.

- Examine the words in sample B. Are any of them spelled incorrectly? (no) Which answer should you choose? (choice 5, no mistake) Find the answer spaces for sample B at the bottom of the page and fill in answer choice 5.

- Now work by yourself to finish the rest of the page in the same way that we did the sample. Mark your answer choices at the bottom of the page.

Spelling Skills (SAT)

SPP 73

- Turn to page _____ in your test booklet. (Check to make sure that everyone has found the right page.)

- On this page you will look for words with spelling mistakes. Look at the directions at the top of the page. Read them to yourself as I read them aloud. (Read the directions to your students.)

- Look at sample A. Read the four words. Which word is spelled incorrectly? What is the correct answer? (B) Yes, B is the right answer because the word lavender is spelled incorrectly. Who can tell me how it should be spelled? (l-a-v-e-n-d-e-r) Find the answer spaces for sample A at the bottom of the page and fill in answer choice B.

- Now look at sample B. Read the four words. Which word is spelled incorrectly? What is the correct answer? (J) Yes, J is the right answer because the word melody is spelled incorrectly. Who can tell me how it should be spelled? (m-e-l-o-d-y) Find the answer spaces for sample A at the bottom of the page and fill in answer choice J.

- Work by yourself to finish the rest of the page in the same way that we did the sample. Mark your answer choices at the bottom of the page.

Teacher Scripts

Spelling

Spelling Skills (SAT)

SPP 74

- Turn to page _____ in your test booklet. (Check to make sure that everyone has found the right page.)

- On this page you will be looking for the word that is spelled incorrectly for the way it is used in a phrase. Look at the directions at the top of the page. Read them to yourself as I read them aloud. (Read the directions to your students.)

- Look at sample A. Which underlined word is spelled incorrectly for the way it is used in the phrase? Which answer did you choose? (A) Yes, A is the right answer because the word hole is spelled incorrectly. How should the word be spelled in this phrase? (w-h-o-l-e) Find the answer spaces for sample A at the bottom of the page and fill in answer choice A.

- Now look at sample B. Which underlined word is spelled incorrectly for the way it is used in the phrase? Which answer did you choose? (F) Yes, F is the correct answer because the word knew is spelled incorrectly. How should the word be spelled in this phrase? (n-e-w) Find the answer spaces for sample B at the bottom of the page and fill in answer choice F.

- Now work by yourself to finish the rest of the page in the same way that we did the samples. Mark your answer choices at the bottom of the page.

Spelling Skills (MAT)

SPP 75

- Turn to page _____ in your test booklet. (Check to make sure that everyone has found the right page.)

- On this page you will be looking for words with spelling mistakes. Look at the directions at the top of the page. Read them to yourself as I read them aloud. (Read the directions to your students.)

- Look at sample A. Read the sentence with the underlined words to yourself. Find the underlined word that has a spelling error. If there is no error, choose the last answer, no mistake. Which word has a spelling error? (the first one) Answer A, a-s-s-i-n-m-e-n-t, has a spelling error and should be spelled a-s-s-i-g-n-m-e-n-t. Find the answer spaces for sample A at the bottom of the page and fill in answer choice A.

- Now do sample B. Find the underlined word that has a spelling error. If there is no error, choose the last answer, no mistake. Which answer choice is correct? (H) Yes, all of the words are spelled correctly. Find the answer spaces for sample B at the bottom of the page and fill in answer choice H.

- Now work by yourself to finish the page. In each item, read the sentence and look at the underlined words. Choose the word that has a spelling error. If there is no error, choose the last answer, no mistake. Mark your answer choices at the bottom of the page.

Teacher Scripts

Language Mechanics: Capitalization (CAT/CTBS) SPP 76

- Turn to page _____ in your test booklet. (Check to make sure that everyone has found the right page.)

- On this page you will be looking for mistakes in capitalization. Look at the directions at the top of the page. Read them to yourself as I read them aloud. (Read the directions to your students.)

- Look at the sentence in sample A. It is divided into four parts. Read the first part of the sentence. Is there a word in this part that needs a capital letter? (no) Read the second part. Is there a word in this part that needs a capital letter? (no) Read the third part. Do you see a word in this part of the sentence that should begin with a capital letter? (yes) Which word is it? (bay) Why should bay begin with a capital letter? (It is part of the name of a city; city names always begin with capital letters.) What letter is under the third part of the sentence? (C) Find the answer spaces for sample A at the bottom of the page and fill in answer space C.

- Now look at sample B. Read the word that comes after the sentence. What is it? (none) The word none has a letter under it. You should mark the answer space for the word none only if another capital letter is not needed in the sentence. Look at the sentence in sample B. Read each part to yourself and look for a word that should begin with a capital letter. Is there a word in any of the four parts of the sentence that needs a capital letter? (no) What should you do? (mark the answer space for none) Find the answer spaces for sample B at the bottom of the page and mark answer space K.

- Do the rest of the page by yourself. Do items 1 through 8 in the same way that we did the samples. Mark your answer choices at the bottom of the page.

Language Mechanics: Capitalization (ITBS) SPP 77

- Turn to page _____ in your test booklet. (Check to make sure that everyone has found the right page.)

- On this page you will be looking for capitalization mistakes. Look at the directions at the top of the page. Read them to yourself as I read them aloud. (Read the directions to your students.)

- Look at sample A. Each item in this lesson contains one or two sentences written on three lines. Read line 4 in sample A. (no mistakes) You should choose this answer only if an item does not have a capitalization mistake. Now read line 1 of sample A. Is there a capitalization mistake in this line? (no) Read line 2. Do you see a mistake in capitalization? (Yes, the word "she" should begin with a capital letter.) Why? (The first word of a sentence always begins with a capital letter.) Find the answer spaces for sample A at the bottom of the page and mark answer space 2 because there is a capitalization mistake in line 2.

- Now look at sample B. Read the item to yourself line by line and look for a capitalization mistake. Did you find a mistake? (no) What should you do if an item does not have a mistake in capitalization? (mark answer space 4, no mistakes) Find the answer spaces for sample B at the bottom of the page and mark answer space 4 because there are no capitalization mistakes.

- Now work by yourself to finish the rest of the page in the same way that we did the samples. Mark your answer choices at the bottom of the page.

Teacher Scripts

Language Mechanics: Capitalization (SAT)

SPP 78

- Turn to page _____ in your test booklet. (Check to make sure that everyone has found the right page.)

- On this page you will be looking for the words that are correctly capitalized. Look at the directions at the top of the page. Read them to yourself as I read them aloud. (Read the directions to your students.)

- Look at sample A. Read the sentence. Which group of words is capitalized correctly? (B) Yes, B is the correct answer because the words in the names of states always begin with capital letters. Find the answer spaces for sample A at the bottom of the page and mark answer space B.

- Now look at sample B. Read the sentence. Which group of words is capitalized correctly? (J) Yes, J is the correct answer because the important words in a title always begin with capital letters. Find the answer spaces for sample B at the bottom of the page and mark answer space J.

- Do the rest of the page by yourself. Do items 1 through 8 in the same way that we did the samples. Mark your answer choices at the bottom of the page.

Language Mechanics: Punctuation (CAT/CTBS)

SPP 79

- Turn to page _____ in your test booklet. (Check to make sure that everyone has found the right page.)

- On this page you will be looking for the correct punctuation for each sentence. Look at the directions at the top of the page. Read them to yourself as I read them aloud. (Read the directions to your students.)

- Look at sample A. Read the sentence. Now look at the punctuation marks under the sentence. Does one of the punctuation marks belong in the sentence? (yes) Which one? (the comma) Where is the comma needed? (after the word hamburgers) Why? (Commas are used to separate words in a series.) What letter is next to the comma? (B) Find the answer spaces for sample A at the bottom of the page and mark answer space B.

- Now look at sample B. Read the word at the end of the row of punctuation marks. What is the word? (none) The word none has a letter in front of it. You should mark the answer space for the word none only if no other punctuation mark is needed in the sentence. Read the sentence in sample B to yourself. Then check to see if the sentence needs one of the punctuation marks given in the row of answer choices. Mark the space for none if the punctuation is correct. Which answer space did you mark? (K, none) Why? (The sentence is correct; no more punctuation marks are needed.)

- Do the rest of the page by yourself. Do items 1 through 8 in the same way that we did the samples. Mark your answer choices at the bottom of the page.

Teacher Scripts

Language Mechanics: Punctuation (CAT/CTBS)

- Turn to page _____ in your test booklet. (Check to make sure that everyone has found the right page.)
- On this page you will be looking for correct punctuation. Look at the directions at the top of the page. Read them to yourself as I read them aloud. (Read the directions to your students.)
- Look at the sentence with the underlined part in sample A. Now look at only the underlined part. The words *our favorite teacher* are a parenthetical phrase which explains part of the sentence. How should you punctuate a parenthetical phrase in a sentence? (Put a comma before and after the phrase to set it off from the rest of the sentence.) Look at the underlined part of the sentence again. Is the punctuation correct? (no) Why not? (A comma is used only before the phrase our favorite teacher; a comma is missing after the phrase.) Look at the answer choices. Examine them carefully and find the one that shows the correct punctuation for the underlined part of the sentence. Which one did you choose? (choice B) Yes, choice B shows commas being correctly used to set off the parenthetical phrase in the sentence. Mark answer space B for sample A.
- Now look at sample B. Read the last answer choice. What is it? (correct as it is) You should mark the answer space for correct as it is only if the underlined part of the sentence already has the correct punctuation. Does the underlined part of the sentence have the correct punctuation? (yes) What should you do? (mark the answer space for correct as it is) Find the answer spaces for sample B at the bottom of the page and mark answer space K.
- Do the rest of the page by yourself. Do items 1 through 6 in the same way that we did the samples. Mark your answer choices at the bottom of the page.

Language Mechanics: Punctuation (ITBS)

- Turn to page _____ in your test booklet. (Check to make sure that everyone has found the right page.)
- On this page you will be looking for punctuation mistakes. Look at the directions at the top of the page. Read them to yourself as I read them aloud. (Read the directions to your students.)
- Each item on this page contains one or two sentences written on three lines. Which answer should you choose if an item does not have a punctuation mistake? (answer 4, no mistakes)
- Look at sample A. Read the item to yourself line by line and stop if you find a line with a punctuation mistake. Read line 1. Is there a punctuation mistake in this line? (no) Read line 2. Do you see a mistake? (Yes, an apostrophe is missing between the letters t and s in the word let's.) That's right. The word let's is a contraction of the words let and us, so an apostrophe should be used in place of the letter that was left out. Find the answer spaces for sample A at the bottom of the page and mark answer space 2.
- Now look at sample B. Read the item to yourself line by line and stop if you find a line with a punctuation mistake. Did you find a mistake? (yes, in line 2) What is the mistake? (the use of a comma after the word centers) Yes, you do not need to pause after the word centers, so a comma should not be used there. Find the answer spaces for sample B at the bottom of the page and mark answer space 2 because there is a punctuation mistake in line 2.
- Do the rest of the page by yourself. Do items 1 through 10 in the same way that we did the samples. Mark your answer choices at the bottom of the page.

Teacher Scripts

Language Mechanics: Punctuation (SAT)

SPP 82

- Turn to page _____ in your test booklet. (Check to make sure that everyone has found the right page.)

- On this page you will be looking for correct punctuation. Look at the directions at the top of the page. Read them to yourself as I read them aloud. (Read the directions to your students.)

- Look at sample A. Read the sentence. Which answer shows the correct punctuation? (C) Yes, C is the correct answer because a comma should be used after an introductory word or phrase in a sentence. Find the answer spaces for sample A at the bottom of the page and mark answer space C.

- Now look at sample B. Read the sentence. Which answer has the correct punctuation? (F) Yes, F is the correct answer because a comma should be used before a quotation, and quotation marks are used to show words that are being said. Find the answer spaces for sample B at the bottom of the page and mark answer space F.

- Do the rest of the page by yourself. Do items 1 through 8 in the same way that we did the samples. Mark your answer choices at the bottom of the page.

Language Mechanics: Capitalization and Punctuation

SPP 83

- Turn to page _____ in your test booklet. (Check to make sure that everyone has found the right page.)

- On this page you will be looking for the answer that shows the correct capitalization and punctuation. Look at the directions at the top of the page. Read them to yourself as I read them aloud. (Read the directions to your students.)

- Look at sample A. Read the sentences. Which one is correctly written without any capitalization or punctuation errors? (the second one, choice B) Yes, the second sentence is written correctly. There are no capitalization or punctuation mistakes. Find the answer spaces for sample A at the bottom of the page and mark answer space B.

- Now look at sample B. This is a different type of item. Read the sentence with the underlined part. Then look at the answer choices. Find the answer choice that shows the correct capitalization and punctuation for the underlined part. If the part is correct, choose "correct as it is." Which answer did you choose? (J) Yes, the underlined part is correct. Find the answer spaces for sample B at the bottom of the page and mark answer space J.

- Do the rest of the page by yourself. For items 1 through 3, choose the sentence that has the correct capitalization and punctuation. For numbers 4 through 6, choose the answer choice that shows the correct capitalization and punctuation for the underlined part. Choose "correct as it is" only if the underlined part has no errors. Mark your answer choices at the bottom of the page.

Teacher Scripts

Language Mechanics: Applied Mechanics (1)

SPP 84

- Turn to page _____ in your test booklet. (Check to make sure that everyone has found the right page.)

- On this page you will be correcting errors in capitalization, punctuation, and spelling in a letter. Look at the directions at the top of the page. Read them to yourself as I read them aloud. (Read the directions to your students.)

- Read the question for sample A and look at all of the answer choices. Now find line 2 in the letter. Which answer choice is the best revision for line 2? (answer C) Yes answer C is correct. The word believe is misspelled. Mark answer space C for sample A in the answer rows at the bottom of the page.

- Do the rest of the page by yourself. Decide which revisions are necessary in the letter. If the indicated part of the letter is correct, choose "Make no change." Mark your answer choices at the bottom of the page.

Language Mechanics: Applied Mechanics (2 and 3)

SPP 85, 86

- Turn to page _____ in your test booklet. (Check to make sure that everyone has found the right page.)

- On this page you will be deciding whether each underlined part has an error in spelling, capitalization, or punctuation. If the underlined part is correct, you will choose "no error."

- Read the passage at the top of the page. Is there an error in the underlined part for sample A? (yes, punctuation) Correct, a comma is missing from the underlined part. At the bottom of the page, mark answer C for sample A.

- Now do sample B. Which answer should you choose? (J) Yes, the underlined part is correct. Mark answer space J for sample B.

- Work by yourself to finish the page. When you reach the arrow, go on to the next page and work until you come to the stop sign at the bottom of the page.

Teacher Scripts

Language Expression: Usage

SPP 87

- Turn to page _____ in your test booklet. (Check to make sure that everyone has found the right page.)

- On this page you will be looking for words that correctly complete sentences. Look at the directions at the top of the page. Read them to yourself as I read them aloud. (Read the directions to your students.)

- Look at sample A. Read the sentence with the blank. Now examine the answers under the sentence. Which answer sounds the best and correctly completes the sentence? (choice C, herself) What is the complete sentence? (She helped herself to food from the buffet table.) Mark answer space C for sample A.

- Now look at sample B. Read the sentence with the blank. Consider the answers under the sentence. Which answer sounds the best and correctly completes the sentence? (choice F, shook) What is the complete sentence? (Jodie wanted to know what was in the package so she shook it.) Mark answer space F for sample B.

- Do the rest of the page by yourself. Do items 1 through 8 in the same way that we did the samples. Mark your answer choices at the bottom of the page.

Language Expression: Usage

SPP 88

- Turn to page _____ in your test booklet. (Check to make sure that everyone has found the right page.)

- On this page you will be looking for words that are being used incorrectly. Look at the directions at the top of the page. Read them to yourself as I read them aloud. (Read the directions to your students.)

- Look at the sentences written on the three lines in sample A. What does it say in line 4? (no mistakes) You should choose this answer only when an item does not have a usage mistake. Read the answer choices to yourself. Which answer did you choose? (B) The second line has a mistake. The word tore should be torn. Find the answer spaces for sample A at the bottom of the page and mark answer space B.

- Now look at sample B. Read the item to yourself line by line and search for a mistake. Choose the last answer if there is no mistake. (pause) Which answer did you choose? (M) All of the lines are correct so you should choose the last answer choice, no mistakes. Fill in answer M for sample B in the answer spaces at the bottom of the page.

- Do the rest of the page by yourself. Read items 1 through 10 to yourself word by word. Choose the line that has an error as your answer. If the item has no errors, choose no mistakes as your answer. Mark your answer choices at the bottom of the page.

Teacher Scripts

Language Expression: Applied Usage

SPP 89

- Turn to page _____ in your test booklet. (Check to make sure that everyone has found the right page.)

- On this page you will be correcting errors in word usage. Look at the directions at the top of the page. Read them to yourself as I read them aloud. (Read the directions to your students.)

- Read the question for sample A and look at all of the answer choices. Now read the first sentence of the selection. Does the sentence need any of the revisions suggested by the answer choices? (no) What should you do? (Choose answer D, Make no change.) Yes, answer D is correct. Mark answer space D for sample A.

- Do the rest of the items by yourself. Decide which revisions are necessary. If the indicated part of the selection is correct, choose "Make no change." Mark your answers at the bottom of the page.

Language Expression: Correct Words

SPP 90

- Turn to page _____ in your test booklet. (Check to make sure that everyone has found the right page.)

- In this lesson you will be looking for the correct ways of saying parts of sentences. Look at the directions at the top of the page. Read them to yourself as I read them aloud. (Read the directions to your students.)

- Look at the sentences with the underlined parts in the samples. Now look at the fourth answer. What is it? (no change) You should choose this answer only when the underlined part of the sentence does not need to be changed.

- Read sample A. Which part of the sentence is underlined? (to practice) Which part of the sentence is similar to practice? (playing) The parts playing and to practice do not match because the forms of the verbs are different. So, the underlined part of the sentence should be changed. Look at the answers. Which answer can you eliminate? (answer 4, no change) Now read the sentence again with each answer in place of the underlined part. Only one of the answers will match the word playing and make the sentence correct. Which answer makes the sentence correct? (answer 1, practicing) Yes, practicing matches the word playing in the sentence. Mark answer space 1 for sample A.

- Look at sample B. Read the sentence. Does the underlined part sound right in the sentence? (yes) That's right. The singular present-tense verb for 'is' is correctly used in the sentence. What should you do now? (mark answer space 4, no change) Fill in the space at the bottom of the page.

- Do the rest of the page by yourself. Do items 1 through 8 in the same way that we did the samples. Mark your answer choices at the bottom of the page.

Teacher Scripts

Language Expression: Grammar and Syntax | SPP 91, 92 |

- Turn to page _____ in your test booklet. (Check to make sure that everyone has found the right page.)
- On this page you will be answering questions about sentences and the words in them. Look at the directions at the top of the page. Read them to yourself as I read them aloud. (Read the directions to your students.)
- Look at the two sentences above the samples. Read them to yourself as I read them aloud. Sentence 1: Mr. Johnson is going to the football game. Sentence 2: I am going to the football game. Now read the question and answer choices for sample A. Which word is used as an adjective in the sentence? (football) Yes, football modifies the noun game. Fill in answer choice B for sample A at the bottom of the page.
- Now look at sample B. Read the question and the answer choices. To find the subject of a sentence, you might ask yourself who or what is performing the action in the sentence or, in this case, who is going to the football game. What is the subject of the sentence? (Mr. Johnson) Which answer choice should you choose? (choice E, Mr. Johnson) Find the answer spaces for sample B at the bottom of the page and mark answer space E.
- Do the rest of the page by yourself. When you come to the arrow at the bottom of the page, continue on to the next page and go on until you get to the stop sign. Do items 1 through 14 in the same way that we did the samples. Mark your answer choices at the bottom of the pages.

Language Expression: Sentences | SPP 93 |

- Turn to page _____ in your test booklet. (Check to make sure that everyone has found the right page.)
- On this page you will be looking for subjects, predicates, and complete sentences. Look at the directions at the top of the page. Read them to yourself as I read them aloud. (Read the directions to your students.)
- Look at sample A. Read the sentence. Four parts of the sentence are underlined. Which underlined part is the simple subject of the sentence? (streetlights) Yes, the sentence is about streetlights. What letter is under the word streetlights? (B) Find the answer spaces for sample A at the bottom of the page and mark answer space B.
- Look at sample B. Read the sentence. Four parts of the sentence are underlined. Which underlined part is the simple predicate of the sentence? (arrives) Yes, arrives is the simple predicate, or verb, of the sentence; it tells what the subject, the train, does. What letter is under the word arrives? (H) Find the answer spaces for sample B at the bottom of the page and mark answer space H.
- Now look at sample C. There are four answer choices. You are to find the complete sentence— the one that is not a fragment or a run-on. Read the first sentence. Is it a complete sentence? (no) Why not? (It does not express a complete thought.) Read the second sentence. Is it a complete sentence? (yes) Why? (It contains a subject and a verb and expresses one complete thought.) What letter is in front of the correct answer? (B) Mark answer space B for sample C because choice B is a complete sentence.
- Do the rest of the page by yourself. Read the directions for each group of items and do items 1 through 10 in the same way that we did the samples. Mark your answer choices at the bottom of the page.

Teacher Scripts

Language Expression: Sentence Combining

SPP 94

- Turn to page _____ in your test booklet. (Check to make sure that everyone has found the right page.)

- On this page you will be looking for the sentence in each item that is the best combination of two or three other sentences.   Look at the directions at the top of the page. Read them to yourself as I read them aloud. (Read the directions to your students.)

- Look at sample A. Read the two underlined sentences. These two sentences can be combined into one sentence. The new sentence must have the same meaning as the underlined sentence and should not repeat the words that are in both sentences. Now carefully read the four answer choices. Look for the sentence that is the best combination of the two underlined sentences. Which sentence is the best combination of the sentences? (choice B, People and animals live in family groups.) Find the answer spaces for sample A at the bottom of the page and mark answer space B.

- Do the rest of the page by yourself. Do items 1 through 3 in the same way that we did the sample. Mark your answer choices at the bottom of the page.

Language Expression: Sentence Completion

SPP 95

- Turn to page _____ in your test booklet. (Check to make sure that everyone has found the right page.)

- On this page you will be answering questions about a passage. Look at the directions at the top of the page. Read them to yourself as I read them aloud. (Read the directions to your students.)

- Read the question for sample A and look at all of the answer choices. Now find line 3 in the selection. Which answer choice is the best word to be added to line 3? (answer D) Yes, answer D is correct. Mark answer D for sample A at the bottom of the page.

- Do the rest of the page by yourself. Do items 1 through 4 in the same way that we did the samples. Mark your answer choices at the bottom of the page.

Teacher Scripts

Language Expression: Paragraphs and Topic Sentences | SPP 96

- Turn to page _____ in your test booklet. (Check to make sure that everyone has found the right page.)
- On this page you will be looking for topic sentences. Look at the directions at the top of the page. Read them to yourself as I read them aloud. (Read the directions to your students.)
- Look at sample A. There is a blank at the beginning of the paragraph. It shows that the topic sentence is missing. Read the paragraph and then read the four answer choices. Look for the sentence that tells the main idea of the paragraph; this is known as the topic sentence. You may want to reread the paragraph after you read each answer choice to help you decide if the sentence tells the main idea of the paragraph. (pause) Which answer choice is the topic sentence of the paragraph. (C) Yes, the paragraph tells why food is one of the most important daily needs. Find the answer spaces for sample A at the bottom of the page and mark answer space C.
- Work by yourself to finish the rest of the page. Mark your answer choices at the bottom of the page.

Language Expression: Paragraphs and Sentence Sequence | SPP 97

- Turn to page _____ in your test booklet. (Check to make sure that everyone has found the right page.)
- On this page you will be putting the sentences of paragraphs in their correct orders. Look at the directions at the top of the page. Read them to yourself as I read them aloud. (Read the directions to your students.)
- Look at sample A. There are four sentences. Each sentence has a number in front of it. Let's read sentence 1 . . . sentence 2 . . . sentence 3 . . . sentence 4. The four sentences make a paragraph but the sentences are not in the correct order. Think about the order in which the events in the paragraph, happened and look for key words that will help you figure out the correct order for the sentences. Now read the sentences to yourself. Which sentence should come first in the paragraph? (sentence 3) Which sentence should come second? (sentence 2) Which sentence should come next? (sentence 4) Which sentence should come last? (sentence 1) The correct order is sentence 3, sentence, 2, sentence 4, and sentence 1. Read the sentences in the correct order. Now look at the answer choices under the sentences. They show the numbers 1, 2, 3, and 4 in different orders. The numbers stand for the numbers of the sentences. Which answer choice shows the numbers in the correct order? (choice C) Find the answer spaces for sample A at the bottom of the page and mark answer space C.
- Work by yourself to finish the rest of the page. Do the items in the same way that we did the sample. Mark your answer choices at the bottom of the page.

Language Expression: Transitions | SPP 98

- Turn to page _____ in your test booklet. (Check to make sure that everyone has found the right page.)
- On this page you will be looking for the words or sentences that will help the ideas in the story flow more smoothly. Look at the directions at the top of the page. Read them to yourself as I read them aloud. (Read the directions to your students.)
- Read the question in sample A and look at the answer choices. Now find lines 2 and 3 in the story. The beginning and end of the sentence you are supposed to be examining can be found in parentheses after the question. Which answer choice is the best revision for the sentence? (answer D) Yes, answer D is correct. Inserting the word Meanwhile improves the sentence. Mark answer space D for sample A at the bottom of the page.
- Now finish the page by yourself. Decide which answer choice helps the ideas in the story flow more smoothly. Mark your answer choices at the bottom of the page.

Teacher Scripts

Language Expression: Writing (TAAS)

Note:

- Both the Grade 7 TAAS test and the Grade 9 TAAS test include four student-generated writing samples: descriptive, informative, classificatory, and persuasive. An additional category, comparative writing, is added at the ninth grade level. Each sample includes a page of instructions and guidelines to help the students get organized. The teacher reads these aloud while the students read along. Any prewriting instructions that you are accustomed to giving your students would be appropriate. Students are encouraged to use scratch paper to brainstorm and make notes.

- The tests include instructions and time for prewriting and writing a first draft. Writing samples are scored with a rubric. If you use the writing process, both you and your students will be familiar with this procedure.

- The scoring emphasis is on content. The only time for concern about errors in mechanics is when there are so many of them that it is hard to read the piece.

Language Expression: Descriptive Writing (TAAS)

| SPP 99, 100 |

- Turn to page _____ in your test booklet. (Check to make sure that everyone has found the right page.)

- In this lesson you will be writing a description of the most interesting place you have ever visited. Read the directions and the tips on the Student Prewriting Page to yourself as I read them aloud. Use this page to brainstorm and organize your ideas. (Allow time for the students to complete their prewriting.)

- Turn to the next page, the Student Draft Page. Read the directions, which are repeated here, and the tips to yourself as I read them aloud. Use this page to write your composition.

- Use your best English skills, but do not worry about making mistakes. The most important thing is to write clearly about the place that you are describing. Use the notes that you made on the Student Prewriting Page to stay organized.

Language Expression: Informative Writing (TAAS)

| SPP 101, 102 |

- Turn to page _____ in your test booklet. (Check to make sure that everyone has found the right page.)

- In this lesson you will be writing about how to prepare a hot dog. Read the directions and the tips on the Student Prewriting Page to yourself as I read them aloud. Use this page to list all of the steps that you should take and then organize them in order from first to last. (Allow time for the students to complete their prewriting.)

- Turn to the next page, the Student Draft Page. Read the directions, which are repeated here, and the tips to yourself as I read them aloud. Use this page to write your composition.

- Use your best English skills, but do not worry about making mistakes. The most important thing is to write clear step-by-step directions. Use the notes that you made on the Student Prewriting Page to stay organized.

Teacher Scripts

See the writing note about the TAAS tests on the previous page.

Language Expression: Classificatory Writing (TAAS)

SPP 103, 104

- Turn to page _____ in your test booklet. (Check to make sure that everyone has found the right page.)

- In this lesson you will be writing about what it would be like to represent your school at an international convention for students. Read the directions and the tips on the Student Prewriting Page to yourself as I read them aloud. Use this page to brainstorm and organize your ideas. (Allow time for the students to complete their prewriting.)

- Turn to the next page, the Student Draft Page. Read the directions, which are repeated here, and the tips to yourself as I read them aloud. Use this page to write your composition.

- Use your best English skills, but do not worry about making mistakes. The most important thing is to write about the good and bad points of your situation. Use the notes that you made on the Student Prewriting Page to stay organized.

Language Expression: Persuasive Writing (TAAS)

SPP 105, 106

- Turn to page _____ in your test booklet. (Check to make sure that everyone has found the right page.)

- In this lesson you will try to convince readers to agree with your point of view through your writing. Read the directions and the tips on the student Prewriting Page to yourself as I read them aloud. Use this page to brainstorm and organize your ideas. (Allow time for the students to complete their prewriting.)

- Turn to the next page, the Student Draft Page. Read the directions, which are repeated here, and the tips to yourself as I read them aloud. Use this page to write your composition.

- Use your best English skills, but do not worry about making mistakes. The most important thing is to convince your readers that your position on the issue is sensible. Use the notes that you made on the Student Prewriting Page to stay organized.

Language Expression: Comparative Writing (TAAS)

SPP 107, 108

- Turn to page _____ in your test booklet. (Check to make sure that everyone has found the right page.)

- In this lesson you will consider opposing points of view and support one of the sides. Read the directions and the tips on the Student Prewriting Page to yourself as I read them aloud. Use this page to brainstorm and organize your ideas. (Allow time for the students to complete their prewriting.)

- Turn to the next page, the Student Draft Page. Read the directions, which are repeated here, and the tips to yourself as I read them aloud. Use this page to write your composition.

- Use your best English skills, but do not worry about making mistakes. The most important thing is to write clearly so that your reader will understand your position about the proposed solutions. Use the notes that you made on the Student Prewriting Page to stay organized.

Teacher Scripts

Language Expression: Writing (NJ EWT)

Note:

- The New Jersey Grade 8 Early Warning Test includes three student-generated writing samples: solving a problem, cause and effect, and opinion. Each one includes a page of instructions and guidelines to help the students get organized. The teacher reads these aloud while the students read along. Any prewriting instructions that you are accustomed to giving your students would be appropriate. Students are encouraged to use scratch paper to brainstorm and make notes.
- The tests include instructions for prewriting and writing. Writing samples are scored with a rubric. If you use the writing process, both you and your students will be familiar with this procedure.
- The scoring emphasis is on both content and mechanics (complete sentences, capitalization, spelling, punctuation, and word use).

Language Expression: Solving a Problem (NJ EWT) SPP 109

- Turn to page _____ in your test booklet. (Check to make sure that everyone has found the right page.)
- In this lesson you will show how well you can explain your solution to a problem. Read the General Directions, the Writing Situation, and Directions for Writing to yourself as I read them aloud.
- Use one side of a sheet of paper to organize your ideas. You may use up to four sides to write your letter. However, you do not have to use all four sides. Follow the directions on this page and try to write clearly, using your best English skills. Do you have any questions? You may start writing now.

Language Expression: Cause and Effect (NJ EWT) SPP 110

- Turn to page _____ in your test booklet. (Check to make sure that everyone has found the right page.)
- In this lesson you will be writing your ideas about the cause of a problem that many young people have. Read the General Directions, the Writing Situation, and Directions for Writing to yourself as I read them aloud.
- Use one side of a sheet of paper to organize your ideas. You may use up to four sides to write your essay. However, you do not have to use all four sides. Follow the directions on this page, and try to write clearly, using your best English skills. Do you have any questions? You may start writing now.

Language Expression: Opinion (NJ EWT) SPP 111

- Turn to page _____ in your test booklet. (Check to make sure that everyone has found the right page.)
- In this lesson you will be writing your ideas about an important change in a law that affects young people. Read the General Directions, the Writing Situation, and Directions for Writing to yourself as I read them aloud.
- Use one side of a sheet of paper to organize your ideas. You may use up to four sides to write your essay. However, you do not have to use all four sides. Follow the directions on this page, and try to write clearly, using your best English skills. Do you have any questions? You may start writing now.

Teacher Scripts

Work-Study Skills: Library and Dictionary Skills   SPP 112

- Turn to page _____ in your test booklet. (Check to make sure that everyone has found the right page.)

- On this page you will be using your dictionary skills, and you will be looking for the best sources for different types of information. You will also be finding information on a library catalog card. Look at the directions at the top of the page. Read them to yourself as I read them aloud. (Read the directions to your students.)

- Look at sample A. What do dictionary guide words tell you? (the first and last words on a dictionary page) And how are words listed in a dictionary? (in alphabetical order) What guide words are given in this question? (kipper, kitten) If a word is on a page with these guide words, it comes between kipper and kitten in alphabetical order. Now look at the four words under the question. Check each word against the guide words. Which word would be on a dictionary page that has kipper and kitten as guide words? (answer C, kitchen) Mark answer space C for sample A at the bottom of the page.

- Now look at sample B. Read the question carefully to yourself. Are there any key words in the question that will help you find the answer? (government of France) Now read the answer choices. Which source would give you information about the government of France? (answer G, the encyclopedia) Yes, an encyclopedia contains general information about the countries of the world. Mark answer space G for sample B at the bottom of the page.

- Do the rest of the page by yourself. Do items 1 through 4 in the same way that we did the samples. Then read the directions above the library catalog card and do items 5 and 6. Mark your answer choices at the bottom of the page.

Work-Study Skills: Alphabetizing   SPP 113

- Turn to page _____ in your test booklet. (Check to make sure that everyone has found the right page.)

- On this page you will be putting words in alphabetical order. Look at the directions at the top of the page. Read them to yourself as I read them aloud. (Read the directions to your students.)

- Look at the four words in sample A. If you put the words in alphabetical order, which one would come first? (answer B, beach) Yes, beach would come first in alphabetical order. Find the answer spaces for sample A at the bottom of the page and mark answer space B.

- Now look at the four words for sample B. Which of these words would come last in the dictionary? Remember, if words start with the same letter, look at the second or even the third letter to put them in alphabetical order. Which word would be last? (answer H, zero) Find the answer spaces for sample B at the bottom of the page and mark answer space H.

- Do the rest of the page by yourself. Read the directions for each section and then do the items in the same way that we did the samples. Mark your answer choices at the bottom of the page.

Teacher Scripts

Work-Study Skills: Table of Contents   SPP 114

- Turn to page _____ in your test booklet. (Check to make sure that everyone has found the right page.)

- On this page you will be using a table of contents to answer questions. Look at the directions at the top of the page. Read them to yourself as I read them aloud. (Read the directions to your students.)

- Look at the table of contents on the top left side of the page. Read the information above the table and in the table itself.

- Look at sample A. Read the question. What key words will help you answer this question? (Brazilian . . . dances) Now look at the answers. They are chapter numbers. Check the answer choices. In which chapter would you find out about Brazilian folk dances? (chapter 4, "Carnival Dances in Brazil") So which answer is correct? (4) Find the answer spaces for sample A at the bottom of the page and mark answer space 4.

- Now look at sample B. Read the incomplete sentence and the answers. Which answer gives you information that you might find in chapter 3? (answer choice 4) Find the answer spaces for sample B at the bottom of the page and mark answer space 4.

- Do the rest of the page by yourself. Use the table of contents on the left side of the page to do items 1 through 4. Read the information about the table of contents and the table of contents itself before you read the questions. Mark your answer choices at the bottom of the page.

Work-Study Skills: Index   SPP 115

- Turn to page _____ in your test booklet. (Check to make sure that everyone has found the right page.)

- On this page you will be using an index from a book to answer questions. Look at the directions at the top of the page. Read them to yourself as I read them aloud. (Read the directions to your students.)

- Look at the index on the top left side of the page. Read the information above the index and the information in the index itself.

- Look at sample A. Read the question. What key word will help you answer the question? (sun) Now look at the answers; they are page numbers. On which page should you start to read about the sun? (155) So which answer is correct? (4) Find the answer spaces for sample A at the bottom of the page and mark answer space 4.

- Now look at sample B. Read the question and the answers. Which answer gives you the page number for information about physical geography? (answer choice 3, 76) Find the answer spaces for sample B at the bottom of the page and mark answer space 3.

- Do the rest of the page by yourself. Use the index on the left side of the page to do items 1 through 4. Read the information about the index and the index itself before you read the questions. Mark your answer choices at the bottom of the page.

Teacher Scripts

Work-Study Skills: Dictionary Skills

SPP 116

- Turn to page _____ in your test booklet. (Check to make sure that everyone has found the right page.)

- On this page you will be using entries from a dictionary to find information. Look at the directions at the top of the page. Read them to yourself as I read them aloud. (Read the directions to your students.)

- Look at sample A. To the left of the sample question there is a dictionary entry for the word novice. Read the dictionary entry. Then read the question for sample A and find its answer in the entry. Which answer did you choose? (B, noun) Right. Novice is a noun. Find the answer spaces for sample A at the bottom of the page and mark answer space B.

- Now use the next dictionary entry to answer questions 1 through 5 by yourself. Mark your answer choices at the bottom of the page.

Work-Study Skills: Outlines

SPP 117

- Turn to page _____ in your test booklet. (Check to make sure that everyone has found the right page.)

- On this page you will be answering questions about outlines. Look at the directions at the top of the page. Read them to yourself as I read them aloud. (Read the directions to your students.)

- Look at the outline on the top left side of the page. You will use this outline to answer the question in sample A. What are the key words in the question? (heading, Geography) Look at the outline. What is the answer to the question? (answer B, Physical Features) Find the answer spaces for sample A at the bottom of the page and mark answer space B.

- Now study the outline below on the left. Use it to answer questions 1 through 3 by yourself. Mark your answer choices at the bottom of the page.

176

Teacher Scripts

Work-Study Skills: Key Terms
SPP 118

- Turn to page _____ in your test booklet. (Check to make sure that everyone has found the right page.)

- On this page you will be deciding which word or phrase you should use to find information in a reference source. Look at the directions at the top of the page. Read them to yourself as I read them aloud. (Read the directions to your students.)

- Look at sample A. Read the question and decide which key term you should use to find the diameter of the planet Mercury. Which answer did you choose? (B, Mercury) Right. The words planet, diameter, and size would be too general. Find the answer spaces for sample A at the bottom of the page and mark answer space B.

- Look at sample B. Read the question and decide which key term you should use to find out about Bastille Day. Which answer did you choose? (M, Bastille Day) Right. Most important holidays are listed by their own names. Find the answer spaces for sample B at the bottom of the page and mark answer space M.

- Do the rest of the page by yourself. Do items 1 through 8 in the same way that we did the samples. Mark your answer choices at the bottom of the page.

Work-Study Skills: Bibliography
SPP 119

- Turn to page _____ in your test booklet. (Check to make sure that everyone has found the right page.)

- On this page you will be using a bibliography to answer questions. Look at the directions at the top of the page. Read them to yourself as I read them aloud. (Read the directions to your students.)

- Look at sample A. Study the entry from a bibliography and then answer the question. Who published this book? (answer B, Little, Brown, and Co.) Right. In this bibliography the publisher is listed after the city in which it was published. Find the answer spaces for sample A at the bottom of the page and mark answer space B.

- Do the rest of the page by yourself. Read the bibliography and do items 1 through 5 in the same way that we did the sample. Mark your answer choices at the bottom of the page.

Teacher Scripts

Work-Study Skills: Maps

SPP 120

- Turn to page _____ in your test booklet. (Check to make sure that everyone has found the right page.)

- On this page you will be using the information on the maps to answer questions. Look at the directions on the top of the page. Read them to yourself as I read them aloud. (Read the directions to your students.)

- Look at the map below the directions on the left side of the page. Read the explanation above the map. Now take a little time to examine the map and notice where things are located.

- Now look at sample A. Read the question and look for the key words. Key words are the words in the question that will help you find the answer. What are the key words in sample A? (City Hall . . . courthouse) Look at the map. Notice the scale in the top left corner. Then find City Hall and the courthouse. Now check each answer for sample A and find the answer that tells how far Mr. Weeks walks. Which answer did you choose? (answer 3, 3 miles) Find the answer spaces for sample A at the bottom of the page and mark answer choice 3.

- Now look at sample B. Read the question to yourself and look for the key words. What are the key words in the question? (Route 120 from the east . . . north . . . first exit) Look at the map and find the answer. What is the first exit? (Fifth St.) Which answer choice is correct? (answer 3) Find the answer spaces for sample B at the bottom of the page and mark answer space 3.

- Do the rest of the page by yourself. Use the map on the left side of the page to do items 1 through 4. Be sure to read the information above the map before you answer the questions. Mark your answer choices at the bottom of the page.

Work-Study Skills: Graphs

SPP 121

- Turn to page _____ in your test booklet. (Check to make sure that everyone has found the right page.)

- On this page you will be using the information on the graphs to answer questions. Look at the directions at the top of the page. Read them to yourself as I read them aloud. (Read the directions to your students.)

- Look at the graph below the directions on the left side of the page. Read the title of the graph. Now look at the labels and lines on the graph. What does the solid line represent? (the Rialto Theater) What does the dashed line represent? (the Barkley Theater) Now read question A. This question has key words that will help you. What are they? (How many more . . . on Wednesday) Find the line for Wednesday on the graph. About how many patrons were at the Rialto on Wednesday? (600) How many patrons were at the Barkley? (400) So, how many more patrons were at the Rialto than at the Barkley on Wednesday? (200) Look at the answers. What is the number of the correct answer? (2) Find the answer spaces for sample A at the bottom of the page and mark answer space 2.

- Now look at sample B. Read the question. What are the key words? (greatest theater attendance) Figure out the answer. On which day did the most people attend the theater? (Friday) Which answer should you mark? (answer 4) Find the answer spaces for sample B at the bottom of the page and mark answer 4.

- Do the rest of the page by yourself. Use the graph in the middle of the page to do items 1 through 4. Be sure to read the title of the graph before you answer the questions. Mark your answer choices at the bottom of the page.

Teacher Scripts

Math Computation: Addition

SPP 122, 123

- Turn to page _____ in your test booklet. (Check to make sure that everyone has found the right page.)

- In this lesson you will be figuring out the answers to addition problems. Look at the directions at the top of the page. Read them to yourself as I read them aloud. (Read the directions to your students.)

- Look at sample A. What are you being asked to do? (add 216.01 and 2.37) Look at the five answer choices. What are they? (21.838, 218.38, 218.48, 449.01, none of these) You should mark the answer circle for none of these only if the right answer is not given as one of the answer choices. Now do the problem. Use scratch paper if you need to. Add carefully. What is the answer to 216.01 plus 2.37? (218.38) What letter is next to the answer 218.38? (B) Find the answer spaces for sample A at the bottom of the page and mark answer space B.

- Now look at sample B. What are you being asked to do? (add $7 \frac{5}{9}$ and $2 \frac{2}{9}$) Use scratch paper if you need to. Remember to line the problem up so that one number is directly under the other. Now do the problem. Add carefully. What is the answer to $7 \frac{5}{9}$ plus $2 \frac{2}{9}$? ($9 \frac{7}{9}$) Is $9 \frac{7}{9}$ one of the answer choices? (no) Since the right answer to the problem is not given as an answer choice, you should mark the answer space for none of these. What letter is next to none of these? (K) Find the answer spaces for sample B at the bottom of the page and mark answer space K.

- Do the rest of the page by yourself. Do items 1 through 8 in the same way that we did the samples. When you come to the arrow at the bottom of the page, go on to the next page and keep working until you come to the stop sign. If you need to, rewrite and figure the problems on scratch paper. Mark your answer choices at the bottom of the page.

Math Computation: Subtraction

SPP 124, 125

- Turn to page _____ in your test booklet. (Check to make sure that everyone has found the right page.)

- In this lesson you will be figuring out the answers to subtraction problems. Look at the directions at the top of the page. Read them to yourself as I read them aloud. (Read the directions to your students.)

- Look at sample A. What are you being asked to do? (subtract 5.90 from 36.08) Look at the five answer choices. What are they? (0.18, 3.018, 30.18, 31.18, and none of these) You should mark the answer choice for none of these only if the right answer is not given as one of the answer choices. Now do the problem. Use scratch paper if you need to. Subtract carefully. What is the answer to 36.08 minus 5.90? (30.18) What letter is next to the answer 30.18? (C) Find the answer spaces for sample A at the bottom of the page and mark answer space C.

- Now look at sample B. What are you being asked to do? (subtract $6 \frac{1}{12}$ from $15 \frac{5}{6}$) Now do the problem. Use scratch paper if you need to. Remember to find the least common denominator for the fractions before you subtract. Subtract carefully. What is the answer to $15 \frac{5}{6}$ minus $6 \frac{1}{12}$? ($9 \frac{3}{4}$) Is $9 \frac{3}{4}$ one of the answer choices? (no) Since the right answer to the problem is not given as an answer choice, you should mark the circle for none of these. What letter is next to none of these? (K) Find the answer spaces for sample B at the bottom of the page and mark answer space K.

- Do the rest of the page by yourself. Do items 1 through 8 in the same way that we did the samples. When you come to the arrow at the bottom of the page, go on to the next page and keep working until you come to the stop sign. If you need to, rewrite and figure the problems on scratch paper. Mark your answer choices at the bottom of the page.

Teacher Scripts

Math Computation: Multiplication

SPP 126, 127

- Turn to page _____ in your test booklet. (Check to make sure that everyone has found the right page.)

- In this lesson you will be figuring out the answers to multiplication problems. Look at the directions at the top of the page. Read them to yourself as I read them aloud. (Read the directions to your students.)

- Look at sample A. What are you being asked to do? (multiply 79 by 30) Look at the five answer choices. What are they? (109, 237, 2170, 2370, and none of these) You should mark the answer space for none of these only if the right answer is not given as one of the answer choices. Now do the problem. Use scratch paper if you need to. Multiply carefully. What is the answer to 79 times 30? (2370) What letter is next to the answer 2370? (D) Find the answer spaces for sample A at the bottom of the page and mark answer space D.

- Now look at sample B. What are you being asked to do? (multiply 0.3 by 0.8) Now do the problem. Use scratch paper if you need to and multiply carefully. What is the answer to 0.3 times 0.8? (.24) Is .24 one of the answer choices? (no) Since the right answer to the problem is not given as an answer choice, you should mark the circle for none of these. What letter is next to none of these? (K) Find the answer spaces for sample B at the bottom of the page and mark answer space K.

- Do the rest of the page by yourself. Do items 1 through 8 in the same way that we did the samples. When you come to the arrow at the bottom of the page, go on to the next page and keep working until you come to the stop sign. If you need to, rewrite and figure the problems on scratch paper. Mark your answer choices at the bottom of the page.

Math Computation: Division

SPP 128, 129

- Turn to page _____ in your test booklet. (Check to make sure that everyone has found the right page.)

- In this lesson you will be figuring out the answers to division problems. Look at the directions at the top of the page. Read them to yourself as I read them aloud. (Read the directions to your students.)

- Look at sample A. What are you being asked to do? (divide 603 by 3) Look at the five answer choices. What are they? (201 R1, 201, 204, 204 R3, and none of these) You should mark the answer space for none of these only if the right answer is not given as one of the answer choices. Now do the problem. Use scratch paper if you need to. Divide carefully. What is the answer to 603 divided by 3? (201) What letter is next to the answer 201? (B) Find the answer spaces for sample A at the bottom of the page and mark answer space B.

- Now look at sample B. What are you being asked to do? (divide .36 by 6) Now do the problem. Use scratch paper if you need to and divide carefully. What is the answer to .36 divided by 6? (.06) Is .06 one of the answer choices? (no) Since the right answer to the problem is not given as an answer choice, you should mark the circle for none of these. What letter is next to none of these? (K) Find the answer spaces for sample B at the bottom of the page and mark answer space K.

- Do the rest of the page by yourself. Do items 1 through 8 in the same way that we did the samples. When you come to the arrow at the bottom of the page, go on to the next page and keep working until you come to the stop sign. If you need to, rewrite and figure the problems on scratch paper. Mark your answer choices at the bottom of the page.

Teacher Scripts

Math Computation: Ratios and Percents SPP 130, 131

- Turn to page _____ in your test booklet. (Check to make sure that everyone has found the right page.)

- In this lesson you will be figuring out the answers to problems involving ratios and percents. Look at the directions at the top of the page. Read them to yourself as I read them aloud. (Read the directions to your students.)

- Look at sample A. What are you being asked to do? [solve a ratio, 1 is to 5 as (blank) is to 10] Look at the answer choices. The last choice is none of these. You should mark the answer circle for none of these only if the right answer is not given as one of the answer choices. Now work the problem. Use scratch paper if you need to. Work carefully. What is the answer? (choice B, 2) Yes, 2 is the correct answer. One is to 5 as 2 is to 10, or 1/5 is equal to 2/10. Find the answer spaces for sample A at the bottom of the page and mark answer space B.

- Now look at sample B. What are you being asked to do? (find what percent of 10 is 5) Be sure to use scratch paper to calculate carefully. What is the answer? (50, 5 is 50% of 10) Yes, the answer is 50. Five is 50% of 10. Which answer choice should you fill in? (J) Find the answer spaces for sample B at the bottom of the page and mark answer space J.

- Do the rest of the page by yourself. Do items 1 through 8 in the same way that we did the samples. When you come to the arrow at the bottom of the page, go on to the next page and keep working until you come to the stop sign. If you need to, rewrite and figure the problems on scratch paper. Mark your answer choices at the bottom of the page.

Teacher Scripts

Math Concepts/Applications: Numeration

SPP 132

- Turn to page _____ in your test booklet. (Check to make sure that everyone has found the right page.)

- On this page you will be looking for the answers to problems about numbers. Look at the directions at the top of the page. Read them to yourself as I read them aloud. (Read the directions to your students.)

- Look at sample A. Read the question. The question contains key words and numbers. Key words and numbers are the important words and numbers in a problem that will help you to find its answer. Read the question in sample A to yourself and look for the key words and numbers. What are they? (8, 198,234, stand for) What does the 8 in 198,234 stand for? (8 thousands or 8000) Look at the answer choices. Which is the correct answer choice? (choice C, 8000) Find the answer spaces for sample A at the bottom of the page and mark answer space C.

- Now look at sample B. Read the problem. Look for the key words and numbers. Remember, key words and numbers are the important words and numbers in a problem that will help you to find its answer. What are the key words and numbers in this problem? (68,231, nearest hundred) To round a number to the nearest hundred, look in the tens place. If the digit is 5 or greater, the number will be rounded up. If the digit is less than 5, the number will be rounded down. What digit is in the tens place in 68,231? (3) Should you round up or down? (down) So the answer will be less than 68,231. What is 68,231 to the nearest hundred? (choice H, 68,200) Find the answer spaces for sample B at the bottom of the page and mark answer space H.

- Do the rest of the page by yourself. Do all of the items in the same way that we did the samples. Use scratch paper if you need to. Mark your answer choices at the bottom of the page.

Math Concepts/Applications: Number Sentences

SPP 133

- Turn to page _____ in your test booklet. (Check to make sure that everyone has found the right page.)

- On this page you will be answering questions about number sentences. Look at the directions at the top of the page. Read them to yourself as I read them aloud. (Read the directions to your students.)

- Look at sample A. Read the problem. In this problem you are being asked to find the value of n that makes the number sentence true. Look at the number sentence again. 5n means 5 times an unknown number. Now do the problem. Use scratch paper if you need to. Five times what number minus 10 equals 25? (7) Look at the answer choices. What letter is next to the answer 7? (B) Find the answer spaces for sample A at the bottom of the page and mark answer space B.

- Now look at sample B. Read the problem and study the number sentence. You are being asked to find the number that goes in the box to make the number sentence true. Look at the number sentence again and compute the left side of the sentence. How much is 8 x 7? (56) Now compute the rest of the sentence. What number times 28 equals 56? (2) Look at the answer choices. What letter is next to the answer 2? (G) Find the answer spaces for sample B at the bottom of the page and mark answer space G.

- Do the rest of the page by yourself. Do all of the items in the same way that we did the samples. Use scratch paper if you need to. Mark your answer choices at the bottom of the page.

Teacher Scripts

Math Concepts/Applications: Number Theory

- Turn to page _____ in your test booklet. (Check to make sure that everyone has found the right page.)

- On this page you will be looking for answers to questions about numbers. Look at the directions at the top of the page. Read them to yourself as I read them aloud. (Read the directions to your students.)

- Look at sample A. Read the question. Now look for the key words and numbers in the question. What are key words and numbers? (the important words and numbers in a problem that help you find its answer) What are the key words and numbers in this question? (another name, 6.7) Look at the answer choices. What is another name for 6.7? ($6\frac{7}{10}$) Yes, $6\frac{7}{10}$ is the same as 6.7. What letter is next to $6\frac{7}{10}$? (C) Mark answer space C for sample A.

- Now look at sample B. Read the question. What are the key words and numbers in the question? (another way, writing, $\frac{1}{5}$) Now look at the answer choices. Which one shows another way of writing the fraction $\frac{1}{5}$? ($1 \div 5$) Yes, $\frac{1}{5}$ can be written as $1 \div 5$. Which answer choice should you mark? (choice J, $1 \div 5$) Find the answer spaces for sample B at the bottom of the page and mark answer space J.

- Do the rest of the page by yourself. Do items 1 through 6 in the same way that we did the samples. Look for the key words and numbers. Use scratch paper if you need to. Mark your answer choices at the bottom of the page.

Math Concepts/Applications: Whole Numbers and Integers

- Turn to page _____ in your test booklet. (Check to make sure that everyone has found the right page.)

- On this page you will be working with special numbers such as factors and multiples, estimates, and negative numbers. Look at the directions at the top of the page. Read them to yourself as I read them aloud. (Read the directions to your students.)

- Look at sample A. Read the question. Look for the key words and numbers in the question. What are they? (best estimate, 47 times 51) You need to find the numbers that will give the best or closest estimate for 47 times 51. Look at the answer choices carefully to find the rounded numbers that are the closest to 47 and 51. What is the correct answer? (choice C, 50 x 50) Find the answer spaces for sample A at the bottom of the page and mark answer C.

- Look at sample B. Read the problem What must you do to find the answer? Subtract -5 from 8. Now subtract. What is the value of p? (13) Find the answer spaces for sample B at the bottom of the page and mark answer space J.

- Do the rest of the page by yourself. Do items 1 through 8 in the same way that we did the samples. Look for the key words and numbers. Use scratch paper if you need to. Mark your answer choices at the bottom of the page.

©Teacher Created Materials, Inc.   183   #2132 How to Prepare. . . Standardized Tests

Teacher Scripts

Math Concepts/Applications: Geometry and Measurement SPP 136–140

- Turn to page _____ in your test booklet. (Check to make sure that everyone has found the right page.)

- On this page you will be looking for the answers to questions about figures, measurement, and time. Look at the directions at the top of the page. Read them to yourself as I read them aloud. (Read the directions to your students.)

- Look at sample A. Read the question. What is the key word in the question? (parallel) What do you know about parallel lines? (No matter how far they are extended, they will never intersect with each other.) Now look at the figure carefully. Which two lines look as though they are parallel? (line EF and line GH) Look at the answer choices. Which one is the correct answer? (choice B, EF and GH) Find the answer spaces for sample A at the bottom of the page and mark answer space B.

- Now look at sample B. Read the question. What are the key words and numbers in this question? (area, 6 meters wide, 8 meters long) What should you do to find the area of the room? (multiply 6 meters by 8 meters) Now do the problem. Do not forget to use scratch paper. What is the area of the living room? (48 square meters) Find the answer spaces for sample B at the bottom of the page and mark answer space H.

- Now work by yourself. When you come to the arrow at the bottom of the page, continue on to the next page. Do all of the items in the same way that we did the samples. Stop when you reach the stop sign. Mark your answer choices at the bottom of each page.

Math Concepts/Applications: Temperature SPP 141

- Turn to page _____ in your test booklet. (Check to make sure that everyone has found the right page.)

- On this page you will be using thermometers to answer the questions. Look at the directions at the top of the page. Read them to yourself as I read them aloud. (Read the directions to your students.)

- Look at sample A. Read the question and look at the thermometer. What is the correct answer? (76°) Look at the four answer choices. Which one is correct? (D) Find the answer spaces for sample A at the bottom of the page and mark answer space D.

- Do the rest of the page by yourself. Mark your answer choices at the bottom of the page.

Teacher Scripts

Math Concepts/Applications: Probability and Statistics

SPP 142

- Turn to page _____ in your test booklet. (Check to make sure that everyone has found the right page.)

- On this page you will be using charts and graphs to answer the questions. Look at the directions at the top of the page. Read them to yourself as I read them aloud. (Read the directions to your students.)

- Look at sample A. Read the question and look at the graph. What is the correct answer? (20 inches) Look at the four answer choices. Which one is correct? (B) Find the answer spaces for sample A at the bottom of the page and mark answer space B.

- Do the rest of the page by yourself. Mark your answer choices at the bottom of the page.

Math Concepts/Applications: Estimation

SPP 143

- Turn to page _____ in your test booklet. (Check to make sure that everyone has found the right page.)

- On this page you will be estimating the answers to questions.   Look at the directions at the top of the page. Read them to yourself as I read them aloud. (Read the directions to your students.)

- Look at sample A. Read the question. What are the key words in this problem? (about how much) Now look at the answer choices. Which one shows about how much you will spend for lunch in a month? (choice C, $90) Yes, $90 is the best choice because, if you round 28 up to 30 or 31 down to 30 and multiply by $3.00, the answer will be $90. Find the answer spaces for sample A at the bottom of the page and mark answer space C.

- Now look at sample B. Read the question. What are the key words in this question? (estimate, area, triangle) How do you find the area of a triangle? (1/2 the base times the altitude or base times altitude divided by 2) Remember, you are being asked to estimate, so what should you do next? (round 6.2 and 5.8 to the nearest meter) Now do the problem. Use scratch paper if you need to. What is the approximate area of the triangle? (18 square meters, choice H) Find the answer spaces for sample B at the bottom of the page and mark answer space H.

- Do the rest of the page by yourself. Do items 1 through 6 in the same way that we did the samples. Mark your answer choices at the bottom of the page.

Teacher Scripts

Math Concepts/Applications: Strategies

SPP 144

- Turn to page _____ in your test booklet. (Check to make sure that everyone has found the right page.)

- On this page you will be figuring out how to solve problems. Look at the directions at the top of the page. Read them to yourself as I read them aloud. (Read the directions to your students.)

- Look at sample A. Read the question. Which answer is correct? (D) Yes, D is the correct answer. Line AB is one edge of the cube. With this information, you could find the area of one side and the total surface area of the cube. Find the answer spaces for sample A at the bottom of the page and mark answer space D.

- Do the rest of the page by yourself. Do items 1 through 6 in the same way that we did the samples. Mark your answer choices at the bottom of the page.

Math Concepts/Applications: Problem Solving and Data Analysis

SPP 145

- Turn to page _____ in your test booklet. (Check to make sure that everyone has found the right page.)

- On this page you will solve problems. Look at the directions at the top of the page. Read them to yourself as I read them aloud. (Read the directions to your students.)

- Look at sample A. Read the question. How can you find the land area of the estate? (subtract the area of the pools from the total area of the estate) Which answer choice is correct? (C) Yes, find the answer spaces for sample A at the bottom of the page and mark answer space C.

- Now look at sample B. Read the question. Which answer is correct? (H) Yes, if you subtract the amount of change ($6.17) and the known prices from $20, the remaining amount will be the price of the fourth thing. Find the answer spaces for sample B at the bottom of the page and mark answer space H.

- Do the rest of the page by yourself. Do items 1 through 4 in the same way that we did the samples. Mark your answer choices at the bottom of the page.

Teacher Scripts

Math Concepts/Applications: Reasonable Answers

- Turn to page _____ in your test booklet. (Check to make sure that everyone has found the right page.)

- On this page you will be choosing the answers that make the most sense. Look at the directions at the top of the page. Read them to yourself as I read them aloud. (Read the directions to your students.)

- Look at sample A. Read the question. One way to work this problem is to first round 198 to the nearest hundred and then divide by 10. What is the correct answer? (choice C, 20) Find the answer spaces for sample A at the bottom of the page and mark answer space C.

- Now look at sample B. Read the question. Which answer is correct? (H) Yes, if there are too many students for one bus, they will need two buses. Find the answer spaces for sample B at the bottom of the page and mark answer space H.

- Do the rest of the page by yourself. Do items 1 through 4 in the same way that we did the samples. Use scratch paper if you need to. Mark your answer choices at the bottom of the page.

Math Concepts/Applications: Pre-Algebra

SPP 147

- Turn to page _____ in your test booklet. (Check to make sure that everyone has found the right page.)

- On this page you will be solving pre-algebra problems. Look at the directions at the top of the page. Read them to yourself as I read them aloud. (Read the directions to your students.)

- Look at sample A. Read the question. Now look at the answer choices. Which one is correct? (choice A, point P) Find the answer spaces for sample B at the bottom of the page and mark answer space A.

- Do the rest of the page by yourself. Do items 1 through 4 in the same way that we did the samples. Use scratch paper if you need to. Mark your answer choices at the bottom of the page.

©Teacher Created Materials, Inc.   187   #2132 How to Prepare. . . Standardized Tests

Student Practice Pages

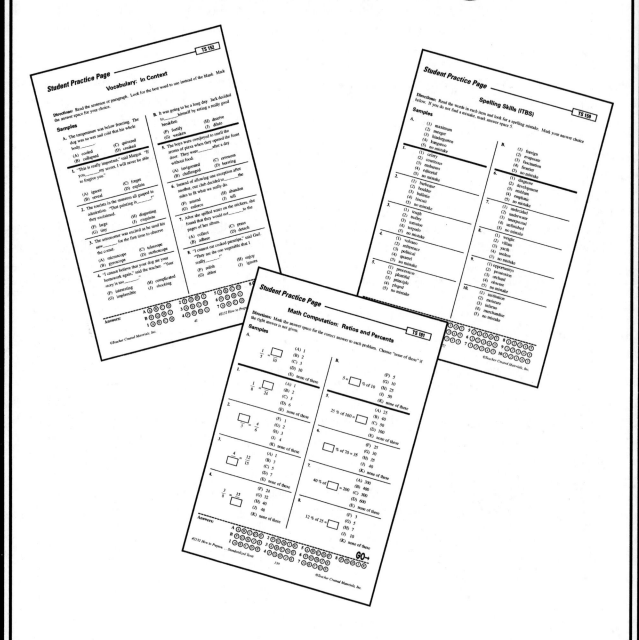

Student's Name _____

Starting Date _____

Teacher Scripts

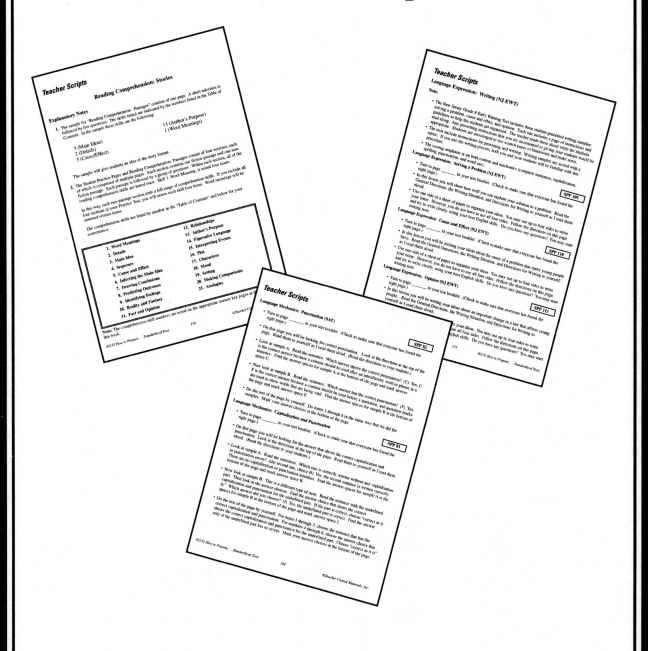

Teacher's Name _____

Starting Date _____

Spelling List

This is a list of selected words that you may wish to add to your spelling program. Many of them appear on the tests as the tested words or as distracters.

abandon	affection	appearance
accept	aggressive	appetite
acceptable	album	application
access	alert	apprehension
accessory	all	apprentice
accident	alligator	approach
accidentally	alphabet	appropriate
accommodate	already	aquarium
according	although	argument
accurate	amateur	arrangement
accusation	amazement	assistance
ache	amend	assurance
achieving	amidst	athlete
acre	analysis	attempt
activate	analyze	attendance
active	ancestor	attorney
adapt	anchor	audience
address	animal	auditorium
adjoins	animation	authority
adjust	anniversary	automatic
adjustable	announce	available
admission	announcer	avalanche
adult	annual	avert
advantageous	antiseptics	award
advertisement	apologize	awl

Spelling List (cont.)

baby	born	cancel
background	borrower	capability
balanced	boulder	capable
ball	bound	capsule
banana	braid	caption
barbecue	brake	captive
bare	break	carnival
bargain	bridle	carriages
barred	brief	castle
basis	brilliant	catalog
bowl	broadcast	cause
be	buddy	causing
bear	budget	cease
beat	bulletin	celery
bee	buoyant	challenge
beet	bushel	challenging
behavior	buy	character
beneficial	by	characteristic
berry	cactus	charity
biscuit	cafeteria	chatterbox
blew	calculate	chime
blister	calendar	chimney
blizzard	calories	chisel
blue	calves	
bored	campus	
boredom	canal	

Spelling List (cont.)

civilization	consistently	currency
civilized	constant	custody
clinic	contestant	customer
colony	continent	dagger
column	continuous	daisies
combine	contribution	days
comedy	convenient	daze
comics	convince	dealt
coming	coolly	decimal
commerce	coordinate	decorate
community	coral	defeated
comparable	cotton	defense
compare	couch	definite
compass	council	delicacy
compete	courteous	delivery
competition	coward	dependent
competitive	creak	descended
conceal	credit	destined
concentrate	creek	destroy
concur	critical	destruction
confess	crocodile	detection
congratulate	cruise	detention
conquer	crumble	development
consent	culture	diagnose
conserve	curiosity	
conspicuous	curious	

Spelling List *(cont.)*

dictionary	dozen	envious
die	dropping	environmental
difference	duel	equator
different	duplicate	equipped
dining	dye	essential
director	eagerly	establish
disappoint	earth	esteem
disappointment	earthquake	estimate
discuss	eased	evaporate
discussion	editing	event
dismissal	editor	every
dismissed	editorial	evidence
dissatisfied	effect	evil
distance	eighth	exact
distinguish	elated	examination
distress	embarrass	example
distribute	emblem	excellent
divert	emphatic	exception
dividend	empire	excitement
documents	emotion	excuse
doe	employees	exhale
donation	encourage	exhaust
doorknob	encyclopedia	exist
dormitory	enemy	expedition
doubtful	enormous	
dough	enthusiasm	

Spelling List (cont.)

experience	filthiest	fractured
experimental	flagpole	fragrance
explain	flew	fragrant
explanation	flier	framework
express	florist	freedom
expression	flounder	frequent
exterior	flour	friction
facial	flower	friend
factor	flue	frightened
fair	focus	fringe
fantasy	foliage	frontier
fascination	force	frustrated
fashion	foreign	fundamentally
fatigue	foretell	furious
faucet	forfeits	furnace
fault	forgetting	fury
feat	formation	gait
February	formerly	gallon
federal	forth	game
ferocious	fortress	garage
fertilizer	fortuneteller	gate
festival	fossil	gentlemen
fiction	foul	genuine
fictional	fountain	germs
fiery	fourth	
fifteenth	fowl	

Spelling List *(cont.)*

gestured	harvest	homesick
ghost	hastily	hopeless
girl	hay	horrible
glare	headquarters	horrid
glistening	heal	horrified
governor	health	horse
gradual	hear	hostage
gradually	heat	however
graduation	heavily	howled
grammar	heed	hue
grate	heel	humor
gravity	height	humorous
great	heir	hungry
greedy	helicopter	icicle
green	helpful	identify
griddle	here	idle
grievance	hesitate	illuminated
growth	hew	illusion
guarantee	hey	imagination
guidance	hi	imagine
guessed	high	immense
guilt	hilarious	impolite
gymnasium	historic	impress
hamburgers	historical	
hanger	hoarse	
harness	holiday	

Spelling List (cont.)

impulse	intersection	ledger
inconsiderate	interval	legal
indicate	introduction	legible
individual	inventory	legislature
industrial	irresistibly	leopard
industries	isolated	liberty
inevitable	jealous	librarian
inferior	jogging	license
inferno	journalist	lie
infirmary	journey	likeness
inflate	judgment	liquid
inform	junction	litter
injury	justice	little
inland	kangaroo	livelihood
innocent	kindergarten	loaf
insects	knead	logical
insistent	knelt	loosen
instantly	knew	losing
institution	label	loyalty
instruments	laboratory	lye
intense	landmark	machine
interference	lavender	made
interior	league	magazine
international	leather	magic
interrupt	leave	
interruption	lecture	

Spelling List *(cont.)*

main	minute	need
maintain	mischief	needless
manage	misfortune	neigh
mane	misplaced	neighborhood
margin	misprint	nephew
marginally	mission	nervous
masquerade	modern	neutral
material	modify	new
maximum	moisture	no
meager	moon	noisy
meanwhile	morning	normal
measure	mosquitoes	normally
measurement	motion	notify
meat	motivate	numeral
mechanical	motivation	oaths
medical	multiple	obey
medium	muscles	object
meet	musician	obligations
melody	mutiny	obscure
memory	mysterious	obvious
merchandise	mystery	occasion
merciful	napkin	occur
messenger	narrow	often
metal	natural	
microscope	nay	
minor	necessary	

Spelling List *(cont.)*

oh	pail	pleasant
omitted	palace	please
onion	pale	pleasure
operate	pamphlet	pledged
opossum	paragraph	plentiful
opponent	parallel	political
opportunity	parrot	politician
oppose	particle	politics
opposite	pastimes	pollution
orbiting	patient	popular
orchard	peal	pores
ordinary	peel	portable
ore	perfume	portrait
organ	permission	possession
origin	permitted	possible
ought	perpetual	posture
ourselves	personally	practically
outfit	persuade	prairie
outfitted	petition	praise
overgrown	phases	prays
owe	physical	precautions
ownership	physically	precede
oxygen	physician	predict
pacific	piece	
package	pigeons	
packet	pleas	

Spelling List (cont.)

present	quart	reliable
preservation	quotation	relied
present	radio	relief
president	read	religious
pressure	realistic	renewed
principles	realistically	repeated
privacy	realize	represent
private	rebellion	republic
privilege	receipt	requirements
procedure	reception	requisition
procession	recklessness	research
products	recognize	resentment
profit	recollect	reservation
promote	recommend	residential
pronunciation	recorded	residue
property	recreation	resistance
prophecy	reed	resource
proposing	reference	response
protected	referred	restaurants
publication	regular	restrict
publish	reigned	retreat
punctuation	reigns	retrieve
punishment	reins	
purposeful	reject	
quantity	relative	
quarrel	release	

Spelling List (cont.)

revenue	sandals	sermon
reverse	sandwich	sew
review	satellite	shark
revised	sauce	shear
revision	scarce	sheer
revive	scarcely	shipments
rewrite	scent	shore
rhyme	schedule	shoulder
rhythm	science	shriek
rickety	scientific	shyness
rightful	scissors	sigh
rode	scrambling	sight
rodeo	scribble	signature
root	scroll	similar
route	scrubbing	similarity
rubbish	seam	sincere
rude	searched	siren
rued	seas	site
ruin	security	situation
rumors	seem	skyscraper
rural	sees	sneeze
sail	sense	so
salary	sentence	soldiers
sale	separate	
salesclerk	sequence	
salvaging	serious	

Spelling List *(cont.)*

solution	suggest	term
son	suggestion	termination
sow	sun	terrier
spacious	supervisor	theme
spectacular	supreme	theory
speech	surf	thermostat
spent	surgeon	thirtieth
spicy	suspect	thoroughly
spirit	sweep	thought
stadium	swing	thoughtful
stake	symbol	threw
stampede	sympathetic	through
staple	sympathy	throughout
stationery	system	thunder
steak	tacks	tide
stomach	tail	tied
stopper	tale	tight
stories	tarnished	time
strategy	tax	tissue
stretch	tease	to
strictly	technology	together
studied	tedious	tomato
style	telescope	too
subscribe	television	topic
subtract	temporarily	torpedo
successful	temporary	tough

Spelling List *(cont.)*

tracked	urgent	wedged
tradition	useless	Wednesday
traditional	vacant	weigh
tragedy	valuable	weight
trait	vane	weird
translate	vanilla	whether
treacherous	varnish	which
treasurer	vehicle	whine
triangle	veil	wine
trickled	vein	wisdom
tried	velocity	witch
trolley	velvet	won
tropical	vendor	wonderful
truly	villain	wood
trumpet	violet	woodshed
two	visitor	worthwhile
umbrella	vital	would
umpire	vitamin	wrapped
undecided	vivacious	wrestle
underwater	volcano	wrote
unexpected	wade	yacht
unfinished	waist	yearning
unit	wait	you
university	warehouse	youngster
unknown	waste	youth
unsuccessful	way	
unusual	weather	

Testing Terms

Assessment

Assessment refers to the systematic and purposeful use of one or more of the various methods of testing student progress and achievement.

Alternative Assessment

Alternative assessment involves innovative ways of keeping track of and evaluating student work and progress. Usually contrasted with traditional, objective, standardized, norm-referenced, and paper-and-pencil testing, it includes methods such as portfolio assessment, observation of assigned tasks, and anecdotal records.

Authentic Assessment

Authentic assessment is the observation and scoring of the performance of a task in real life or, if that is impossible, in a situation that closely matches the standards and challenges of real life.

Criterion-Referenced Assessment

This kind of assessment is compared to and based upon behavioral objectives in which the learner's proficiency in an area of the curriculum is determined by his or her degree of success in completing prescribed tasks and not by comparison to the scores of other learners.

Portfolio Assessment

Portfolio assessment is a longitudinal system of assessment that occurs over a period of time and involves chronologically ordered samples of a student's work that can be compared to identify that student's progress. These samples are stored in an individual container of some kind (a portfolio).

Traditional Assessment

A traditional assessment system involves the periodic collection of data about student achievement by means of objective, standardized, norm-referenced, and paper-and-pencil tests.

Evaluation

Evaluation is the process of judging the information or results obtained from assessment for one purpose or another. (If you assess a student's ability to complete a given task in the fall and then again in the spring, you can evaluate the progress he or she has made by comparing the two assessments.)

Testing Terms (cont.)

Information Management

In an information management system, assessment information (test dates, observation checklists, portfolio materials, etc.) regarding student progress is collected, organized, and maintained.

Anecdotal Records

These used to be just lists of teacher observations stated factually and objectively without teacher interpretation or judgment. They were usually kept to document behavior problems. Anecdotal records have, however, taken on a new meaning with new forms of assessment. They have become positive narratives that document the growth and development of students. They are, at least to some extent, subjective since they contain teacher interpretation and judgment. They are often kept in student portfolios and have thus become a part of portfolio assessment.

Checklists

Checklists are convenient forms in a variety of styles. They are designed (or can be designed through the use of task analysis) to help teachers record what they see during observation-based assessment.

Checkpoints

Checkpoints are important assessment points along the way between the beginning and the end of the educational process.

Exit Demonstration (Culminating Activity, Outcome)

Exit demonstration refers to the final culminating activity that proves that a student has mastered an area of the curriculum.

Portfolios

In addition to functioning as a type of assessment, portfolios also function as containers for collecting, organizing, and maintaining student records.

Rubrics

In connection with assessment, a rubric is a scoring guide that differentiates, on an articulated scale, among a group of student samples that respond to the same prompt.

Running Records

A running record is of student miscues (errors) made during the oral reading of a selection.

Testing Terms (cont.)

Standards

Content Standards

These are standards that describe the desired outcomes in various subject areas. (frameworks; curriculum outlines)

Curriculum Standards

The course of study in a given area; an outline of content.

National Standards

A set of standards for the whole country. Currently, a popular movement among one group of educators. Usually understood to include content standards, performance standards, and school delivery standards.

Performance Standards

Standards that define the level and quality of performance that students must exhibit to show mastery of an area of the curriculum.

School Delivery Standards

Standards that indicate whether or not a school has the resources necessary to enable students to meet the performance standards.

Tests

Tests are assessment tools constructed in such a way that achievement can be measured.

Achievement Tests

These are tests designed to assess the amount of information or degree of skill possessed by the test taker, usually objective, standardized, norm-referenced, paper-and-pencil tests.

Cognitive Tests

Cognitive tests are used to assess intellectual functioning.

Norm-Referenced Tests

These tests are based on and judged in comparison with standards determined by testing a selected pool of individuals, forming the standardized sample.

Tests *(cont.)*

Objective Tests

Tests in which each question is stated in such a way that there is only one correct answer, true/false and multiple-choice tests are examples of objective tests.

Paper-and-Pencil Tests

We refer to tests that are designed to be read either orally by the teacher or silently by the student and answered in writing as paper-and-pencil tests.

Performance Tests

Students are asked to perform tasks while their methods and reasoning processes are observed, monitored, and recorded by means of an instrument (such as a checklist). In most cases, the students' methods and reasoning processes are considered of the same or greater value than the actual results or answers.

Proficiency Tests

Proficiency tests are written to test the objectives that are actually being taught. In order to construct a proficiency test, educators first decide on the things that they really want their students to learn (goals and objectives). Teachers then teach these things and test students to see if they have learned the material.

Psycho-Motor/Perception Tests

These tests used to measure visual-motor skills are usually standardized and norm-referenced.

Standardized Tests

(See *Norm-Referenced Tests, page 205.*)

Writing Sample Tests

Students are asked to demonstrate writing abilities by actually writing in response to given prompts. These writing samples are graded with the use of rubrics.
(See *Rubrics, page 204.*)

Answer Key

Page 32

A	B	2	H	5	B	8	F
B	H	3	C	6	F		
1	C	4	J	7	B		

Page 33

A	C	1	C	3	C	5	D
B	F	2	J	4	F	6	H

Page 34

A	D	2	G	5	B	8	F
B	F	3	A	6	G	9	D
1	C	4	J	7	B	10	H

Page 35

A	B	2	J	5	A	8	H
B	J	3	B	6	J	9	D
1	A	4	H	7	B	10	F

Page 36

A	B	2	F	5	D	8	G
B	J	3	B	6	G	9	C
1	D	4	H	7	A	10	F

Answer Key (cont.)

Page 37

A	B	2	G	5	A	8	J
B	H	3	D	6	H		
1	C	4	H	7	B		

- A. B
- B. H
- 1. C
- 2. G
- 3. D
- 4. H
- 5. A
- 6. H
- 7. B
- 8. J

Page 38

- A. D
- B. G
- 1. B
- 2. H
- 3. D
- 4. H
- 5. A
- 6. G
- 7. C
- 8. J

Page 39

- A. D
- B. G
- 1. B
- 2. J
- 3. C
- 4. H
- 5. B
- 6. J

Page 40

- A. A
- B. G
- 1. C
- 2. J
- 3. A
- 4. H
- 5. B
- 6. G

Page 41

- A. C
- B. F
- 1. B
- 2. J
- 3. C
- 4. G
- 5. C
- 6. F
- 7. B
- 8. G

Answer Key (cont.)

Page 42

A ● Ⓑ Ⓒ Ⓓ 1 Ⓐ Ⓑ Ⓒ ● 3 Ⓐ ● Ⓒ Ⓓ 5 Ⓐ ● Ⓒ Ⓓ
B Ⓕ Ⓖ Ⓗ ● 2 ● Ⓖ Ⓗ Ⓙ 4 Ⓕ Ⓖ ● Ⓙ 6 ● Ⓖ Ⓗ Ⓙ

Page 43

A ● Ⓑ Ⓒ Ⓓ 1 Ⓐ Ⓑ ● Ⓓ 3 ● Ⓑ Ⓒ Ⓓ 5 Ⓐ Ⓑ Ⓒ ●
B Ⓕ Ⓖ Ⓗ ● 2 Ⓕ ● Ⓗ Ⓙ 4 Ⓕ ● Ⓗ Ⓙ 6 ● Ⓖ Ⓗ Ⓙ

Page 44

A Ⓐ Ⓑ Ⓒ ● 2 Ⓕ Ⓖ ● Ⓙ 5 Ⓐ Ⓑ Ⓒ ● 8 Ⓕ ● Ⓗ Ⓙ
B Ⓕ ● Ⓗ Ⓙ 3 ● Ⓑ Ⓒ Ⓓ 6 Ⓕ Ⓖ ● Ⓙ 9 ● Ⓑ Ⓒ Ⓓ
1 Ⓐ Ⓑ Ⓒ ● 4 Ⓕ Ⓖ Ⓗ ● 7 Ⓐ Ⓑ Ⓒ ● 10 Ⓕ Ⓖ Ⓗ ●

Page 45

1 Ⓐ Ⓑ ● Ⓓ #3   4 ● Ⓖ Ⓗ Ⓙ #13
2 Ⓕ ● Ⓗ Ⓙ #2   5 Ⓐ Ⓑ Ⓒ ● #1
3 Ⓐ Ⓑ ● Ⓓ #5

Page 47

1 Ⓐ ● Ⓒ Ⓓ #6   4 Ⓕ Ⓖ Ⓗ ● #4   7 ● Ⓑ Ⓒ Ⓓ #1
2 Ⓕ Ⓖ ● Ⓙ #11 5 ● Ⓑ Ⓒ Ⓓ #7   8 ● Ⓖ Ⓗ Ⓙ #1
3 Ⓐ Ⓑ ● Ⓓ #2   6 Ⓕ Ⓖ Ⓗ ● #8

Answer Key (cont.)

Page 50

9 (A) (B) ● (D) #3
10 ● (G) (H) (J) #5
11 (A) ● (C) (D) #9

12 (F) (G) (H) ● #10
13 (A) ● (C) (D) #12
14 ● (G) (H) (J) #16

15 (A) (B) ● (D) #15
16 (F) (G) ● (J) #17

Page 51

17 (A) (B) ● (D) #14
18 ● (G) (H) (J) #18
19 (A) ● (C) (D) #19

20 (F) (G) ● (J) #20
21 ● (B) (C) (D) #21
22 (F) (G) ● (J) #13

23 (A) ● (C) (D) #1
24 (F) ● (H) (J) #1

Page 53

1 (A) ● (C) (D) #3
2 (F) (G) ● (J) #20
3 (A) (B) (C) ● #2

4 (F) (G) ● (J) #11
5 (A) ● (C) (D) #13
6 ● (G) (H) (J) #15

7 (A) (B) (C) ● #1
8 (F) ● (H) (J) #1

Page 56

9 (A) (B) (C) ● #6
10 (F) ● (H) (J) #12
11 (A) (B) ● (D) #4

12 ● (G) (H) (J) #16
13 (A) (B) ● (D) #5
14 ● (G) (H) (J) #7

15 (A) ● (C) (D) #14
16 (F) (G) (H) ● #17

Page 57

17 (A) (B) ● (D) #19
18 (F) ● (H) (J) #9
19 (A) (B) (C) ● #21

20 ● (G) (H) (J) #18
21 (A) (B) ● (D) #10
22 (F) ● (H) (J) #8

23 ● (B) (C) (D) #1
24 (F) (G) ● (J) #1

Answer Key (cont.)

Page 59

1 ● Ⓑ Ⓒ Ⓓ #3   4 Ⓕ Ⓖ ● Ⓙ #13   7 Ⓐ Ⓑ Ⓒ ● #1
2 Ⓕ ● Ⓗ Ⓙ #2   5 Ⓐ Ⓑ ● Ⓓ #7   8 Ⓕ Ⓖ ● Ⓙ #1
3 ● Ⓑ Ⓒ Ⓓ #11   6 Ⓕ ● Ⓗ Ⓙ #20

Page 62

9 Ⓐ Ⓑ ● Ⓓ #4   12 ● Ⓖ Ⓗ Ⓙ #16   15 Ⓐ ● Ⓒ Ⓓ #9
10 Ⓕ Ⓖ Ⓗ ● #5   13 Ⓐ ● Ⓒ Ⓓ #14   16 Ⓕ ● Ⓗ Ⓙ #15
11 Ⓐ ● Ⓒ Ⓓ #12   14 ● Ⓖ Ⓗ Ⓙ #17

Page 63

17 Ⓐ Ⓑ Ⓒ ● #19   20 Ⓕ ● Ⓗ Ⓙ #21   23 ● Ⓑ Ⓒ Ⓓ #1
18 Ⓕ ● Ⓗ Ⓙ #18   21 ● Ⓑ Ⓒ Ⓓ #8   24 Ⓕ ● Ⓗ Ⓙ #1
19 Ⓐ Ⓑ ● Ⓓ #10   22 Ⓕ Ⓖ ● Ⓙ #6

Page 65

1 ● Ⓑ Ⓒ Ⓓ #3   4 Ⓕ Ⓖ ● Ⓙ #8   7 ● Ⓑ Ⓒ Ⓓ #1
2 Ⓕ Ⓖ ● Ⓙ #5   5 Ⓐ Ⓑ ● Ⓓ #11   8 Ⓕ Ⓖ Ⓗ ● #1
3 Ⓐ ● Ⓒ Ⓓ #2   6 Ⓕ ● Ⓗ Ⓙ #21

Page 68

9 Ⓐ ● Ⓒ Ⓓ #6   12 Ⓕ Ⓖ ● Ⓙ #9   15 Ⓐ Ⓑ ● Ⓓ #15
10 ● Ⓖ Ⓗ Ⓙ #10   13 Ⓐ Ⓑ Ⓒ ● #12   16 Ⓕ Ⓖ ● Ⓙ #14
11 ● Ⓑ Ⓒ Ⓓ #4   14 Ⓕ Ⓖ ● Ⓙ #7

Answer Key (cont.)

Page 69

17 (A) (B) ● (D) #17   20 (F) (G) ● (J) #20   23 (A) ● (C) (D) #1
18 (F) (G) (H) ● #19   21 ● (B) (C) (D) #16   24 ● (G) (H) (J) #1
19 (A) ● (C) (D) #13   22 (F) (G) ● (J) #18

Page 70

A (A) ● (C) (D)   2 (F) (G) ● (J)   5 (A) ● (C) (D)   8 ● (G) (H) (J)
B (F) (G) ● (J)   3 (A) ● (C) (D)   6 ● (G) (H) (J)
1 ● (B) (C) (D)   4 (F) (G) (H) ●   7 (A) (B) ● (D)

Page 71

A (A) ● (C) (D)   2 (F) (G) ● (J)   5 (A) (B) ● (D)   8 (F) ● (H) (J)
B ● (G) (H) (J)   3 (A) (B) (C) ●   6 ● (G) (H) (J)   9 (A) (B) ● (D)
1 (A) (B) ● (D)   4 (F) ● (H) (J)   7 ● (B) (C) (D)   10 (F) (G) ● (J)

Page 72

A (1) ● (3) (4) (5)   2 ● (2) (3) (4) (5)   5 (1) (2) (3) ● (5)   8 (1) (2) ● (4) (5)
B (1) (2) (3) (4) ●   3 (1) (2) ● (4) (5)   6 (1) (2) ● (4) (5)   9 ● (2) (3) (4) (5)
1 (1) (2) ● (4) (5)   4 (1) ● (3) (4) (5)   7 (1) (2) (3) (4) ●   10 (1) (2) (3) (4) ●

Page 73

A (A) ● (C) (D)   2 (F) (G) ● (J)   5 (A) (B) ● (D)   8 ● (G) (H) (J)
B (F) (G) (H) ●   3 ● (B) (C) (D)   6 (F) (G) ● (J)   9 (A) (B) ● (D)
1 ● (B) (C) (D)   4 (F) ● (H) (J)   7 (A) ● (C) (D)   10 ● (G) (H) (J)

Answer Key (cont.)

Page 74

A	B	1	2	3	4	5	6	7	8	9	10
A	F	B	J	B	F	B	G	B	H	D	F

Page 75

A	B	1	2	3	4	5	6	7	8
A	H	C	E	A	H	B	F	C	H

Page 76

A	B	1	2	3	4	5	6	7	8
C	K	B	G	C	J	C	G	D	F

Page 77

A	B	1	2	3	4	5	6	7	8	9	10
2	4	3	1	4	4	1	3	1	1	1	3

Page 78

A	B	1	2	3	4	5	6	7	8
B	J	D	J	F	H	F	J	G	F

Page 79

A Ⓐ ● Ⓒ Ⓓ Ⓔ	2 Ⓕ Ⓖ Ⓗ Ⓙ ●	5 Ⓐ ● Ⓒ Ⓓ Ⓔ	8 Ⓕ Ⓖ Ⓗ ● Ⓚ	
B Ⓕ Ⓖ Ⓗ Ⓙ ●	3 Ⓐ ● Ⓒ Ⓓ Ⓔ	6 ● Ⓖ Ⓗ Ⓙ Ⓚ		
1 Ⓐ ● Ⓒ Ⓓ Ⓔ	4 Ⓕ Ⓖ Ⓗ ● Ⓚ	7 Ⓐ Ⓑ ● Ⓓ Ⓔ		

Page 80

A Ⓐ ● Ⓒ Ⓓ Ⓔ	1 Ⓐ Ⓑ ● Ⓓ Ⓔ	3 Ⓐ Ⓑ Ⓒ ● Ⓔ	5 Ⓐ Ⓑ Ⓒ Ⓓ ●	
B Ⓕ Ⓖ Ⓗ Ⓙ ●	2 Ⓕ ● Ⓗ Ⓙ Ⓚ	4 Ⓕ ● Ⓗ Ⓙ Ⓚ	6 ● Ⓖ Ⓗ Ⓙ Ⓚ	

Page 81

A ① ● ③ ④	2 ① ● ③ ④	5 ① ● ③ ④	8 ① ② ● ④
B ① ● ③ ④	3 ① ② ③ ●	6 ● ② ③ ④	9 ① ● ③ ④
1 ① ② ● ④	4 ● ② ③ ④	7 ① ② ③ ●	10 ① ② ③ ●

Page 82

A Ⓐ Ⓑ ● Ⓓ	2 Ⓕ Ⓖ ● Ⓙ	5 Ⓐ ● Ⓒ Ⓓ	8 Ⓕ Ⓖ Ⓗ ●
B ● Ⓖ Ⓗ Ⓙ	3 Ⓐ Ⓑ Ⓒ ●	6 Ⓕ Ⓖ Ⓗ ●	
1 Ⓐ ● Ⓒ Ⓓ	4 ● Ⓖ Ⓗ Ⓙ	7 ● Ⓑ Ⓒ Ⓓ	

Page 83

A Ⓐ ● Ⓒ Ⓓ	1 Ⓐ Ⓑ ● Ⓓ	3 Ⓐ Ⓑ ● Ⓓ	5 Ⓐ Ⓑ ● Ⓓ
B Ⓕ Ⓖ Ⓗ ●	2 Ⓕ ● Ⓗ Ⓙ	4 Ⓕ Ⓖ Ⓗ ●	6 Ⓕ Ⓖ ● Ⓙ

Answer Key (cont.)

Page 84 A Ⓐ Ⓑ ● Ⓓ 1 Ⓐ Ⓑ Ⓒ ● 3 Ⓐ Ⓑ Ⓒ ●
            2 ● Ⓖ Ⓗ Ⓙ 4 Ⓕ ● Ⓗ Ⓙ

Page 85 A Ⓐ Ⓑ ● Ⓓ B Ⓕ Ⓖ Ⓗ ● 1 Ⓐ Ⓑ ● Ⓓ 2 ● Ⓖ Ⓗ Ⓙ

Page 86 3 Ⓐ Ⓑ ● Ⓓ 5 Ⓐ Ⓑ ● Ⓓ 7 ● Ⓑ Ⓒ Ⓓ
            4 Ⓕ Ⓖ Ⓗ ● 6 Ⓕ ● Ⓗ Ⓙ 8 Ⓕ Ⓖ ● Ⓙ

Page 87 A Ⓐ Ⓑ ● Ⓓ 2 Ⓕ ● Ⓗ Ⓙ 5 Ⓐ Ⓑ Ⓒ ● 8 ● Ⓖ Ⓗ Ⓙ
            B ● Ⓖ Ⓗ Ⓙ 3 Ⓐ Ⓑ Ⓒ ● 6 Ⓕ Ⓖ ● Ⓙ
            1 Ⓐ ● Ⓒ Ⓓ 4 Ⓕ ● Ⓗ Ⓙ 7 Ⓐ ● Ⓒ Ⓓ

Page 88 A Ⓐ ● Ⓒ Ⓓ 2 Ⓙ ● Ⓛ Ⓜ 5 ● Ⓑ Ⓒ Ⓓ 8 ● Ⓚ Ⓛ Ⓜ
            B Ⓙ Ⓚ Ⓛ ● 3 Ⓐ Ⓑ ● Ⓓ 6 Ⓙ Ⓚ ● Ⓜ 9 Ⓐ ● Ⓒ Ⓓ
            1 ● Ⓑ Ⓒ Ⓓ 4 Ⓙ ● Ⓛ Ⓜ 7 ● Ⓑ Ⓒ Ⓓ 10 ● Ⓚ Ⓛ Ⓜ

Answer Key *(cont.)*

Page 89

A. A B C ●
1. ● B C D
2. A B ● D
3. A ● C D
4. A B C ●

Page 90

A. ● 2 3 4
B. 1 2 3 ●
1. 1 ● 3 4
2. 1 ● 3 4
3. 1 ● 3 4
4. ● 2 3 4
5. 1 2 ● 4
6. 1 2 3 ●
7. ● 2 3 4
8. 1 2 ● 4

Page 91

A. A ● C D
B. ● F G H
1. A B ● D
2. E F G ●
3. ● B C D
4. ● F G H
5. A B ● D
6. E F ● H

Page 92

7. A ● C D
8. E F ● H
9. ● B C D
10. E F ● H
11. ● B C D
12. E F ● H
13. A B C ●
14. E F ● H

Page 93

A. A ● C D
B. F G ● J
C. A ● C D
1. A ● C D
2. F ● H J
3. ● B C D
4. F G H ●
5. A B ● D
6. F ● H J
7. A B C ●
8. F ● H J
9. A B ● D
10. ● G H J

Page 94   A (A) ● (C) (D)   1 (A) ● (C) (D)   2 (F) (G) ● (J)   3 (A) ● (C) (D)

Page 95   A (A) (B) (C) ●   1 (A) ● (C) (D)   3 (A) (B) ● (D)
                                2 ● (B) (C) (D)   4 ● (B) (C) (D)

Page 96   A (A) (B) ● (D)   1 (A) ● (C) (D)   2 ● (B) (C) (D)   3 (A) (B) (C) ●

Page 97   A (A) (B) ● (D)   1 (A) ● (C) (D)   2 (F) (G) (H) ●

Page 98   A (A) (B) (C) ●   1 ● (B) (C) (D)   2 (A) (B) ● (D)   3 (A) (B) (C) ●

Answer Key (cont.)

Page 112 A. C B. G 1. C 2. J 3. C 4. H 5. A 6. J

Page 113 A. B B. H 1. C 2. F 3. B 4. G 5. D 6. G 7. D 8. F 9. B 10. F

Page 114 A. 4 B. 4 1. 3 2. 1 3. 3 4. 4

Page 115 A. 4 B. 3 1. 1 2. 4 3. 1 4. 3

Page 116 A. B 1. B 2. F 3. B 4. G 5. D

Answer Key (cont.)

Page 117   A Ⓐ ⬤ Ⓒ Ⓓ   1 Ⓐ Ⓑ ⬤ Ⓓ   2 Ⓕ ⬤ Ⓗ Ⓙ   3 ⬤ Ⓑ Ⓒ Ⓓ

Page 118   A Ⓐ ⬤ Ⓒ Ⓓ   2 ⬤ Ⓚ Ⓛ Ⓜ   5 Ⓐ Ⓑ Ⓒ ⬤   8 Ⓙ Ⓚ Ⓛ ⬤
               B Ⓙ Ⓚ Ⓛ ⬤   3 Ⓐ Ⓑ Ⓒ ⬤   6 ⬤ Ⓚ Ⓛ Ⓜ
               1 Ⓐ Ⓑ Ⓒ ⬤   4 Ⓙ ⬤ Ⓛ Ⓜ   7 Ⓐ ⬤ Ⓒ Ⓓ

Page 119   A Ⓐ ⬤ Ⓒ Ⓓ   2 Ⓕ ⬤ Ⓗ Ⓙ   4 ⬤ Ⓖ Ⓗ Ⓙ
               1 Ⓐ Ⓑ ⬤ Ⓓ   3 Ⓐ Ⓑ Ⓒ ⬤   5 Ⓐ Ⓑ ⬤ Ⓓ

Page 120   A ① ② ⬤ ④   1 ⬤ ② ③ ④   3 ① ⬤ ③ ④
               B ① ② ⬤ ④   2 ① ② ⬤ ④   4 ① ② ③ ⬤

Page 121   A ① ⬤ ③ ④   1 ① ② ⬤ ④   3 ⬤ ② ③ ④
               B ① ② ③ ⬤   2 ⬤ ② ③ ④   4 ① ② ③ ⬤

Answer Key (cont.)

Page 122

A (A) ● (C) (D) (E) 2 (F) ● (H) (J) (K) 5 (A) (B) ● (D) (E) 8 (F) (G) (H) ● (K)
B (F) (G) (H) (J) ● 3 (A) (B) (C) (D) ● 6 (F) ● (H) (J) (K)
1 (A) (B) ● (D) (E) 4 (F) (G) (H) ● (K) 7 (A) (B) ● (D) (E)

Page 123

9 (A) (B) (C) ● (E) 12 ● (G) (H) (J) (K) 15 (A) (B) ● (D) (E) 18 (F) ● (H) (J) (K)
10 (F) ● (H) (J) (K) 13 (A) (B) ● (D) (E) 16 (F) ● (H) (J) (K)
11 (A) (B) (C) ● (E) 14 (F) ● (H) (J) (K) 17 (A) (B) (C) (D) ●

Page 124

A (A) (B) ● (D) (E) 2 (F) (G) ● (J) (K) 5 (A) ● (C) (D) (E) 8 (F) ● (H) (J) (K)
B (F) (G) (H) (J) ● 3 (A) (B) (C) ● (E) 6 ● (G) (H) (J) (K)
1 ● (B) (C) (D) (E) 4 (F) ● (H) (J) (K) 7 (A) (B) ● (D) (E)

Page 125

9 (A) ● (C) (D) (E) 12 (F) (G) ● (J) (K) 15 ● (B) (C) (D) (E) 18 (F) ● (H) (J) (K)
10 (F) ● (H) (J) (K) 13 ● (B) (C) (D) (E) 16 ● (G) (H) (J) (K)
11 (A) (B) (C) ● (E) 14 ● (G) (H) (J) (K) 17 (A) ● (C) (D) (E)

Page 126

A (A) (B) (C) ● (E) 2 ● (G) (H) (J) (K) 5 (A) ● (C) (D) (E) 8 (F) ● (H) (J) (K)
B (F) (G) (H) (J) ● 3 (A) ● (C) (D) (E) 6 (F) (G) (H) ● (K)
1 (A) (B) ● (D) (E) 4 (F) (G) ● (J) (K) 7 (A) ● (C) (D) (E)

Page 127

9 Ⓐ Ⓑ Ⓒ ● Ⓔ	12 Ⓕ Ⓖ Ⓗ ● Ⓚ	15 ● Ⓑ Ⓒ Ⓓ Ⓔ	18 Ⓕ Ⓖ Ⓗ ● Ⓚ
10 Ⓕ ● Ⓗ Ⓙ Ⓚ	13 Ⓐ ● Ⓒ Ⓓ Ⓔ	16 Ⓕ Ⓖ Ⓗ ● Ⓚ	
11 Ⓐ Ⓑ Ⓒ ● Ⓔ	14 ● Ⓖ Ⓗ Ⓙ Ⓚ	17 Ⓐ ● Ⓒ Ⓓ Ⓔ	

Page 128

A Ⓐ ● Ⓒ Ⓓ Ⓔ	2 Ⓕ Ⓖ ● Ⓙ Ⓚ	5 Ⓐ Ⓑ Ⓒ ● Ⓔ	8 Ⓕ Ⓖ ● Ⓙ Ⓚ
B Ⓕ Ⓖ Ⓗ Ⓙ ●	3 Ⓐ ● Ⓒ Ⓓ Ⓔ	6 ● Ⓖ Ⓗ Ⓙ Ⓚ	
1 Ⓐ Ⓑ ● Ⓓ Ⓔ	4 Ⓕ Ⓖ Ⓗ ● Ⓚ	7 Ⓐ Ⓑ Ⓒ ● Ⓔ	

Page 129

9 Ⓐ Ⓑ ● Ⓓ Ⓔ	12 Ⓕ ● Ⓗ Ⓙ Ⓚ	15 Ⓐ Ⓑ Ⓒ ● Ⓔ	18 Ⓕ ● Ⓗ Ⓙ Ⓚ
10 ● Ⓖ Ⓗ Ⓙ Ⓚ	13 Ⓐ ● Ⓒ Ⓓ Ⓔ	16 Ⓕ ● Ⓗ Ⓙ Ⓚ	
11 Ⓐ ● Ⓒ Ⓓ Ⓔ	14 Ⓕ ● Ⓗ Ⓙ Ⓚ	17 ● Ⓑ Ⓒ Ⓓ Ⓔ	

Page 130

A Ⓐ ● Ⓒ Ⓓ Ⓔ	2 Ⓕ ● Ⓗ Ⓙ Ⓚ	5 Ⓐ ● Ⓒ Ⓓ Ⓔ	8 ● Ⓖ Ⓗ Ⓙ Ⓚ
B Ⓕ Ⓖ Ⓗ ● Ⓚ	3 Ⓐ Ⓑ ● Ⓓ Ⓔ	6 Ⓕ Ⓖ Ⓗ Ⓙ ●	
1 Ⓐ Ⓑ ● Ⓓ Ⓔ	4 Ⓕ Ⓖ ● Ⓙ Ⓚ	7 Ⓐ Ⓑ ● Ⓓ Ⓔ	

Page 131

9 Ⓐ ● Ⓒ Ⓓ Ⓔ	12 Ⓕ Ⓖ Ⓗ Ⓙ ●	15 ● Ⓑ Ⓒ Ⓓ Ⓔ	18 Ⓕ ● Ⓗ Ⓙ Ⓚ
10 Ⓕ ● Ⓗ Ⓙ Ⓚ	13 Ⓐ Ⓑ ● Ⓓ Ⓔ	16 Ⓕ ● Ⓗ Ⓙ Ⓚ	
11 ● Ⓑ Ⓒ Ⓓ Ⓔ	14 Ⓕ Ⓖ ● Ⓙ Ⓚ	17 Ⓐ Ⓑ ● Ⓓ Ⓔ	

Answer Key (cont.)

Page 132   A Ⓐ Ⓑ ● Ⓓ   1 Ⓐ Ⓑ ● Ⓓ   3 Ⓐ Ⓑ Ⓒ ●   5 Ⓐ ● Ⓒ Ⓓ
             B Ⓕ Ⓖ ● Ⓙ   2 Ⓕ ● Ⓗ Ⓙ   4 Ⓕ ● Ⓗ Ⓙ

Page 133   A Ⓐ ● Ⓒ Ⓓ   1 Ⓐ Ⓑ ● Ⓓ   3 Ⓐ ● Ⓒ Ⓓ   5 Ⓐ Ⓑ ● Ⓓ
             B Ⓕ ● Ⓗ Ⓙ   2 Ⓕ Ⓖ ● Ⓙ   4 Ⓕ Ⓖ ● Ⓙ   6 Ⓕ Ⓖ ● Ⓙ

Page 134   A Ⓐ Ⓑ ● Ⓓ   1 ● Ⓑ Ⓒ Ⓓ   3 Ⓐ Ⓑ ● Ⓓ   5 Ⓐ ● Ⓒ Ⓓ
             B Ⓕ Ⓖ Ⓗ ●   2 Ⓕ ● Ⓗ Ⓙ   4 Ⓕ Ⓖ ● Ⓙ   6 Ⓕ Ⓖ Ⓗ ●

Page 135   A Ⓐ Ⓑ ● Ⓓ   2 Ⓕ ● Ⓗ Ⓙ   5 ● Ⓑ Ⓒ Ⓓ   8 Ⓕ Ⓖ Ⓗ ●
             B Ⓕ Ⓖ Ⓗ ●   3 ● Ⓑ Ⓒ Ⓓ   6 Ⓕ Ⓖ Ⓗ ●
             1 Ⓐ ● Ⓒ Ⓓ   4 ● Ⓖ Ⓗ Ⓙ   7 Ⓐ Ⓑ ● Ⓓ

Page 136   A Ⓐ ● Ⓒ Ⓓ   1 Ⓐ Ⓑ Ⓒ ●   2 Ⓕ Ⓖ Ⓗ ●   3 Ⓐ Ⓑ ● Ⓓ
             B Ⓕ Ⓖ ● Ⓙ

222

Answer Key (cont.)

Page 137   4 Ⓕ Ⓖ ● Ⓙ   6 ● Ⓖ Ⓗ Ⓙ   8 Ⓕ Ⓖ Ⓗ ●
                5 Ⓐ Ⓑ Ⓒ ●   7 Ⓐ Ⓑ ● Ⓓ

Page 138   9 Ⓐ ● Ⓒ Ⓓ   11 ● Ⓑ Ⓒ Ⓓ
              10 Ⓕ Ⓖ ● Ⓙ   12 Ⓕ Ⓖ ● Ⓙ

Page 139   13 Ⓐ Ⓑ Ⓒ ●   15 Ⓐ Ⓑ ● Ⓓ   17 Ⓐ Ⓑ Ⓒ ●
              14 Ⓕ ● Ⓗ Ⓙ   16 Ⓕ Ⓖ Ⓗ ●   18 Ⓕ Ⓖ ● Ⓙ

Page 140   19 Ⓐ ● Ⓒ Ⓓ   21 Ⓐ Ⓑ Ⓒ ●
              20 Ⓕ ● Ⓗ Ⓙ   22 Ⓕ ● Ⓗ Ⓙ

Page 141   A Ⓐ Ⓑ Ⓒ ●   1 Ⓐ Ⓑ ● Ⓓ   2 Ⓕ ● Ⓗ Ⓙ

Answer Key (cont.)

Page 142   A (A) ● (C) (D)   2 (F) ● (H) (J)   4 (F) ● (H) (J)
             1 (A) ● (C) (D)   3 (A) (B) ● (D)

Page 143   A (A) (B) ● (D)   1 (A) (B) ● (D)   3 (A) ● (C) (D)   5 (A) (B) (C) ●
             B (F) (G) ● (J)   2 ● (G) (H) (J)   4 (F) ● (H) (J)   6 (F) (G) ● (J)

Page 144   A (A) (B) (C) ●   1 ● (B) (C) (D)   3 (A) (B) ● (D)   5 ● (B) (C) (D)
                               2 (F) ● (H) (J)   4 ● (G) (H) (J)   6 (F) ● (H) (J)

Page 145   A (A) (B) ● (D)   1 (A) ● (C) (D)   3 (A) ● (C) (D)
             B (F) (G) ● (J)   2 (F) ● (H) (J)   4 (F) ● (H) (J)

Page 146   A (A) (B) ● (D)   1 (A) (B) ● (D)   3 (A) (B) ● (D)
             B (F) (G) ● (J)   2 (F) (G) ● (J)   4 (F) (G) ● (J)

Page 147   A ● (B) (C) (D)   1 (A) (B) ● (D)   3 ● (B) (C) (D)
                               2 (F) (G) (H) ●   4 (F) (G) (H) ●